TIME and the

HIGHLAND MAYA

Barbara Tedlock

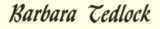

TIME and the

Revised Edition

HIGHLAND MAYA

Albuquerque
UNIVERSITY *of* NEW MEXICO PRESS

This book was published with the assistance of subsidies from the National Endowment for the Humanities and the Mellon Foundation, Inc.

Library of Congress Cataloging-in-Publication Data

Tedlock, Barbara.
    Time and the highland Maya / Barbara Tedlock.—Rev. ed.
      p.   cm.
    Includes bibliographical references and index.
    ISBN 0-8263-1342-6
    1. Quichés—Calendar. 2. Quichés—Religion and mythology.
3. Quichés—Astronomy. 4. Shamanism—Guatemala—
Momostenango. 5. Momostenango (Guatemala)—Social
conditions. I. Title.
F1465.2.Q5T43   1992
299'.784—dc20
                                             91-44651
                                                  CIP

Contents

Maps

Illustrations

All photographs were taken by Barbara and Dennis
Tedlock.

Tables

Acknowledgments

Several persons, both here and in Guatemala, have given me valuable help and encouragement during various stages of the research and the writing of this book. I am especially grateful to my husband-colleague Dennis Tedlock, who has shared with me the many hours of fieldwork, the strains of apprenticeship, many of his photographs, and his editorial expertise. I am also greatly indebted to Robert M. Carmack, who introduced me to Guatemala and read and critiqued large portions of this manuscript. The section in chapter 2 on Momostecan history would not have been possible without his historical knowledge, of which he freely gave. The map of Momostenango is based on the survey work which he and a group of his graduate students did during the early 1970s. I am also most grateful to Dell Hymes, who read and discussed a paper of mine based on the information in chapter 5; he suggested, on the strength of my linguistic data, that I dare to make the suggestions concerning Mayan hierographic decipherment that are given in chapter 5.

I am also most grateful to the following friends and colleagues who have freely given their time and criticisms: Lyle Campbell, Duncan Earle, Peter T. Furst, Beth Hadas, Edward T. Hall, John Hawkins, David H. Kelley, Timothy Knab, Floyd Lounsbury, June Nash, Benjamin Paul, Flavio Rojas Lima, Paula Sabloff, Douglas W. Schwartz, and Mary Elizabeth Smith. My greatest debt is to the daykeepers of Momostenango, who shared their lives—hopes, dreams, and realities—with me during the late 1970s. May they withstand the turbulent 80s in Guatemala.

Finally, I acknowledge the financial support given to me during the main period of residence in Guatemala (1975–76) by the Graduate School of the State University of New York at Albany. Later, in 1979, Tufts University awarded me a Faculty

Fellowship, making it possible for me to return to Guatemala for the summer. A Weatherhead Resident Fellowship at the School of American Research in Santa Fe, New Mexico, during 1980–81, gave me the time, space, and a beautiful environment in which to complete this manuscript.

Foreword

While the Classic and contemporary Mayan obsession with time has long been recognized, Barbara Tedlock sharply refocuses our vision of time's reading in the highland Guatemala realm of the Quiché. Combining anthropological fieldwork with formal apprenticeship to a diviner in Momostenango and grounding herself in a "human intersubjectivity" whose primary medium is language, she enters into the Quiché context of communicative interaction known as *ch'obonic*, to divine, to understand.

Her study of the practical knowledge of a master diviner questions and refutes most of the assumptions made by ethnographers to date. Tedlock challenges and dismantles accepted distinctions: between priestly and shamanistic statuses; between "good" and "evil" day names and blood movements (allegedly dualistic); between opposed solar (365-day) and divinatory (260-day) calendars. She finds that none of these can be thus separated in the practice of divination. She demonstrates, against years of misreading, that there is no "first day" to the present calendar and disposes of scholarly fixation on an etymologically constructed symbol system for the days. She finds that this fixation has obscured a far more important mnemonics system referring to ritual practices associated with each day and ultimately linking divination with the most important categories of the social structure. Instead of the accepted view, she offers an integrated picture of rigorous, rational interpretation of the irrational "speaking" of possessed persons and objects as well as the dialectical rather than dualistic relationship between paired terms in divinatory interpretation.

Indigenous theories of the diviner's body as microcosm; the counting of the days conceived as a "speaking of the calendar" tied, by way of the four Year-bearers, to the mountains of the four directions; the correspondences between blood lightning in the body and sheet lightning on the mountain lakes; the taking over of the seeds by the days of the calendar that they might give their messages; the "borrowing" of the world's powers by the diviner and his respectful payment; the reaching down and climbing up into the limits of earthly space in the placing of shrines; the sounding of dead voices, epic battles of bygone times, attachments and resentments of ancestral souls—these are some of the rewards of the practical mastery Tedlock apprenticed herself to, providing us with a knowledge we both respect as science and delight in as poetry.

Many doors are opening now in the privileged house of anthropology on new possibilities of dialogue and creativity between the humanities and the sciences. Barbara Tedlock has now opened a door upon our understanding of time in the order of the Mayan cosmos, an understanding many of us shall be mining in these exciting days when so much in Mayan studies seems to be on the brink of collective decipherment and revelation. This is a beautifully precise articulation of a fundamental facet of the mystery, bright as the time-hallowed red seeds of the *tz'ite*, gentle and expert as the movements of the diviner's hands, clear and sharp as his crystals, the world's officers marshalling the seeds. Tedlock has us all in her debt on the "white and yellow" road of knowledge.

Nathaniel Tarn

Preface to the Revised Edition

In the twelve years since the manuscript of this book was originally accepted for publication, there have been major developments in Mayanist research and profound political and social changes in highland Guatemala. With the recent discovery of hundreds of previously unknown artifacts and important advances in hieroglyphic decipherment, Mayan civilization has entered into world history.[1] During this same time, numerous scholars have turned their attention to the study of the Postclassic and Colonial periods in order to explain the remarkable success and longevity of Mayan culture in the face of disease, invasion, war, and oppressive colonial policies.[2]

Guatemala, which has the largest segment of the Mayan population (four million), underwent a civil war during the eighties. Guerrilla takeovers of rural hamlets triggered massive levels of state violence, including death-squad executions and military counterinsurgency attacks. Mayan leaders and outside observers have felt that the government used its counterinsurgency campaign as a thin disguise for ethnocide, if not genocide, against the Mayan population.[3] The bitter irony is that the overwhelming majority of the infantry used by the military in its counterinsurgency war were Mayans themselves. Rural communities that were located in the vicinity of the base of operation for the Guerrilla Army of the Poor (EGP) and the Revolutionary Organization of People in Arms (ORPA) suffered the most intense violence, while those that were more removed from these centers of resistance to the state suffered sporadic violence and/or economic hardship.[4] Mayan communities located in the department of Totonicapán, although they were well within the original area of ORPA organization, did not suffer directly from either death-squad or military violence, but they did have to contend with severe economic deprivation. Such was the case with Momostenango, the community that serves as the ethnographic focus of this account. It had been a relatively wealthy community, supporting itself primarily through woolen-blanket weaving and long-distance trading. During the extreme violence of the early 1980s, merchants found it dangerous to travel to Chichicastenango, Antigua, Guatemala City, and other Central American countries to sell their wares. Even the short trip to the neighboring town of San Francisco el Alto became problematic, after buses were stopped and merchants were harangued and sometimes robbed by guerrillas.

After several night raids on the town center by guerrillas, who left behind spray-painted slogans on the walls of the municipal offices and leaflets containing death threats against numerous wealthy merchants and town leaders, three unidentifiable bodies were found on the road leading to San Francisco el Alto. At this point Momostecan exmilitary men, many of whom were traditionalists, decided to fight back. They captured a car containing six guerrillas and participated in armed confrontations with other guerrilla groups along the northwest borders of the municipality. By demonstrating that their community was organized, ready, and willing to fight guerrillas, they kept the national military and its scorched-earth counter-insurgency campaign out of Momostenango.[5]

At the height of the violence, the Guatemala Scholars Network, which I joined upon its foundation in 1980, issued a ban on social science research in Guatemala. This was done in order to protect Mayan consultants from the possibility that in the course of interacting with outsiders, they might falsely be accused by military informers of subversion. Dennis Tedlock and I both honored this ban, staying away from Momostenango for fear of endangering the lives of our associates there. The prohibition on research was lifted in 1987. During the summer of 1988 we returned to the field for the first time in nearly a decade. We visited the man who had taken us on as apprentices in 1976 and caught up on our obligations as initiated daykeepers. Although Momostenango never appeared on any of the Amnesty International lists of communities suffering massacres, we nonetheless feared that horrible things might have happened. We were relieved to find all of the people we knew alive and well, although notably poorer.

In the fall of 1989, we again returned to Momostenango, this time in order to make offerings and renew our divining bundles at the 8 Batz' ceremony. During this visit we found that there were many more people from other highland Mayan communities crowding into the shrines than there had been when we lived there during the seventies. And although everyone was poorer than before, the traditionalists were involved in constructing a cement-block chapel next to the important earth shrines at Ch'uti Sabal ("Little Declaration Place"). They had decided to build this chapel after a Protestant alcalde, appointed by General Efraín Ríos Montt, had barred members of the *cofradías* and the organization of priest-shamans from using the municipal offices in the town center for religious purposes. All day long on 8 Batz', each person who entered the shrines was asked for contributions to help with construction expenses.

Two new chapters in this book, numbers eight and nine, include materials concerning Mayan calendars and astronomy that I collected during my original and more recent field trips. In the afterword, which is also new, I discuss some of the political and cultural consequences of the civil war and the subsequent Mayan diaspora, with special attention to the emergence of a transnational Pan-Mayan culture and ethnic identity. Momostenango, partly because it was not devastated by the military, has become a major pilgrimage site, where people not only arrive to worship but to learn traditional Mayan cosmology. Momostecan priest-shamans today are actively involved in teaching indigenous methods of timekeeping and astronomy to Mayans from other highland Guatemalan communities. My own teacher has been elevated to the position of head priest-shaman for the ward of Santa Isabel (see map, chapter 2), which contains two of the most important local earth shrines, Ch'uti Sabal and Nima Sabal. As a result of his own more intense involvement in the practice of traditional religion, he has recently been instructing people, at various levels of knowledge, in Mayan healing, dream interpretation, calendrics, and cosmology. As his former student, I hope to be able to help spread this traditional knowledge by means of a Spanish-language edition of the present book. Mayan readers are passionately interested in the history, use, and interpretation of their own calendars and astronomy.

Barbara Tedlock

9 Ix in the year 5 E, or May 20, 1991
East Aurora, New York

TIME and the

HIGHLAND MAYA

1.

Introduction

The ancient Maya were great horologists, students of time. They measured the lunar cycle and solar year; lunar and solar eclipses; and the risings of Venus and Mars with great accuracy. In many cases, their measurements were more accurate than those of the Europeans who conquered them. But unlike the Europeans, the Maya were interested not only in the quantities of time but also in its qualities, especially its meaning for human affairs. We have been quick to understand their astronomy, but our efforts to inhabit their symbolic world have proved much more difficult and demanding. The very foundation of their calendar, composed of myriad overlays of cycles of differing lengths and portents, rests on a cycle of 260 named and numbered days. The length of this cycle has no obvious correlation with astronomical events, and the names of its days and their divinatory interpretations are largely lacking in astronomical references.

Among the Lowland Maya of Yucatán, the ancient ways of reckoning and interpreting time are known from inscriptions on thousands of stone monuments, from the few ancient books that survived the fires of Spanish missionaries, and from early colonial documents. But the contemporary indigenous people of that region have long since forgotten how to keep time in the manner of their ancestors. With the Highland Maya, and especially those of the western highlands of Guatemala, the situation is reversed. Here, the archaeological monuments are bare of inscriptions, and not one of the ancient books escaped the flames, though the content of a few such books was transcribed into alphabetic writing and preserved in colonial documents. But it is among the Highland Maya rather than among their Lowland cousins that time continues to this day to be calculated and given meaning according to ancient methods. Scores of indigenous Guatemalan communities, principally those speaking the Mayan languages known as Ixil, Mam, Pokomchí, and Quiché, keep the 260-day cycle and (in many cases) the ancient solar cycle as well (chapter 4).

One Guatemalan community is famous above all others for public rituals that are centered outside the physical and calendrical precincts of the Church, and that is the Quiché town of Momostenango. Its reputation as a major ceremonial center goes back at least to the time of the Spanish conquest (chapter 2). The present study will center on the Quiché in general and Momostenango in particular, but extensive comparisons will be drawn with other Highland

1

Mayan communities, in both Guatemala and Chiapas, Mexico. In addition, there will be occasional excursions into the Lowland Maya and into areas of Mesoamerica that lie beyond the Mayan world.

Everywhere, all the periods or cycles of Mayan time, whether they directly concern the movements of heavenly bodies or seem understandable only as expressions of peculiarly human rhythms, share the same basic unit of measurement: the day. The word for day is *kin* in the language of the Maya of Yucatán and *k'ij*[1] in the languages of the Quiché and nearly all other Highland Maya; in both cases, this word means not only "day" but also "sun." By means of metonymy, it refers to longer periods of time, even including whole aeons,[2] and it can also take on the sense of "time-liness": where we would say, "The time has come," the speaker of a Mayan language says, "The day has come."

The word for "day" is the closest the Mayan languages come to having a term for "time" itself, but it is more than that. A day, each day, has "its face," its identity, its character, that influences its events (chapter 5); a person's luck of the moment, or even his fate in general, is called "the face of his day" *(uwäch uk'ij* in Quiché). One of the commonest forms of Maya divination, centering on the counting out of portions of the 260-day cycle, is sometimes called *k'ijiloxic* in Quiché, literally "being dayed"—in other words, "being timed." One of the Quiché terms for those who are qualified to perform this kind of divination is *ajk'ij* (the Yucatec equivalent was *ah kin*), literally "person whose occupation is the days," that is, "daykeeper" or, more broadly, "timekeeper" (chapter 3).

Further, the Mayan word for "day" serves as a stem in words meaning "worship," as in Quiché *k'ijilabal*, which might be literally translated as the "means of daying," or less literally as the "observance of the days." This same word, *k'ijilabal*, can also mean the "place of daying"—that is, the "place of worship"; as will become apparent later, places of worship change according to what day it is (chapter 3). Here is a temporalization of space, expressed at the cosmic level by the Quiché words for east and west that (unlike the English terms) make overt reference to the motion of the sun: *chirelabal k'ij* ("at the rising of the sun") and *chukajibal k'ij* ("at the setting of the sun"). A similar directional terminology prevails in other Mayan languages, and most of them even give north and south an indirect temporal dimension, that is, they are named by reference to the sun's (or the day's) "right" and "left" sides as it travels (or elapses) westward.

These extensions of the meaning of *kin* and *k'ij* clearly indicate that an ethnography of Mayan time, or ethnohorology, will quickly exceed the limits of mathematically describable time and involve questions of timeliness, destiny, divination, religious ritual, and cosmology, all of which have qualitative or symbolic dimensions that Mayan peoples did not and do not conceive of as separable from the quantitative aspects of time. All of these quantitative and qualitative questions are brought together in a form of Quiché divination that combines the precise counting out of the 260-day cycle (chapter 5) through the use of seeds and crystals with "the speaking of the blood," a shamanic gift possessed by (or possessing) the diviner, whose body is conceived as a microcosm filled with movements that reflect the past and future events of the macrocosm (chapter 6). The term for this combined divinatory process is *ch'obonic* ("to understand"; chapter 7). To study the theory of Quiché divination, then, is not only to study Quiché horology, somatology, and cosmology, but to study Quiché epistemology.

The epistemology of the Quiché daykeeper or diviner, although some of its elements are stated by practitioners in the form of abstract propositions or generalizations, is transmitted to the novice only in the context of actual divinatory events (chapter 3). Divinatory theory is not a static, ideal system that is ontologically prior to divinatory practice; rather, it derives from practice and is demonstrated in practice, as would seem to befit a way of knowing whose principal object is the movements of time. When an ethnographer asks for a description of the Quiché calendar or of calendrical divination, the daykeeper will feel compelled (if the day of the interview is an auspicious one) to bring out his or her divining seeds and crystals and perform a full demonstration, one whose results will be understood to reflect upon the life situation of the ethnographer.

Philosophical Reflections

In my own study of the theory and practice of Quiché calendrical divination, I employed traditional anthropological methodology, but I also chose to undergo formal apprenticeship to a professional diviner. In reflecting on this decision, I can see that it was partly my previous training and fieldwork in ethnomusicology that allowed me to learn to divine instead of only learning *about* divination. In ethnomusicology, learning to perform the foreign music one is attempting to describe is a respected practice. Mantle Hood, the chief proponent of this practice, comments:

> My own experience and that of a number of advanced graduate students working in various parts of the world have convinced us that many of the accumulating errors in descriptive and stylistic studies in the field of ethnomusicology would have been avoided had the investigator learned such skills as how to manipulate a loose-haired bow in one hand and the slender neck of a two-stringed lute in the other or had he slowly and painstakingly learned to execute the microtonal deviations characteristic of the style of the Japanese flute or trained his fingers to respond to the subtle requirements of hand drumming. (Hood 1963:277)

In other words, learning how to perform aids in both description and analysis. Another obvious analogy is with anthropological linguistics: that whole field is founded upon the practice of learning to pronounce sounds and later to produce sentences that the native speaker judges to be correct.

For some, the idea of apprenticeship to a diviner will raise the question of loss of objectivity. But I am in agreement with Sylvia Gronewold, who finds the idea of the anthropologist gone native, never to return, to be an "archetype," a construct of the professional imagination. The favorite example of this archetype has long been Frank Hamilton Cushing, but Gronewold finds that Cushing "was a dedicated professional. Although he became, to an impressive degree, a Zuñi, he did not cease to be an anthropologist."[3] Less well known to the profession is the case of Gladys A. Reichard, who participated both as a patient and as an assistant in Navajo curing ceremonies and who studied the art of Navajo weaving by mastering it.[4] Gary Witherspoon gives her published works first place in the vast anthropological literature on the Navajo.[5] Both Cushing and Reichard learned the appropriate native languages exceptionally well. Linguistic knowledge is often held up as a measure of professional seriousness in anthropology, but it is also a measure of anthropological participation.

What lies behind the belief that "going native" is a real danger to the anthropologist is the logical construction of the relationship between objectivity and subjectivity, between self and other, between scientist and native, as an analytical opposition. The implication is that the native way of knowing is somehow incompatible with the scientific way of knowing, and that the domain of objectivity is the sole property of the outsider. I count myself among those anthropologists, growing in number, who reject such an analytical construction. Solon T. Kimball, for example, notes that "the time may have arrived when we are ready to undertake systematic observations of the processes of induction and involvement in another culture."[6] Bennetta Jules-Rosette, who joined an African church in the process of studying it, writes that "through continued observation, I began to develop a repertoire of knowledge and expectations, or a common culture, that was shared with participants and created in interaction with them."[7] In his introduction to her book, Victor Turner observes that "to each level of sociality corresponds its own knowledge, and if one wishes to grasp a group's deepest knowledge one must commune with its members [and] speak its Essential We-talk (to combine the vocabularies of Martin Buber and Alfred Schutz)."[8] Johannes Fabian holds a similar position, declaring that anthropological investigation must enter "a context of communicative interaction through the one medium which represents and constitutes such a context: *language.*"[9]

In Schutz's terms, the "We-talk," or "context of communicative interaction," referred to by Turner and Fabian belongs not to the realm of "objectivity" or "subjectivity" but to that of "human intersubjectivity," and it is this realm, as a field of investigation, that distinguishes the "social" from the "natural" sciences.[10] In my own fieldwork, I entered the particular context of communicative interaction called *ch'obonic* in Quiché, learning how to talk about calendrical divination and to talk the divinatory language itself. The present account of Quiché calendrical and divinatory theory and practice rests on a foundation of human intersubjectivity. In this sense, it belongs to the human, rather than the natural, sciences.

One of the consequences of entering the intersubjective field is that it changes the relationship between "theory," which previously belonged solely to the "objective" domain of the anthropologist, and "practice," which belonged solely to the "subjective" domain of the native. As Pierre Bourdieu has pointed out, the "objectivist" anthropologist, starting from the observation of practice, sets an ideal "constructed object" as his theoretical goal. Once he has reached this goal, he can only see the continuing (and changing) practices of the natives as an imperfect falling away from the ideal, as if his own theory were ontologically prior to native practice. In place of an opposition between theory *and* practice, Bourdieu proposes the development of a theory *of* practice, grounded in the direct study of what he calls the "practical mastery" or "practical knowledge" of the native.[11] In these terms, the present study, rather than terminating in the construction of an abstract, ideal "object," retains the "practical knowledge" of the Quiché calendrical diviner as a central concern. It does not have as its final object the erection of a calendrical "symbol system," to be understood apart from the questions asked of diviners. Further, in learning how divinatory knowledge is actually transmitted from an experienced calendar diviner to a novice, I have taken a step beyond Bourdieu. The present work is a contribution to the study not only of practical knowledge but also of practical epistemology.

The Fieldwork

The present study is based on three periods of fieldwork in Guatemala, the first from June to August of 1975, the second from February through December of 1976, and the third from June to August of 1979. The methods included ethnographic survey, formal (structured) and informal (unstructured) interviewing, the reading of an ethnohistorical document with consultants, the discussion of modern ethnographies and previously reported ethnographic "facts" with consultants, participant observation, and apprenticeship.

The ethnographic survey was conducted in five Quiché communities—San Cristóbal Totonicapán, Chinique, Chichicastenango, San Pedro Jocopilas, and Santa Catarina Ixtahuacán—at various times during the last four months of 1976 and during the summer of 1979. This work was saved for last, when I knew enough of Quiché language, religion, world view, and medicine to participate within the native context. In Momostenango, the town in which I resided during my first two visits to Guatemala, I conducted informal and formal interviews with a fairly wide range of Quiché men and women including weavers, merchants, farmers, town officials, and various religious specialists, ranging from members of the Catholic Action movement to dozens of priest-shamans. I also read and discussed a 1722 ethnohistorical document, a calendar written in the Quiché language,[12] with a literate Momostecan elder; in addition, I checked certain problems in the document with several other people in Momostenango and Chinique.

Tapes were made during all formal and some informal interviews, as well as during the reading of the ethnohistorical document. Tapes were also made during the long hours of dialogue with my teacher during the apprenticeship. In all, 125 ninety-minute cassettes were produced on my portable Sony TC-55. As soon as possible after the interviews or dialogues, the tapes were translated into literal English and written down in notebooks. During subsequent interviews and lessons, vocabulary items, important concepts, and prayers were discussed again or checked with other consultants. Those other consultants included a wide range of priest-shamans, not only from the town center but also from the outlying districts of Los Cipréses, Santa Ana, Xequemeyá, and Canquixajá. They included representatives of every level of the divinatory hierarchy (see chapter 3), up to and including one of the two head priest-shamans for the entire community. In all, the formal fieldwork produced 2,513 written pages recorded in nine notebooks.

In the middle stages of my work in Momostenango, my husband and I undertook formal training as calendar diviners; we were initiated in August of 1976. We later had occasion to perform calendrical divinations for Quichés who solicited our services (chapter 3 contains a discussion of the training, initiation, roles, and status of calendar diviners). The unusual opportunity to learn divination was provided by a gifted, socially prominent priest-shaman who noticed our intense interest in the topic and my cooperativeness in answering the questions he asked during the calendrical divinations he performed for me during a serious illness. His high status and reputation for stability enabled him to risk potential public and private criticism for accepting foreigners as students. My husband and I were trained and initiated together because it was divined that our joint indiscretions had caused my illness and because our teacher had a series of dreams that recommended the "united service" *(tunulic chac)* for us.

My learning of divinatory practice involved a role not yet formally discussed in the sociological and anthropological literature on the topic of fieldwork, namely, participant-as-observed. In many ways, this was the most painful part of my fieldwork, since educated outsiders (except for linguists) are not used to being closely tested on their day-to-day comprehension of the information they are accumulating. As a product of modern American education, I had little ability to remember things I was told without writing them down. Another problem was to learn to do whatever was asked in formal training quickly and efficiently, without constant internal and external questioning of the request or command. Later, of course, I was free to analyze the enculturation techniques that were used upon us, but while I was in training, I simply had to act.

Much has been written on the topic of liminality in *rites de passage*,[13] but the experience of liminality is more painful than one would be led to believe. My teacher repeatedly told us that our fellow North Americans in the area—a Peace Corps volunteer, an anthropologist and his visiting girl friend, and a linguist—were all "enemies of the training" and should be avoided. This, in addition to the pressures of the training itself, left us quite exhausted by the time four and a half months had passed and we were ready for initiation. Now that some time has passed, I can see that this liminal stage, during which I was neither a North American nor a Mesoamerican, neither an anthropologist nor a diviner, was absolutely necessary to the training.

Shortly after beginning formal training, I realized that my teacher's personal commitment to completing our training was extremely serious. If we failed as students, he failed, and our social disgrace was his. Furthermore, I realized that our physical appearance alone would attract a lot of attention during the public initiation we were being groomed for. Clearly, we had to be star pupils (or so we thought), able to greet people properly; to count the 260-day calendar rapidly (backward and forward) without stumbling, interpreting its meanings; and to improvise prayers in Quiché. We also had to know how to make offerings properly and in the right order, and how to handle the divining paraphernalia.

The taping of the hours of dialogue with our teacher, which I played back, wrote down, and used to generate further questions, had an ironic result: when the great day came, we were overprepared. In my observations of and conversations with novices who were initiated at the same time as ourselves, I found that although they, too, had met with their teachers on so-called permission days (chapter 3) and had been drilled on the calendar (chapters 4 and 5) and the "speaking of the blood" (chapter 6), our overall knowledge was greater than theirs. In fact, none of the novices who were within our hearing range on the initiation days even attempted to pray aloud. Instead, their teachers simply did everything for them, including even the burning of the offerings. In discussing this with experienced diviners later, I found that they were unperturbed by the initial lack of knowledge demonstrated by these novices. They declared that we had worked so hard because "our ancestors were ignorant and could not help us." Consequently, we had had to use a machine and to be drilled more thoroughly than a Quiché novice would. Our method of learning was described as "a struggle."

Nonetheless, our grasp of so many of the mnemonic devices of calendrical interpretation (chapter 5) and of the precise meanings of the "speaking of the blood" (chapter 6) was a marvel to several diviners. It was our tape-assisted precocity that led to the appearance of clients, though clients who were themselves diviners were not overly impressed and used the divining situation to test us. Testing also occurred whenever we went to the shrines on the obligatory days for offerings and prayer (chapter 3). Priest-shamans who did not know us personally would greet us and tell us that it was nice to see us "today, 1 Came," when it was actually 8 Came or 1 Toj on the Quiché calendar. We learned to correct them politely, after which they treated us with respect, but there are so many diviners in Momostenango that this testing process never really ended. The most serious challenge came from one of the two "mother-fathers of the town" (*chuchkajawib rech tinimit*), a head priest-shaman for the entire municipality. He greeted us on the road from a shrine one day, and, after naming that day falsely and being corrected, he asked who had trained us. We gave him the name of our teacher immediately, without thinking. Later I wondered whether we should have withheld his name, but when I told him about the incident, he said that no harm was done. He was correct, and this particular confrontation simply served as my introduction to the town priest-shaman, a man whom I would later have occasion to interview.

I should add that many diviners who had already heard about us opened conversations with expressions of approval rather than with tests, and that no direct opposition was ever expressed by anyone. As for our roles as anthropologists, those returned in full as soon as the liminal period was over, on the day of initiation. From my teacher's point of view, there was never any question of having to make a final choice between being an anthropologist and becoming a calendrical diviner. Among the Quiché, new roles are properly added to old ones, not substituted for them.

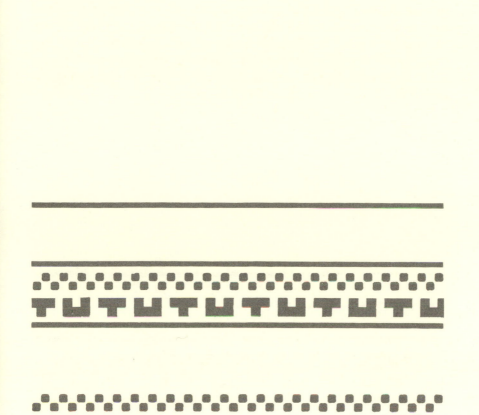

2.

Momostenango

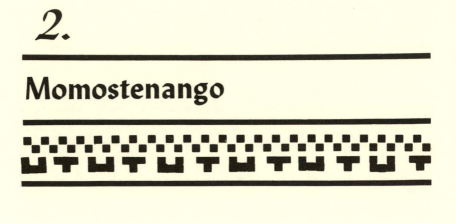

Momostenango is located in the cool, tropical highlands of midwestern Guatemala. It is one of the eight predominantly mono-lingual Quiché-speaking municipalities *(municipios)* that make up the county *(departamento)* of Totonicapán (see map 1).[1] Quiché—along with Cakchiquel, Tzutuhil, Pokomam-Pokomchí, Uspantec, and Kekchí—is a Mayan language of the subgroup known as Qui-chean.[2] At the present time, speakers of Quichean languages num-ber about one million.

To the modern traveler, Momostenango is best known for its fine woolen blankets (fig. 1). In the ethnographic literature, its chief fame comes from the fact that it is the site of a ritual that comes each nine months on the day named 8 Batz', the largest and best-known ritual in all of Mesoamerica that is scheduled according to the Prehispanic calendar.[3]

History

During the Prehispanic period, soon after the collapse of Tula in highland Mexico and Chichén Itzá in Yucatán, a number of militaristic ruling dynasties claiming Toltec ancestry arose along the Veracruz-Tabasco Gulf Coast. According to various Quichean docu-ments, thirteen separate groups of "Toltec" (epigonal or epi-Toltec) warriors and priests from this area entered the Guatemalan high-lands some ten generations before the Spanish conquest, or around A.D. 1225. The Quiché, under the influence of these epi-Toltec militarists and priests, soon dominated the other epi-Toltec groups (such as the Cakchiquel and Aguacatec) as well as non-Toltec groups (such as the Mam and Ixil), evolving a conquest state. At its height (ca. A.D. 1450) the Quiché kingdom stretched from Soconusco in southern Chiapas to the far northern reaches of Alta Verapaz, including all Quiché-speakers as well as a large number of Uspan-tec, Ixil, Aguacatec, Mam, Pokomam, Tzutujil, and Cakchiquel peoples.[4] The last capital of the Quiché kingdom was at K'umarcaaj (also known by its Nahua name Utatlán), the ruins of which are located just outside the present town of Santa Cruz del Quiché.

Momostenango, which during Prehispanic times was called "Above the Walls" (Chuwa Tz'ak), was once a part of the Mam territory of Otzoya. During the reign of the Quiché King Qu'ikab (ca. A.D. 1450–1490), it was conquered by the Nijaib, one of the four

MEXICO

GUATEMALA

BELIZE

Gulf of
Honduras

Huehuetenango

Santa Cruz Quiché

Quezaltenango

Lake Atitlán

Guatemala City

HONDURAS

Pacific

Ocean

EL
SALVADOR

0   50   100
kilometers

Department of Totonicapán

Area in which Quiché is spoken

Areas of other languages of the
Quichean subgroup of the Mayan family

International boundary

Municipality of Momostenango

Map 1. Guatemala

1. The blanket market in Momostenango.

principal lineages of the Quiché kingdom.[5] Less than a century later (in 1524), during the battle between Quiché and Spanish forces in the Quezaltenango valley, a large group of Quiché (including people from Chuwa Tz'ak) were led by Don Francisco Izquín Nijaib. After his forces were defeated by Alvarado, Chuwa Tz'ak was given in stewardship (*encomienda*) to Juan Pérez Dardón, a captain in Alvarado's force who received tribute from the community. Meanwhile, the Tlaxcalan Indian allies of the Spanish had given the place the Nahua name "Momostenango," from *mumuztli*, meaning "altar of the idols" or "shrine," and *tenango*, meaning "home" or "town." Thirty years after the conquest of Guatemala, representatives of the Nijaib lineage of the former Quiché kingdom described the battle near Quezaltenango in a document written in the Quiché language (but using the Latin alphabet). The patrilineage used this document and three others to make land claims and seek the status of a privileged leader (*cacique*) in the post-Conquest community. Two of these documents are still extant in the book of the Momostecan canton of San Vicente Buenabaj, where the direct descendants of the Nijaib lineage (now called Vicente) still reside.[6]

Although Momostenango, like other indigenous communities, lost a large portion of its population to epidemics immediately following the conquest, much of the community's Prehispanic social organization remained intact because the heads of so many of the local patrilineages were given privileged status by the Spanish. From colonial sources, it appears that Quiché Prehispanic social organization resembled that of central Mexico, with communities divided into four endogamous quarters called *calpules* (from the Nahua *calpulli*, roughly equivalent to a ward) or *parcialidades*, each with its own head or ruler.[7] In Momostenango, the four quarters were renamed after the conquest for the patron saints assigned to them—Santiago, Santa Ana, Santa Isabel, and Santa Catarina—and were continued as administrative divisions, just as were similar quarters in Mexico. Each quarter had its own mayor (*alcalde*) and alderman (*regidor*), apparently representing the principal clans.[8] At first, there were no resident missionaries in the community, though a hermitage was established at the fortified center of Chuwa Tz'ak (now called "Pueblo Viejo"); early missionary work was conducted by visiting Franciscans from the convent of Quezaltenango. It was not until the 1590s, when the town center of

Momostenango was moved from Pueblo Viejo to its present location, that a Franciscan convent was built in the community.

In oral narratives collected in Momostenango during 1975–76, a wealthy indigene named Diego Vicente, a seventeenth-century descendant of Francisco Izquín Nijaib, is credited with moving the town center to its current location and building the church and convent there.[9] He and his sister Francisca are said to have gone to Spain together and petitioned the Crown for the title to much of what is now within the boundaries of Momostenango. After returning with written validation of their title, they gave much silver and gold to the church, including a carved monstrance (or chalice) which is still in the local convent. Diego Vicente then set up estates (haciendas) in several different locations within the community, including Pueblo Viejo, Xequemeyá, San Vicente Buenabaj, and Tierra Colorada. In each one, he established a patrilineage shrine known as the foundation (warabalja, "sleeping house" of the ancestors), where his many descendants still pray and make offerings to him, calling on him by name. He is also said to have made the first silver-tipped staffs or canes of office for the mayors. His memory was publicly honored in 1976 when a bust of him, along with one of Teodoro Cifuentes (a local military leader), was placed at the main entrance to the town center of Momostenango (fig. 2).

The colonial records for seventeenth-century Momostenango show that the population was by then beginning to recover slightly from the initial impact of European diseases and that Spaniards increasingly penetrated the community.[10] One, by the name of Gaspar de los Reyes, got title to two large ranches, one of which included Jutacaj and parts of Canquixajá and Xequemeyá (see map 2). He built his estate on the second ranch and, in 1630, obtained a consignment from the Crown that forced local indigenes to work for him. There was also a large ladino-run[11] cattle ranch in the neighboring Sijá valley, and, in 1689, the Vicente patrilineage complained to the Crown that animals from this ranch were straying into their lands. Early in the same century, the quarter of Momostenango called Santiago, consisting of 457 tribute payers (working-age males), was given as a large land grant to Bartolomé Flores, while the other three quarters, with a total of 250 tribute payers, were given to María de Carranza. This reduction of the municipality into two rather than four sections was paralleled administratively by a royal decree from Philip III in 1618, stating that municipalities

2. Busts of two Momostecan heroes: Teodoro Cifuentes (left) and Diego
Vicente (right).

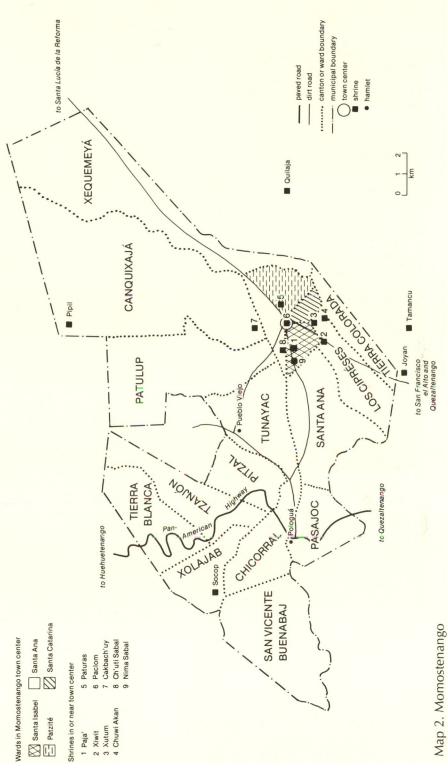

Wards in Momostenango town center

- ⬡ Santa Isabel   □ Santa Ana
- ▤ Patzité   ▨ Santa Catarina

Shrines in or near town center

1 Paja'   5 Paturas
2 Xiwit   6 Paclom
3 Xutum   7 Cakbach'uy
4 Chuwi Akan   8 Ch'uti Sabal
          9 Nima Sabal

— paved road
— dirt road
······· canton or ward boundary
—··—··— municipal boundary
◯ town center
■ shrine
● hamlet

0 1 2
km

XEQUEMEYÁ

CANQUIXAJÁ

PATULUP

TIERRA BLANCA

XOLAJAB

SAN VICENTE BUENABAJ

CHICORRAL

TZANJUÓN

PITZAL

TUNAYAC

PASAJOC

SANTA ANA

LOS CIPRESES

TIERRA COLORADA

■ Pipil
■ Quilaja
■ Tamancu
■ Joyan
■ Socop

● Pueblo Viejo
● Pologuá

Pan-American Highway

to Santa Lucía de la Reforma
to Huehuetenango
to Quezaltenango
to Quezaltenango
to San Francisco el Alto and Quezaltenango

Map 2. Momostenango

with more than eighty houses were to have two mayors and four aldermen. The result was that Momostenango's four mayors were reduced to two while the four aldermen remained. At some point after this reduction, Santiago became the patron saint of the community at large.

The records for the eighteenth and nineteenth centuries show that Momostecans were far from passive spectators in the violent changes that the Spaniards were making in all areas of their lives. Throughout this period, they maintained a nearly constant struggle against civil and religious domination. At certain stages, this struggle meant armed uprisings against tribute payment, and at others, it meant the removal of priests who tried to ban Prehispanic ritual practices. During and immediately after the Guatemalan struggle for independence (1811–21) local rebellions increased. A group of Momostecan rebels who numbered nearly six hundred, including militant women leaders, established political relations with all the indigenous pueblos in the immediate region, including San Bartolo Aguas Calientes, Santa María Chiquimula, San Francisco el Alto, San Cristóbal Totonicapán, and San Miguel Totonicapán. They participated in the nativistic rebellions in San Miguel Totonicapán, which included the crowning of Atanasio Tzul as King of the Quichés. Shortly thereafter, hundreds of Momostecans objected to the newly organized Federation of Central America. In 1824 they joined in a movement to annex much of western Guatemala, including Momostenango, to Mexico. In Robert M. Carmack's opinion, the many rebellions of the eighteenth and nineteenth centuries constituted a nativistic liberation movement in which Momostecans were attempting to free themselves from excessive taxation, ladino mayors, priests who ridiculed indigenous religious rituals, blockage of free communication and trade between municipalities, and restrictions on the buying and selling of municipal land.[12]

During the nineteenth century, this Momostecan nativistic and militaristic spirit was directly rewarded by the national government of Guatemala. In 1868, Momostecans fought with Justo Rufino Barrios in an attack against government soldiers in Huehuetenango. When Barrios became president of the republic in 1871, he granted title to 149 square kilometers of the fertile coffee-producing piedmont region above Retalhuleu to the 380 Momostecan families who had long been farming there.[13] This land grant officially became the municipality of El Palmar in 1873. By

1950, there were 8,509 residents of the municipality, most of them Quiché-speakers who proudly considered themselves to be of *la raza de Momostenango*—that is, of Momostecan descent and cultural heritage. The Momostecan heritage claimed by these Palmareños includes the patron saint Santiago Apostal (St. James the Apostle), who, since he carries a sword in his right hand, is a particularly fitting patron for these militaristic people; dozens of outdoor potsherd altars named after similar altars in Momostenango itself; and calendrical rites centering around the day 8 Batz'.[14] Once every 260 days, on 8 Batz', a few Palmareños still make the pilgrimage to Momostenango itself in order to visit the more powerful altars of their ancestral community.

During the early twentieth century, President Manuel Estrada Cabrera gave Momostecans land in the Ixil municipalities of Chajul and Nebaj.[15] As in the case of the El Palmar lands, this was a reward for extraordinary military service. The day 8 Batz' is celebrated in Nebaj by local calendar diviners who learned the custom in Momostenango.[16] At the present time, Momostecans are the majority of the population in one of the sixteen Nebaj rural cantons, and each year several of them make the pilgrimage to Momostenango to celebrate 8 Batz' at the original shrines.

The Momostecan combination of militarism and nativism came to national attention again in 1906, during the war with El Salvador. On this occasion, two indigenous Momostecan regiments led by Teodoro Cifuentes, the famous ladino military hero from Momostenango (fig. 2), were placed in the front lines and became the decisive force in winning the war.[17] According to oral narratives, these men were able to win because they were accompanied by both the patron saint, Santiago, who flew over their heads on his horse with his sword raised to urge them onward, and priest-shamans who performed indigenous rituals, before and during the battle, to protect the soldiers against bullets and thus render them victorious. As a result of the victory, the Momostecans were received as national heroes in Guatemala City and were further honored by being selected as the elite guard for President Estrada Cabrera.[18] Some five hundred Momostecan soldiers served in this capacity at La Palma, the presidential residence in Guatemala City, successfully defending Cabrera during many attempted coups until he finally fell in 1920. They later served President Ubico (in office from 1931 to 1944) in the same capacity. During these duties in

Guatemala City, Momostecan soldiers were given permission to construct outdoor pottery and stone shrines on the grounds of La Palma, where they conducted indigenous religious rituals, burning great mounds of copal incense and sacrificing chickens on appropriate days of the Prehispanic calendar.

Ethnography

The conduct of rituals in accordance with the Prehispanic calendar, carried out on a generous scale and without any effort at secrecy, has long been an identifying characteristic of Momostecan culture. The very name Momostenango, "town of altars," calls attention to the most distinctive characteristic of the municipality— the extraordinarily large number of outdoor shrines still in use by thousands of adherents of the indigenous religion (fig. 3). But because the indigenous men of Momostenango wear "Western" clothes and (in many cases) speak enough Spanish to do business with ladinos, while the majority of the women (although still mostly monolingual) have stopped wearing their traditional blouse (huipil), the municipality would be classified by Richard N. Adams as "modified" rather than "traditional."[19] Yet such markers as the celebration of 8 Batz', the political and religious importance of the local priest-shamans, and the existence of approximately three hundred land-holding patrilineages make Momostenango much more traditional than many other Guatemalan communities whose inhabitants wear their distinctive costumes (traje típico) but do not practice such elaborate ritual.

According to the census of 1973, the population of Momostenango consisted of 43,245 persons; of these, fewer than 2 percent were ladinos.[20] For administrative purposes, the municipality is divided into the four wards of the town center—Santa Ana, Patzité, Santa Catarina, and Santa Isabel—with a total population of 5,298. The municipality also includes fourteen rural cantons—Tunayac, Santa Ana, Los Cipréses, Tierra Colorada, Xequemeyá, Canquixajá, Patulup, Pitzal, Tzanjón, Tierra Blanca, Xolajab, Chicorral, Buenabaj, and Pasajoc—with a population of 37,947 (fig. 4 and map 2).

The settlement pattern consists largely of dispersed hamlets; the urbanized area at the center is even smaller than the population

3. The earth shrine in the main plaza of Momostenango.

4. A rural area of Momostenango in the canton of Los Cipréses.

figure would indicate since even the wards include rural hamlets. The hamlet is the smallest social group that identifies an indigenous person's geographic origin. Each hamlet has a topographic name; since in many cases its lands belong to a single clan, it may also carry the name of that clan. The remotest hamlets are an eight-hour walk from the town center. In 1937, Momostenango was classified as a particular type of municipality with a "vacant" center, meaning that its center consisted of a church, courthouse, and marketplace, with homes owned by indigenes but occupied only on market days, during religious celebrations, or during a term of political office; at other times, the indigenes lived and worked at their country homes.[21] Today, however, Momostenango has enough indigenes living permanently in the town center to be classified as intermediate between the vacant center type, in which almost no one lives permanently in the center, and a "nucleus" type of municipality, in which most of the population lives in the center (fig.5).

Even with this demographic shift toward a more nucleated community, the clan (alaxic, "to be born") and lineage (xe'al, "root," or alaxic, "to be born") are still the fundamental social units.[22] The clan structure is patrilineal, with both males and females affiliated to and receiving their surname from their father's clan at birth. There is a strong prohibition against marrying anyone from one's own or one's mother's patriclan, even where the exact genealogical connections are not known. Most clans retain the knowledge of the name of a founding ancestor; otherwise, the only individual names that are retained are those of the members of one's own immediate lineage. Generally, genealogical connections between the various lineages and the founding ancestor of the larger clan are incompletely known, especially when clan membership numbers in the thousands and the lineages are dispersed in two or more cantons. The symbolic importance of the clan is underscored in ritual obligations, scheduled according to the 260-day calendar, that bring together people of the same clan at the same altar in the public shrines of the town center. But in terms of daily interaction and the local round of traditional indigenous religious rituals, the lineage is more important than the clan.

With an area of nearly three hundred square kilometers, Momostenango has a population density of approximately one hundred forty persons per square kilometer. Although the cool, humid highland areas of Mesoamerica have supported a relatively dense pop-

5. The urbanized center of Momostenango.

ulation since Classic times (between eight and sixteen persons per square kilometer), the present population of Momostenango is so much higher that only about one-fourth of the necessary food can be grown within the community. As a result, Momostecans have migrated over the years to other areas of the country in search of farm land. One of the earliest migrations was the one to El Palmar, where coffee and two crops of corn can be grown in a single year. Also, there have long been Momostecan enclaves in Chajul, Nebaj, and San Pedro Jocopilas. Most recently, nearly three hundred Momostecan families migrated into the Ixcán Grande area of Hue-huetenango. All of these areas are lower in altitude and thus afford a longer agricultural season. Momostenango lies from one to three thousand meters above sea level; this great variation in altitude means that such diverse crops as wheat, potatoes, corn, beans, squash, *huisquil*, chile, apples, pears, peaches, plums, avocados, lemons, limes, and oranges can all be grown within the municipality. However, most of the agricultural land is above twenty-three hundred meters where only one annual harvest is possible.[23] The indigenous farmers (*ajchaquib*), by combining milpa agriculture with the raising of cash crops and wage labor, are able to provide a minimal living for their families.

Milpa agriculture involves preparatory burning of fields followed by digging up the earth with large-bladed hoes; planting maize and beans together in groups, with squashes added between rows; and piling up earth around the roots as the plants grow. This is the typical mode of cultivation not only in Momostenango but throughout the Guatemalan highlands. The combination of these plants in the same field helps prevent erosion and guarantees some harvest, no matter what the rainfall pattern.

In milpa agriculture as practiced in Momostenango, men's and women's roles are separate but interdependent. The men do the burning, hoeing, and planting of the seeds. The women cover the seeds with compost made from leaves and from the manure of the pigs that they raise. As the plants grow, the women spend much of their time cultivating, piling up the dirt around the roots, and cleaning the field of unwanted weeds. In the weeding, they are extremely careful to leave useful wild plants, for some are edible greens and others provide dyes and dye fixatives for wool. Still others bear large burrs that are bound together to make carding combs. At harvest time, the men go into the fields and do the bulk of the work. On the other hand, cash-crop agriculture, such as growing wheat (which often depends on plows and horses), is an exclusively male occupation.

Many farmers must do seasonal work on the ladino-owned plantations (*fincas*) on the Pacific Coast in order to meet the subsistence needs of their families. A slightly better living is enjoyed by families who combine milpa agriculture and raising pigs and chickens with one of the other traditional indigenous occupations—spinning, weaving, or merchandizing. Spinning, which also involves dyeing and carding, is primarily a female occupation in this community; weaving, especially of woolen blankets, is primarily male. There are three main types of weavers—blanket weaver (*ajquemal c'ul*), napkin or handkerchief weaver (*ajquemal su't*), and blouse weaver (*ajquemal po't*). Of the more than four thousand weavers in Momostenango, only about thirty men and women make the *su't*, a square of cotton cloth worn by women on their heads or as a cape, or the *po't*, the traditional red and yellow striped blouse (*huipil*) that all the women of the community once wore (fig. 6).

The great majority of the weavers specialize in making woolen blankets on large foot-looms (fig. 7). Momostenango is the center of foot-loom weaving in all of Central America, and its current reputation as a relatively wealthy indigenous community is directly related to the weaving industry. As early as 1770, Momostenango was reported to be a municipality of "rich Indians" who made, wore, and sold woolens.[24] The emphasis on weaving in this region arose from several environmental and demographic factors. These include the lack of total self-support from agriculture (resulting from overpopulation and the extremely leached soils and eroded surfaces) and the environmental advantage of dozens of hot springs (necessary to the felting process in blanket production). The process, which consists of soaking a blanket in hot water, treading it, slapping it on a rock, and wringing it, is generally performed by two adult men. The wool is grown in the nearby municipality of Santa María Chiquimula and in the county of Huehuetenango; it is brought in bulk form into the town center and sold to spinners and weavers on market days (Wednesday and Sunday; fig. 8). As the occupation of spinner is almost exclusively female and that of weaver almost exclusively male, these two occupations are part of a mutually dependent subsistence economy. The blanket, depend-

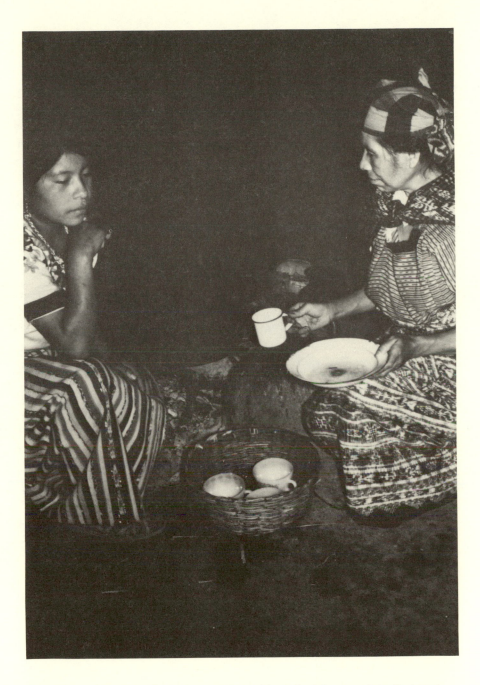

6. A Momostecan wife (in the traditional *huipil* of the municipality) and her teenage daughter (in a stylish embroidered *huipil)* kneeling before the cooking fire.

7. Foot-loom blanket weaving.

ing on quality and market conditions, sells for anywhere between eight and thirty-five *quetzals* (dollars) to wholesalers and occasional tourists on the streets of the town center each market day. Since a mother, father, and one son or daughter, all working part-time, can produce three blankets a week, families who weave can afford to buy what food they themselves are not producing, as well as luxury items such as radios and watches.

Merchants *(ajc'ay)* travel to markets in other rural communities and to the two main cities in the nation (Guatemala City and Quezaltenango), selling as much clothing, blankets, unprocessed foods, livestock, and cheap manufactured items as they can carry by means of the tumpline and can manage on the bus. There are a few women merchants, but they tend not to travel as far as the men nor to carry as valuable a load.

Outside these indigenous occupations, there exists a small group of individuals, primarily male, who engage in what were once purely ladino occupations: carpentry, tailoring, butchery, and baking. An even smaller number of indigenes has amassed enough capital to own and run trucks and a bus line, or to buy and sell clothes and blankets in large quantity throughout Central America. One Momostecan carries blankets as far north as Chicago; another owns a store in Costa Rica, where he and his family spend half the year; and several own small stores locally, in Quezaltenango, or in Guatemala City. These Momostecans have emerged as a new indigenous elite; through a series of alliances with more traditional farming and weaving families, they have begun to dominate the governing of the municipality.

There are five major corporate groups that conduct the political and much of the religious life of Momostenango. These groups include the the Municipal Corporation, the Auxiliary Organization, the elders, the hierarchy of priest-shamans, and the religious confraternities. The Municipal Corporation is the primary decision-making body prescribed by Guatemalan law. The chief administrator of this body is the mayor *(alcalde)*; below him are two city managers *(síndicos)* and four aldermen *(regidores)*. With the exception of one of the two city managers and the third and fourth aldermen, these paid officials are elected by the local population every four years.

The mayor acts as the chief administrator and judge of the town. Since the mid-1950s, this post has been held by an indige-

8. The Wednesday vegetable market in Momostenango.

nous person, except for brief periods during the 1960s when ladinos were appointed to the post by military governments. Below the mayor are two ranked city managers called first city manager *(síndico primero)* and second city manager *(síndico segundo)*. The first city manager, usually a ladino, is the legal representative of the community before various national agencies such as the INFOM (Agency for Municipal Development) and the Hacienda (Treasury). He is also responsible for national, urban, and rural matters such as road building and upkeep, tourism, education, and modern agricultural practices. The second city manager, who is always an indigene, takes part in some of these same affairs. He is also the head of the Auxiliary Organization. Next come the four aldermen, who are concerned with the budget, urbanization, education, public health, tourism, farming, and road repair. The first alderman, who, like the mayor, has been indigenous since the 1950s, is the person who acts as the mayor when the latter is unavailable. Thus, although he has less apparent authority than the city managers, he is potentially quite powerful. There are several other important positions, including a treasurer, police chief, military commissioner, and market administrator.

The second group of officials, the Auxiliary Organization *(auxiliatura)*, unlike the first is neither paid (with the exception of its secretary) nor officially recognized by the Guatemalan national government. These officials constitute the traditional civil hierarchy of the municipality, which in both its internal organization and many of its functions duplicates the Municipal Corporation. Most legal disputes and administrative processes that directly affect the indigenous majority of the community pass through this organization. Its highest office is that of mayor, also referred to by indigenes (in Spanish) as *timón* ("plow shaft") or (in Quiché) as *ilol katinimit* ("seer of our town"). The holder of this office is simultaneously second city manager in the Municipal Corporation. Below him are two assistants *(rach'il)*, eighteen auxiliary mayors *(alcaldes auxiliares)*—one for each of the four wards of the town center plus one for each of the fourteen cantons—and two drummers *(ajk'ojom)*, who serve as town criers. The two assistants are simultaneously the third and fourth aldermen of the Municipal Corporation. Unlike the first and second aldermen, who can substitute for the mayor of the Municipal Corporation, these men cannot substitute for the mayor of the Auxiliary Organization. Instead, the sacred authority of this office passes to one of the four auxiliary mayors from the wards of the town center. On the bottom level are twenty police-men and messengers (*ajch'amiy*, "those of the staff"). These are young men who are doing their first public service for the commu-nity, while the auxiliary mayors, assistants, and drummers are middle-level positions filled by middle-aged men who have already served either as local policemen or else as soldiers in the Guate-malan military.

The office of mayor, the plow shaft (*timón*) or seer (*ilol*) in this organization, is a crucially important one for the entire indigenous community. The man selected for it has already served in a middle-level position with the Auxiliary Organization, is an elder in the community, is nearly always at least a middle-level member of the hierarchy of priest-shamans, and has often served as an officer in the Guatemalan military. His duties include mediating between local customary law and national law, burning copal incense at outdoor altars, and collecting money and making the arrangements for community-wide celebrations. This overlapping of modern and ancient civil and religious duties is typical of the offices in the Auxiliary Organization. The drummers, for example, who make important announcements from hilltops surrounding the munici-pality as well as from the local radio station, combine these duties with visits to the most important water sources of the town, where they burn copal incense and petition the Day Lords of the Prehis-panic Quiché calendar to send rain.

A third corporate group in Momostenango, the elders (*ajaw-ab*), consists of approximately two hundred fifty men who choose the officials of the Auxiliary Organization. As the most respected members of the indigenous community, they are bowed to and addressed as father (*tat*) by men who are not elders, as well as by all women and children. Although there is no formal ranking of elders, certain of them, who because of leadership qualities influ-ence the group more than others, are known as road guides (*c'amal be*). Becoming an elder, which is a lifetime commission rather than a temporary office in Momostenango, depends on a complex of ascribed as well as achieved characteristics. The ascribed character-istics are advanced age, male sex, and position in a high-ranking family—that is, the patrilineage in question must either be wealthy or number many civil, military, or religious leaders among its members. The achieved characteristics include the fulfillment of the series of statuses within the hierarchy of the Auxiliary Organization previously discussed.[25] Besides selecting the officials in the Auxiliary Organization, the elders meet four times annually to arrange community-wide religious rituals and whenever else they may be needed to resolve any political or religious crises. Their decisions are consensus decisions, arrived at (except in their selection of civil officials) with the help of a process of divination involving the 260-day sacred calendar.

A fourth corporate group consists of a hierarchy of priest-shamans known as "mother-fathers" (*chuchkajawib*); with approximately three hundred initiated male members, they are chosen by calendrical divination and serve for life. At the top of the hierarchy are two "mother-fathers of the town" (*chuchkajawib rech tinimit*). When a vacancy arises (through a death), the successor is chosen through calendrical divination performed by the second level of this hierarchy, the canton priest-shamans (*chuchkajawib rech canton*). Membership in this group, with one position for each canton, is also determined through calendrical divination, this time performed by the third level of the hierarchy, the patrilineage priest-shamans (*chuchkajawib rech alaxic*), one for each of the approximately three hundred patrilineages in the community. A patrilineage priest-shaman is chosen (again through divination) by a small group of three to six priest-shamans from neighboring patrilineages. When a patrilineage priest-shaman moves up to the canton or town level, he retains his duties at the lower levels.

The two town priest-shamans are responsible for rituals that affect the health and economic prosperity of the entire community. They greet the Mam ("Year-bearer") of the indigenous 365-day solar calendar every year and pass the silver-tipped staff of office of each ranked official of the Auxiliary Organization through the giant bonfire they light each New Year's Day (which currently falls on March 1). In addition, each of the town priest-shamans makes a pilgrimage into the mountains on special days of the 260-day calendar.

The fourteen canton priest-shamans, like the two town priest-shamans, greet the Mam each year, but they do this at lower, closer-in hilltops than the town priest-shamans. On occasion, one or more of them may accompany a town priest-shaman on his ritual pilgrimages and thus help preserve the knowledge of the proper ritual and cycle of visits. They themselves make similar pilgrimages into the nearby hills.

The nearly three hundred patrilineage priest-shamans serve as the headmen and priests of their individual lineages. Their specific duties include settling marriage and land disputes, training and initiating the *ajk'ij* ("daykeepers," a group of approximately ten thousand men and women who practice the indigenous religion), curing, introducing infants to the world, marrying, performing burial and commemorative ceremonies for the dead, and carrying out local planting and harvesting rituals according to the 260-day calendar.

The fifth major corporate group in Momostenango consists of twenty Catholic confraternities *(cofradías)*, which are known in Quiché as the "thirteen groups" *(oxlajuj ch'ob)*.[26] They include, in approximate order of importance, Corpus Christi (also called "Señor de Resurrección"), Santiago (the patron saint), María Concepción, San Antonio Xepom, Santa Cruz (includes Santo Entierro), Capetado, San José, Virgen de Dolores, San Francisco de Asís, Galuna, Santa Ana, Santa Bárbara (includes San Simón), San Luís Gonzaya, San Miguel Arcángel, Jesús Nazareno (also called Jesús de Merced), San Nicolás Tolentino, San Antonio Pologuá, Virgen de Rosario, Virgen de Guadalupe, and Corazón de Jesús. The offices in the individual confraternities include three male and two female levels: for the males there are the mayor *(alcalde)*, deputy *(teputado)*, and steward *(mayordomo* or *mortoma)*; for the females there are the woman leader *(chuchaxel)* and the girl leader *(alaxel)*. The exception is the confraternity for San Miguel Arcángel, which has no female offices.

The overall leadership of the religious confraternities consists of the mayors of the three most important groups: Corpus Christi, Santiago, and María Concepción. These mayors handle all confraternity recruitment as well as the organization and coordination of the annual saints' birthdays, Holy Week, and All Saints Day. In this community, unlike other indigenous Guatemalan communities described by anthropologists, the elders do not appoint people to confraternity positions, nor do men who are ascending the achievement ladder toward eldership generally serve in confraternities. In fact, there is so little competition for these positions that it does not take many years for an interested man to become mayor in one of the three main confraternities, and, once he does so, he may remain in that position for many years. There is also a tendency for certain of the confraternities to be localized within the rural cantons—for example, Jesús Nazareno and Santa Cruz are maintained solely in Xequemeyá; San Nicolás Tolentino and San José are in Tunayac; and Dolores, Corazón de Jesús, San Miguel Arcángel, and San Luís Gonzaya are in Santa Ana. The list of office holders in these confraternities is quite stable, with little rotation of personnel.

As elsewhere in Mesoamerica, one may speak of a "civil-religious hierarchy" in Momostenango. However, the bridge between religious and governmental duties is provided not by the confraternities[27] but by the hierarchy of priest-shamans. In fact, men who are actively working toward the respected position of elder in the community tend to avoid the confraternities altogether and instead undergo training and initiation as priest-shamans. When asked about the importance of the confraternities, one elder said he had never had time for them, given all his duties as a lineage priest-shaman and political office holder (he served one year as auxiliary mayor for the ward of Santa Isabel and four years as both second city manager in the Municipal Corporation and mayor in the Auxiliary Organization). He then explained the relationship between eldership and the hierarchy of priest-shamans in this way:

> Here there are about two hundred and fifty elders. He who comes out of being auxiliary mayor is now an elder. I am an elder by the service I did. Now, in the matter of the customs there are no "elders." No, these are priest-shamans—but I think they are the same thing that elders are [laughs]. Yes, the majority of elders are priest-shamans.

The customs (costumbres) to which he is referring consist of a large complex of community-wide rituals performed in accordance with the Prehispanic Quiché calendars, together with other rituals that follow the Gregorian calendar. These two types of ritual, however, do not constitute a simple dualistic opposition between Pre-Conquest and Post-Conquest ritual, or between paganism and Christianity. Rather, there are always "Catholic" elements in pagan ritual, and "pagan" elements in Catholic ritual. For example, although the famous 8 Batz' celebration takes place largely at outdoor shrines and hearths, it includes a visit to the parish church. Conversely, the image of San Antonio Pologuá is removed from the

church each year on August 14–24 and taken to twenty-two different earth shrines where copal is burned in its honor (fig. 9). The
various confraternities wash the clothing and change the flowers of
their respective saints according to the Prehispanic 260-day Quiché
calendar, while many priest-shamans preface their divinations with
the Lord's Prayer. The term "syncretism" has been used throughout
the anthropological literature on Mesoamerica to label such combinations of Prehispanic and Posthispanic elements.

Besides the largely indigenously controlled corporate groups
in Momostenango, there exist several associations controlled by
ladinos, including the local school system, medical clinic, five Protestant churches, and the lay Bible study groups organized by Catholic Action. The school system, consisting of twenty-one schools
and one stenographic academy, is combined with the systems of
three neighboring municipalities to make up one district under the
Ministerio de Educación Pública de Guatemala. The teachers are
nearly all ladino monolinguals (Spanish speakers), and the entering
students are nearly all indigenous monolinguals (Quiché speakers).
As the community leaders have pointed out repeatedly in official
reports, very few indigenous pupils become literate, even when
they attend the local schools for the full six compulsory years. As a
result of the poor quality of education offered and considerable
pride in Quiché culture (a heritage that is ignored in the curricu-
lum), only 2,147 students (less than one-fifth of the school-age
population) were enrolled in the local schools as of 1969.[28] Instead,
it is the two years of obligatory military service (beginning at the
age of eighteen) that provides Momostecan boys the main opportunity to become literate. Girls, on the other hand, rarely learn to
read and write. The stenographic academy teaches typing and other
office skills to forty pupils per year, but these are primarily ladinos.

The medical clinic has a monolingual ladino doctor and ladino
nurses, but it serves primarily indigenous patients. There is also a
group of indigenous paramedics loosely connected to the clinic;
they bring the ability to administer penicillin shots, as well as a few
other simple skills, to the people in the rural cantons. But since
most are not initiated Quiché curers and thus lack the requisite
power and authority to heal, they are ignored by a large proportion
of the rural population. Several indigenous midwives have received
training in Western procedures for child delivery in a hospital in
Huehuetenango, but once again, because they are rarely initiated

9. A shrine dedicated to San Antonio Pologuá, on a hill above the Momostecan hamlet of that name. The man in the kilt is a pilgrim from Nahualá.

curers they have few patients. It is the initiated indigenous Quiché midwives *(iyom)* who deliver most of the babies.

There are five local Protestant missions—Seventh Day Adventist, Primitive Methodist, Pentecostal, Jehovah's Witness, and Mormon—but they have had few converts and little impact on the religious beliefs or practices of the community. The Seventh Day Adventists are the most successful both in terms of their number of converts (approximately one hundred fifty) and in their medical outreach program. One of the two ladino pharmacists in the community is a Seventh Day Adventist who has succeeded in helping hundreds of indigenous Momostecans by diagnosing illnesses and prescribing medicines.

Recent Changes

Unlike the schools, medical clinic, and Protestant sects, the Catholic Action (Acción Católica) movement has had a major impact on the indigenous population of Momostenango. This new brand of international Roman Catholicism, aimed at underdeveloped nations with anticlerical laws, entered Guatemala in 1945. In its Guatemalan form, it promulgated a doctrine emphasizing belief in one all-powerful God, playing down the importance of the saints, and making a frontal attack on all indigenous customs that involve the veneration of natural objects or are scheduled according to the Prehispanic calendar. The movement was overtly aimed at separating "true" Catholics from the practitioners of rites with "pagan" elements. There is ample evidence that its short-term effect in many parishes was to weaken the traditional civil-religious hierarchy and to seriously factionalize the community.[29]

In Momostenango, Catholic Action was introduced by a ladino priest in 1946. The main inducements for conversion were and still are agricultural and health benefits consisting mainly of free insecticide, fertilizer, and medicines for the members, who are known as *catequistas*. The requirements for conversion, as defined by the local priest, include avoidance of participation in the "idolatry" and ritual drunkenness of the local confraternities, marriage in the church, attendance at weekly catechism classes and mass, and the surrender (to the priest) of all calendrical divining equipment, together with the contents of the *mebil*, a traditional household shrine that consists mainly of archaeological relics. At the high point of this movement, during the mid-1950s, nearly one-fifth of the indigenous community had converted from traditional Catholicism to this new orthodoxy. Then, in 1954, when the priest felt confident that he had converted enough "pagans," he dared to lock the doors of the church on 8 Batz', the initiation day for new diviners or daykeepers *(ajk'ij)*. As a result, hundreds of patrilineage priest-shamans and their initiates could not enter the church in order to visit Santiago, San Antonio Pologuá, and the Momostecan ancestors who are buried beneath the floor. That night the priest-shamans convened the elders, who decided to send a delegation to the church to confront the priest. The delegation, consisting primarily of patrilineage heads, informed the priest that he must leave Momostenango or be killed. He fled.

Soon thereafter, Momostenango was sent the current priest, who, in the eyes of the elders, is just as bad as the previous one. One of the major complaints they have is that his catechism classes and prayer meetings keep teenagers out late in the evening, setting up courting situations that undermine the traditional system of arranged marriages between the men and women of neighboring patrilineages. As members of the hierarchy of priest-shamans, the elders also openly disagree with the parish priest and his converts on religious doctrine. As the result of numerous confrontations with Catholic Action converts armed with arguments memorized from catechisms, the priest-shamans and their followers have developed an orally transmitted counter-catechism of their own. In place of the standard trinity of Catholic doctrine, consisting of Father, Son, and the Holy Ghost, they argue for a trinity on a much larger conceptual scale, consisting of Tiox (Dios), the Mundo, and Nantat. In this alternative trinity, "Dios" refers to the entire Christian pantheon of *dioses*, including God, Jesus, ghosts, angels, saints, and virgins—together with their physical images in the local parish church and cemetery chapel. "Mundo" refers to the earthly world as a whole, for which reason the Mundo is sometimes addressed as *pachulum Mundo* ("round World"); the plural form, *mundos*, covers the plurality of mountains and volcanoes of the world, in both their physical and spiritual aspects, together with the main altar in the parish church and the grounds of the cemetery. "Nantat" encompasses the ancestors in general, both as *uxlab* ("breath" or "spirit") and as *much'ulic bak, much'ulic ulew, much'ulic poklaj* ("powdered bone, powdered clay, powdered sand") referring to their physical remains.

Given this alternative trinity, in which a mixture of spiritual and material qualities may be found in all three parts, the elders particularly oppose the Catholic priest's violent separation of God, as a purely spiritual entity and the ultimate source of all good, from the material world, a doctrine that leads, as they point out, to the confusion of the very earth itself with the devil. In their view, persons, gods, saints, their own ancestors, and the earth all possess mixtures of positive and negative qualities. For example, San Antonio Pologuá is a great curer of illness as well as a great causer of illness, and priest-shamans can cure disease because they know how to inflict it. This profoundly *dialectical* view of man, nature, and religion, in which dualities complement rather than clash with one another, is different in its very logic from the *analytical* view of the priest, who teaches the *catequistas* that they must finally choose between becoming truly Christian, which is synonymous with all goodness and purity, and leaving themselves in the company of the priest-shamans, who are nothing but evil witches.

The majority of the wealthier indigenous weaving and merchant families of Momostenango have resisted conversion to the new Catholicism, meanwhile consolidating their control over the civil offices in the municipality. A group of them, nearly all elders, recently founded a religious organization that stands outside both Catholic Action and the traditional confraternities, while at the same time reaffirming the importance of saints and of Momostecan cultural identity. It is a brotherhood (*hermandad*), modeled after the ladino brotherhoods of Momostenango and Quezaltenango and devoted to providing band music for the patron saint of Momostenango during his annual feast days.

During the patron saint's feast in 1976, antagonism between the new orthodoxy and the traditional Catholicism of the confraternities came to a head. On July 24, when the religious leadership of the confraternity of the patron saint of Momostenango took the image of Santiago from the church, the deputy (the second most important official in this confraternity) was drunk. That night, he washed the face of the image with hot water and, as a result, some eyelashes fell out. The next day, everyone saw the unhappy result; it was considered a serious moral breach, and the man was jailed. Citing his misconduct, the *catequistas* argued that since they themselves abstain from alcohol as part of their religious duties, they should be allowed to staff the patron saint's confraternity rather than traditional Catholics.[30] After some debate, the elders decided to retain traditional Catholics in the first and third positions in the confraternity but to admit *catequistas* in the second and fourth positions.

The elders feel the new arrangement will work out well, given that both sides agreed which group should fill each position. Since the customs of the priest-shamans are older than those of the Roman Catholic Church, the first *alcalde* in the confraternity should always be a priest-shaman. He, as in the past, will be responsible for carrying out these ancient rituals at outdoor earth shrines on the proper days in the Quiché calendar. During the fiesta, the first and third-ranking members of the confraternity will abstain from sex and give the saint and themselves the proper *traguitos* of liquor, while the two Catholic Action members will be trusted to abstain from alcohol and look out for the image so that no errors will be made because of drunkenness. Catholic Action members are pleased because now they can participate in part of the ancient customs of their native town without being totally under the religious authority of the hierarchy of priest-shamans.

The ideological course of these events can be understood on the same general pattern as the events that led to the formulation of an alternative catechism. The Catholic Action converts made an argument of the analytical kind, demanding that they simply replace the traditional Catholics in the confraternity. The elders met this argument with a dialectical solution, not only interlacing converts and traditionalists in the confraternity's four leadership posts, but pointing out a useful complementarity of ritual abstinences in the Catholic Action avoidance of alcohol and the traditional avoidance of sexual relations. In effect, the dualism between converts and traditionalists shifted from an external opposition between institutions to an internal complementarity within a single institution. Similarly, in the development of the alternative catechism, the good/evil and spiritual/material dualisms were shifted from an external opposition between Christianity and witchcraft or between God and the Devil to an internal complementarity within a religion and a pantheon that encompass the Christian divinities rather than opposing them.

In these recent events, we see an ideological process that must have been repeated many times over the last four centuries in Mesoamerica, with fresh onslaughts of European analytical or oppositional dualism followed by reassertions of Mesoamerican dialectical or complementary dualism. What has commonly been called "syncretism" in Mesoamerica, which is the supposedly unconscious combination of "native" and "European" cultural elements,[31] probably comes about through events much like these, whose results present just such combinations. The exact sources of a particular combination may perhaps become "unconscious"—or better, unknown—with the passage of time, but the creation of a combination has probably always been an intentional process, as it was here.

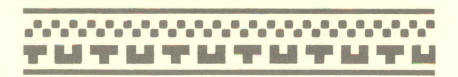

3.

Shamanic Priests

and Priestly Shamans

In Momostenango, the Quiché term *ajk'ij* ("day [sun or time] keeper") is used to refer to the large group of active practitioners of the indigenous religion who are initiated calendar diviners, dream interpreters, and curers. Above them are approximately three hundred heads of the local patrilineages who form the triple-tiered hierarchy of "mother-fathers" *(chuchkajawib)* discussed in the previous chapter. All members of this hierarchy were originally initiated as daykeepers and only later acquired their commissions at the lineage, canton, and town levels. Calendrical divination remains central to the ritual activities of all daykeepers, even when they are also mother-fathers. Furthermore, all daykeepers are empowered to make prayers to the gods and the ancestors on behalf of lay people, even when they are not mother-fathers. If one adopted the analytical method cultural anthropologists use for separating shamans from priests, in which the priest serves as an intermediary between man and the gods while the shaman directly possesses (or is possessed by) supernatural powers in the realm of divination and curing, one would have to refer to all Momostecan daykeepers and mother-fathers as both priests and shamans.[1]

Similar problems abound in the anthropological literature on Mesoamerica. For example, in Santa Eulalia, a Kanhobal Mayan community in the northwestern highlands of Guatemala, one of the ritual specialists called "prayermaker" is appointed for life by the elders to a position called "giver of the road" *(aqon be kalap)* or "in the seat" *(yul cila'),* in which he represents the entire community before the gods. But he is also a diviner: when he must choose other prayermakers (except for him, they serve only for a year), he does so by divination. When these other prayermakers are making their ceremonial rounds, he remains in a house where he both prays for them (in which he is priestly) and divines whether their activities will have the desired effect (in which he is shamanic).[2] In the Mam village of Santiago Chimaltenango (also Mayan), there is a *chimán del pueblo*, appointed for life, with priestly duties much like those of the Santa Eulalia "giver of the road," or the top level of the Momostecan hierarchy. But above all, it is his shamanic ability to look into the future through divination that sets this *chimán* apart from the laity and makes them dependent on him in religious affairs.[3]

One way out of the dilemma posed by the cultural anthropologist's analytical distinction between priest and shaman is to narrow the definition of the latter and thus reduce the scope of the problem. It is common practice among Mesoamericanists to use the Siberian word "shaman" to refer to religious specialists whose skills include divination, but William Madsen questioned the use of this term in his review of the ethnographic evidence for Mesoamerican shamanism.[4] Following Mircea Eliade's Siberian model, he defined the shaman as "an individual who has received power to cure and divine direct from supernatural beings through dreams, visions, or spirit possession."[5] This leaves him within the camp of cultural anthropology, but now the argument rests not on analytical grounds but on the historical authority of Siberian shamanism, which is implicitly "prior" to Mesoamerican shamanism; precision is added to the category "shaman" not by sharpening up its relationship with other categories but by increasing the list of traits needed for membership in the category. In this way, Madsen was able to find that the Valley of Mexico was the only area in all of Mesoamerica where so-called shamans were truly shamans. His detailed example of true shamanism was drawn from his own fieldwork in the Na-huatl-speaking pueblo of San Francisco Tecospa. There he found the following traits characteristic of classical Siberian shamanism: divine election, marriage to a spirit wife, curing and divining with the aid of supernatural beings, punishment by supernatural helpers for disobedience, and the ability to enter the other world.

In reviewing the ethnographic materials from other Mesoam-erican communities, Madsen found the majority of the requisite traits lacking. If he were right, this would represent an historical change, given that Peter T. Furst found a strong thread of shaman-ism running through the Precolumbian religions of Mesoamerica.[6] But, in fact, there is ethnographic evidence from Mayan communities in both Guatemala and Mexico for a number of the shamanic traits Madsen found in his Nahuatl community. For example, marriage to a spirit wife is found in the Mam village of Todos Santos. According to Maud Oakes, the novice *chimán* sits in a "corral" inside a darkened room, praying until he is or is not successful at becoming possessed by a "spirit wife." From this time on, if he is successful, he can sit in this corral and become possessed by this spirit wife at will, divining the future (in a high-pitched feminine voice) for anyone who attends the ceremony.[7] Among the Yucatec Maya, Alfonso Villa Rojas found that in the town of X-cacal (in Quintana Roo), where shamans use the same crystals that he and

Robert Redfield had reported in Chan Kom, the crystal itself is referred to as "a wife."[8]

Chortí diviners of eastern Guatemala and Mam diviners of northwestern Guatemala have been described as receiving "information from a spirit who causes their leg to twitch in code-like response to questions."[9] Madsen did not classify this phenomenon as a shamanic gift of power direct from supernatural beings, but Charles Wisdom's description of a Chortí diviner questioning an intimate spirit in a darkened room reminds one of classic Siberian shamanic séances: "He begins . . . chewing tobacco and then rubbing the saliva on his right leg. Next, he questions the spirit *sahurín* who is in the calf of his right leg. The spirit answers by a twitch in this calf meaning 'yes' and no twitch meaning 'no.'"[10] The Kanhobal shamans of Santa Eulalia receive messages in dreams, through sensations in their hands and legs, and through sounds or voices in their ears which Oliver La Farge called "mediumistic" in character. He described one such shaman this way: "When he was going strong and particularly after a few drinks, Xux gave the impression of being a human radio set, attuned to an ether crackling with supernatural messages."[11]

These are merely examples; direct communication between spirits or gods and the diviner is hardly foreign to modern Mayan peoples. Further, an examination of the recruitment of Mayan diviners reveals the presence of all of the classic ways of becoming a shaman: through sickness, dreams, and ecstasies, as well as inheritance.[12] For example, Sister Blanche M. Leonard collected a first-person account from a Yucatec shaman (*h-men*) that is a classic narration of shamanic recruitment:

> When I was starting out I had a strange experience. Unknown to my father, I set out for the sacred hill and cenote, Tetzik. I fell asleep and had a long dream. Many spirits beat me and punished me. When I woke up I found the divining stone (a crystal) and a special stone, a sacred stone which the Lord of the Field left for me. When I returned home I was sick for nine days and could not speak. (Leonard 1964–65: Appendix)

Lois Paul and Benjamin D. Paul reported that in the Tzutuhil Maya community of San Pedro la Laguna (located in Guatemala on

Lake Atitlán), divine election, whether for a shaman or a midwife, involves the wandering of the future practitioner's spirit into the realm of the supernatural—what Eliade referred to as the "ecstatic journey."[13] In addition, they found that both shamans and midwives typically experience a severe and intractable illness during which spirits visit them, demanding that they become curers and offering to teach them. Later, a practicing shaman divines that the dreamer was destined from birth to be a curer with supernatural connections, and warns him or her to begin practice or else perish.

Among the Tzotzil Mayans of Zinacantán, seers (h'iloletik) obtain ritual power through dreaming or hallucinatory experience, for which reason Evon Z. Vogt felt that they should be classified as shamans.[14] A Zinacanteco who will become a shaman has three dreams that begin when he or she is ten to twelve years old. The soul of the dreamer is summoned by the supernatural counterpart of the ranking cargo holder of the Zinacantán civil-religious hierarchy. He, in turn, declares that the dreamer must become a seer and cure people, and that refusal will mean death.[15] Note that in this case, the principal actor in what is clearly a shamanic dream is a distinctly priestly character.

In San Pedro Chenalho, another Tzotzil community, a combination of dreaming and inheritance prevails. In Calixta Guiteras-Holmes's study of the world view of a particular seer from this community, we learn that his mother was also a seer, and that she wished him to replace her as a healer. He learned to pulse, pray, and prescribe herbs in his dreams: "I know everything by my dreams. I learned to listen to the pulse in my dreams. It was so that my mother learned also."[16] This combination of dreams with heredity fits well with Eliade's summary of the Siberian and Central Asian data, where hereditary shamanism exists side-by-side with a shamanism directly bestowed by the gods and spirits.[17]

Clearly, shamanism—defined in the strictest possible manner by Madsen as necessarily involving direct communication between spirits and the diviner through dreams, visions, or spirit possession—exists in many Mayan communities, and Momostenango will prove no exception (see the next section). Mayan diviners are shamanic in their recruitment, initiation, and practice. Recruitment is both by hereditary transmission of the shamanic profession and the spontaneous "call" or "divine election," just as it is in Asia. Even the narrow historicist definition of shamanism leaves untouched the problem of the combination of shamanic and priestly cultural traits in the same Mesoamerican practitioner. It remains to be seen whether a social anthropological approach to the problem might have a different outcome. In its simplest form, this approach makes an analytical distinction between service to the community, which is priestly, and service to individuals, which is shamanic.

An example of the social anthropological distinction between priest and shaman is provided by the work of Maud Oakes. She reported that the main calendar expert in the Mam village of Todos Santos, as the unofficial head of the community, sets the time of all religious rituals and gives the final word in all important civil and political matters, determining everything with his divining seeds. She referred to him both as "the calendar priest of the pueblo" and as a "shaman-priest," pointing out that his responsibilities are primarily to the community, while the other local "shamans" carry on a private practice; she thus followed a public/private or community/individual dichotomy of priest and shaman.[18] In Jacaltenango, a Jacaltec Mayan community, Oliver La Farge and Douglas Byers described the prayermakers, or "good men" (watc winaq), as the nearest local approach to a permanent and definite priesthood. These specialists serve the community as a whole, while the "born shamans," including curanderos, brujos, and "soothsayers," only serve the people as individuals. But it turns out that both the "good men" and "born shamans" include soothsayers, so that it is not divination that distinguishes the priest from the shaman but rather service to the community as opposed to service to individuals.[19]

Manning Nash adopted the same dichotomy between community and individual service, but instead of applying it within a single society (as previous ethnographers had done), he used it to distinguish between separate societies and ultimately between the northwestern and midwestern highlands of Guatemala, calling the calendar experts of the former area "priests" and those of the latter "shamans."[20] According to his scheme, the continuation of the ancient solar calendar, which he connects with community affairs, is diagnostic of the presence of priests in the northwestern area, while the fact that the midwestern area is limited to the 260-day divinatory calendar is diagnostic of the presence of shamans.[21] He is wrong in finding the solar calendar absent from the latter area (see chapter 4), but what is of greater concern here is his underlying Durkheimian assumption that divination, which is seen as a magical rather than a religious act, will be found in an individual (shamanic) context rather than in a social (priestly) one.[22] W. Lloyd Warner has long since shown the potential social nature of magic, as when the "church" (in Émile Durkheim's sense) of the shaman is the clan.[23] Nash did not raise the possibility that the midwestern highland calendar diviners, whom he felt were not integrated into the formal religious and civil organizations of their communities, might be clan or lineage priests.

If I were to follow Durkheim's priest/shaman analytical distinction, I would then categorize the Momostecan daykeeper as a shaman, since his duties are primarily to individuals, and the mother-father as a priest, since his duties are to his lineage. However, the daykeepers who are particularly gifted diviners are the pool from which new mother-fathers are selected after the death of a particular lineage head. Even when they never actually become mother-fathers, they are often referred to honorifically by that title, and as such they may even be called in to help solve a lineage problem, thus assuming a priestly title and role, if not a priestly status. For their part, lineage heads remain daykeepers even after they become mother-fathers; they serve in a private capacity when they divine and interpret dreams for individuals who are members of their own lineage, thus assuming a role appropriate to their continuing shamanic status.

Any attempt to separate priests from shamans in these communities according to a public/private, or religion/magic dichotomy fails, since the same practitioner could be called, in different contexts, either "priest" or "shaman." If a practitioner performs both shamanic and priestly roles, even though he does not have an institutionalized status with respect to a lineage, clan, or community, then it is misleading to simply designate him or her as a "shaman." In other words, among the Maya the technical terms "shaman" and "priest" are useful, when separated, only as *role* and not as *status* designations. When it comes to status, an interlaced concept of "priest-shaman" or "shaman-priest," depending on the degree and type of public and/or private duties rendered, makes more sense and does less violence to the ethnographic data. Since the ordinary daykeepers of Momostenango are more commonly involved in individual than community-wide rituals, they may be designated as "shaman-priests." On the other hand, mother-fathers, who have many lineage or community rituals to perform, may be designated "priest-shamans."

Recruitment of a Daykeeper

In Momostenango, a daykeeper, or shaman-priest, is recruited in classical shamanic fashion, with "divine election" through birth, illness, and dreams, followed by marriage to a spirit spouse at initiation. The precise day a person is born on the 260-day Quiché sacred calendar—referred to in Quiché as *rajilabal k'ij* ("the day count") or *ch'ol k'ij* ("ordering of days") and referred to in Spanish as *el calendario del Mundo* ("the calendar of the World")—helps to determine whether or not that person might become a daykeeper. If the day of birth *(ru k'ij alaxic)* is Ak'abal, No'j, Can, Came, Aj, E, Quej, K'anil, Ix, or Tz'iquin (see table 2 for a full list of days), then the child receives from the day a kind of soul, called "lightning" *(coyopa)*, that enables him or her to receive messages from the external world, both natural and supernatural, within his or her own body. Since this lightning moves about only in the blood, tissue, and muscles of the person and never leaves the body until death, it is what historians of religion would call a "body soul."

Most frequently, daykeepers describe the sensation of body lightning as feeling as if air were rapidly moving through their flesh in a flickering or undulating manner, similar to the pattern of exterior sheet lightning as it moves at night over the lakes. The lightning of the human body can move as much as once an hour, or sometimes more, throughout the lifetime of the individual, but it is only through training that the person can learn to interpret these movements as a message-bearing code. When diviners are discussing these messages in the Quiché language, they either say *casilob uquiqu'el* ("the blood moves") or *cacha' uquiqu'el* ("the blood speaks"). When speaking in Spanish, they say *brinca la sangre* ("the blood jumps").

A person who is destined to become a daykeeper has a series of dreams *(wachic')* that indicate that he or she must come before the Mundo, or earth deity. Often a prospective daykeeper dreams of being chased by deer, horses, cows, oxen, or bulls, any of which indicate that he or she must arrive to give presents at the shrines of the Mundo, which manifest in dreams as large animals. To dream of a lake below a mountain indicates that the Mundo is calling one to visit first the lake and then the mountaintop, which symbolize the paired public shrines: the low shrine, or "water place" (*uja'l*), and the high shrine, or "mountain place" (*ujuyubal*, fig. 10). To dream simply of a lake indicates that the blood is ready to give answers to a calendar diviner's questions, for as one man put it, "A lake is like a mirror, not moving until one's day comes, and then it begins to move with the lightning." Although a novice experiences blood lightning from early childhood, not until he or she is initiated can it be asked for the answers to questions. Another preinitiation dream involves encounters with the opposite sex. For example, if the divining seeds are destined for a young married man, he may suddenly begin dreaming of having sexual intercourse with a beautiful, dark woman, or he will see a woman (other than his own wife) pregnant with his child. Likewise, if the divining seeds are destined for a woman, she might dream of leaving her husband and marrying another man.

Lincoln reported that an Ixil divining priest who had studied in Momostenango interpreted the following dreams as a "call" to become a calendar diviner. A man who had horrible pains in his knees and legs, day after day, dreamt he was walking on the water of Lake Atitlán and fell in up to his knees. He also dreamt that a snake entered his left foot, went up through his leg, through his head, and down through his right leg and out again. As a result, he studied with the diviner and learned to pray; on the first day of study, all his pains and bad dreams left him.[24] An illness of this sort, with its accompanying dreams, is indeed considered a call to become a diviner in Momostenango. The illness (*yabil*) called "snake" (*cumatz*) is one of the six main illnesses a future daykeeper might experience.

In the snake illness, there are sudden and extremely painful cramps in one or more of the following areas of the body: arms, legs, torso, wrists, elbows, ankles, knees, and neck. The muscles are taut and knotted, while the joints act as if they were dislocated. The person cannot turn, move, or walk about easily. One former sufferer complained that it felt as though there were a pole crosswise through his trunk so that he could not turn his body, and his arm and leg joints hurt so badly he would not allow anyone in his

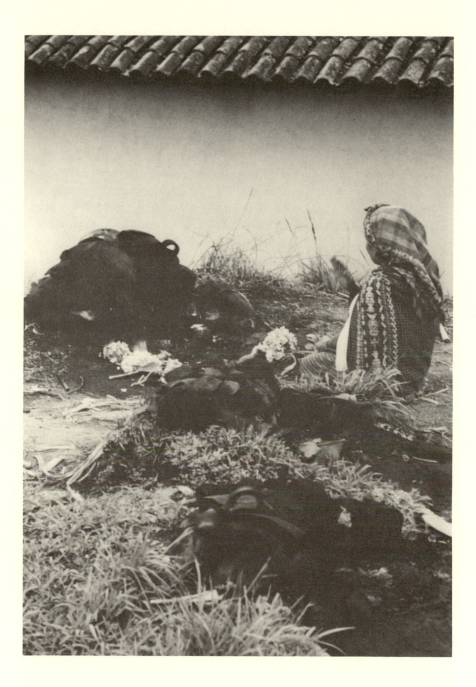

10. A daykeeper at Paclom, one of the mountain-place shrines.

family to touch them. Episodes of seizure by the snake illness are of relatively brief duration, lasting from a few minutes to a couple of days, but they are recurrent.

When a calendar diviner diagnoses snake illness and tells the patient that it is time to begin his or her apprenticeship as a diviner, the symptoms often leave instantly or else soon after training begins. After the diagnosis, the diviner may rub a wild marigold (*parutz'*) over the affected part, throwing it out of the house into the road "so that when another person comes along he will take the snake illness with him." Next, he prescribes that the entire plant be boiled and then rubbed over the affected part; this warms the muscles and relieves the pain. Some diviners use a menthol salve from the pharmacy instead, which has the same effect. But this is only a treatment of symptoms; the cure is for the patient to begin instruction as a daykeeper.

A related diviner's illness is called "before the horse" (*choquej*). The symptoms of the horse illness are extremely painful cramps in the muscles (like a charley horse), particularly in the arms and legs. The affected body parts are rubbed with *aguardiente* to relieve the pain, but the cramps may recur, intermingled with two or three other kinds of illness, until a mother-father or priest-shaman recognizes a whole complex consisting of illnesses, dreams, and a particular birth date and accepts the afflicted person as his apprentice or "burden" (*ëkomal*).

A third cramping illness is "twisted stomach" (*yi'tz'inak pamaj*). Here the stomach (*pam*) and the small and large intestine (*alajtak* and *chomak ixcolob*) churn constantly, causing the person great pain, flatulence, and finally diarrhea. To relieve the symptoms, a tea may be prepared from marigold flowers. This may calm the stomach for awhile, but once again, this is a recurring illness that can only be cured by initiation as a calendar diviner.

These three illnesses—snake, horse, and twisted stomach—often occur serially (and even simultaneously) over three to six months, until the victim is quite weak and unable to work. Friar Francisco Vázques reported that an epidemic of an illness called "snake" (*cumatz*) occurred in Guatemala in 1650, affecting only the Indian population. He described this illness as an attack of violent cramps that started in the stomach and spread throughout the body, affecting both the muscles and the nervous system.[25] This would appear to be a combination of the snake, horse, and twisted stomach illnesses of today, but he also noted that many sufferers had extremely high fevers and that some of them even died from the illness. This makes his *cumatz* epidemic sound more like the pulmonary plague *gucumatz* that swept through Guatemala in 1545–48 and again in 1576–81, greatly reducing the native population.[26] On the other hand, the seventeenth-century Guatemalan chronicler Francisco Antonio de Fuentes y Guzmán described at first-hand a particular case of *cumatz* that seems to resemble the modern non-fatal version. In this case, a young indigenous woman in the town of Mixco, for no apparent reason, began yelling, "*cumatz! cumatz! cumatz!*" and acted "as if a snake were inside her"; then she suddenly went limp, falling into the fire and seriously burning herself.[27] From this example and from the modern occurrences of snake illness in the Guatemalan highlands, the syndrome would seem to be the Highland Maya analog of *amok, latah, imu, pibloktoqu, wintiko, koro, negi negi, boxi*, and *zar*, which are all temporary, recurrent, stereotypic, unsought possessions or "hysterical psychoses" specific to particular cultures.[28]

Besides suffering from the snake, horse, and twisted stomach illnesses, a prospective calendar diviner might be accident-prone, falling down and dislocating his or her bones, one after another. This illness, called "dislocated bone" (*k'ajinak bak*) is treated by a specialist known as a "bone dresser" (*wikol bak*), who is also an initiated calendar diviner. He bathes the affected area in the herb known as "ear of the armadillo" (*uxiquiniboy*), arranges it in its proper place, wraps it with leaves from the *tz'ite* tree and ties it with *tz'ite* splints. But this is considered a remedy rather than a cure, for this, too, is a recurring illness.

The dislocated bone illness may or may not occur together with another affliction, "inebriation" (*k'abaric*), also called the "bought illness" (*lok'om yabil*). The symptoms are usually quite extreme, causing the victim, as one man put it, "to drink like an animal until he falls down." Diviners explain that in both the dislocated bone and inebriation illnesses, the person is suddenly grabbed, pushed, pulled, or sucked to the ground by the Mundo. A further affliction, also classed as an illness (*yabil*), is "loses-his-money" (*tzako' upwak*), in which thieves are described as being "pulled like a magnet" toward the prospective daykeeper. They remove his or her money very easily, even from the innermost pocket of a male or from under the blouse (*huipil*) of a female. As one diviner who had suffered such losses explained it, "It's as if the evil one were commanded by the Mundo, 'Go take it out!'"

What all six illnesses share is the sudden loss of full command of one's body, particularly the loss of the ability to go about in the world. In the snake illness, one has lost the functioning of the joints; one's movements are disjointed. In the horse illness, the leg and arm cramps are so severe that one can neither walk nor work. With the twisted stomach, one cannot leave the house for the constant pain and diarrhea. In inebriation, people fall to the ground and may yell and rage for hours before passing out and lying motionless until the next day. In the dislocated bone illness, even after the treatment by the bone dresser, it is several days before the person can walk about or work again. The loses-his-money illness also immobilizes the sufferer, since, as Momostecans say, "without money one is lost—one cannot go anywhere and there is nothing one can do."

A series of bouts with these debilitating illnesses sends a person to a calendar diviner, who determines whether or not he or she is being "called" to serve the Mundo. If the person has had no clear dreams indicating such a calling, and if the birth date is not favorable, training will not be recommended. If the person has had the proper sort of dreams but his family did not take notice of his or her date of birth on the indigenous calendar, then a calendar diviner will divine what the day was. This has to be done more frequently today than in the past because of the recent popularity of the Catholic Action movement that directly opposed all indigenous ways. Today, many children of Catholic Action converts are undergoing initiation as daykeepers—along with some of the converts themselves, including individuals who gave up being calendar diviners for Catholic Action only to have their earlier dreams and illnesses all over again.

Training of a Daykeeper

Once a calendar diviner has determined that the patient should be trained as a daykeeper, and if he himself is an initiated mother-father or priest-shaman, he will explain to the person the schedule for the "washings" (ch'ajbal) or "permissions" (permisos) that must be done. If the diviner is not a priest-shaman, then he or she will refer the patient to the head priest-shaman (always a male) of the patient's own patrilineage for training and presentation. It is preferred that a husband and wife be trained together, since priest-shamans often find that an illness experienced by one member of a couple has been caused by both of them, and that both suffer as a result of the illness. Likewise, it is desirable for a lay person who marries an initiated daykeeper to undertake the training and to be presented at the same altar as his or her spouse.

Training commences during the period of permissions, which begins on 1 Quej or else on 1 Cawuk, depending on the age, financial ability, and character of the person. If the novice is an adult, able to meet the twenty *quetzals* (dollars) in expenses, and of strong character, then he or she (or both husband and wife together) will be trained and presented in a period of time described by priest-shamans as "nine months," by which is meant nine twenty-day Quiché months rather than nine thirty or thirty-one day Gregorian months. If, however, the person is quite young, or poor, or the priest-shaman has any reservations about his or her abilities, he will do only the first part of the permissions, called the "work-service" *(chac patan)*, before the initiation days, which are 7 Tz'i' and 8 Batz'. At this time, he will present the person to the Mundo as a simple "burner" *(poronel)*, meaning that the person will be able to burn offerings at public shrines but is not yet a full-fledged daykeeper *(ajk'ij)*. Within the next Quiché nine-month period, the trainer will complete the second part of the permissions, known as the "mixing pointing" *(baraj punto)*, so that when the following 7 Tz'i' and 8 Batz' come around, he may present the person with divining seeds and crystals, transforming the novice into a day-keeper or shaman-priest.

During 1976, when my husband and I underwent the training, the two sets of permissions, which follow one another within the same 260-day cycle, fell on 18 days between April 21 and August 16 (table 1). There were eight permissions for the mixing and pointing, with the last day, 8 Came, overlapping the beginning of the ten permissions for the work and service. On permission days bearing the number one *(jun)*, the patrilineage priest-shaman must go to the "one-place" *(junabal)* shrine, also called Paja' ("At the Water"); on days with the number eight *(wajxakib)*, he goes to the "eight-place" *(wajxakibal)* shrine, also called Ch'uti Sabal ("Little Declaration Place"). These are the two public shrines where he will

Table 1. Permission days in 1976

Washing for the mixing and pointing (Ch'ajbal baraj punto)		Washing for the work service (Ch'ajbal chac patan)	
1 Quej	April 21	1 Cawuk	June 12
1 Junajpu	May 4	1 E	June 25
8 Quej	May 11	8 Cawuk	July 2
1 Aj	May 17	1 Can	July 8
8 Junajpu	May 24	8 E	July 15
1 Came	May 30	1 Tijax	July 21
8 Aj	June 6	8 Can	July 28
8 Came	June 19	1 Batz'	August 3
—	—	8 Tijax	August 10
—	—	1 C'at	August 16

formally present his novice on 8 Batz' (see map 2). On these visits, he makes offerings and prayers to the Day Lords, Tiox, the Mundo, and to all the deceased calendar diviners of his lineage.

In the first set of permissions, the four "one" days—1 Quej, 1 Junajpu, 1 Aj, and 1 Came—which span a forty-day period, are for the mixing or rolling *(baraj)*, a word ordinarily used in the sense of rolling tamales. Diviners, with their divining seeds and crystals, are like tamale-makers with their dough: they roll their mixture quickly with one hand, pressing it firmly into the table-top, then they grab a handful and set it aside. The four "eight" days—8 Quej, 8 Junajpu, 8 Aj, 8 Came—spanning a second forty-day period overlapping with the first, are for the *punto*, from the Spanish noun meaning "point of time or space." Diviners think of the *punto* as the last pile of seeds, counted out from what is set aside, which points to the final outcome of the particular mixing in a divination. When I asked two Momostecan calendar diviners if the *baraj punto* could also be called *vara punta*, "pointed stick," as Ruth Bunzel had suggested,[29] they immediately liked the idea, for it reminded them of the staff of office *(tac'alibal)* of the priest-shaman. However, they stressed that the staff is spiritual, not material, and that the Spanish term *vara* is properly applied to a wooden stick with a silver top, carried by civil authorities. Nevertheless, they enjoyed and accepted *vara punta* as a sound play on *baraj punto*, with its enlargement of meaning.

In the second set of permissions, the six "one" days, spanning a sixty-five day period, are for the *chac*, which is the ordinary Quiché word for manual work or labor; the four "eight" days, stretching over forty days, are for the *patan*, from the Quiché verb *patanic*, "to serve." The noun *patan*, or "service," is also the name for the leather band worn where the tumpline, used for carrying heavy loads, crosses the forehead.

On each of these eighteen permission days, both the novice and the teacher must avoid quarreling or having sexual relations with anyone. The ceremonial day begins in the early dawn, after the morning star has risen. Theoretically, offerings and prayers can be made at any time during the day, but if a calendar diviner is seen at the public shrines at exactly 12:00 noon, he or she is suspected of witchcraft. The ideal is to rise at 4:00 or 5:00 A.M. and go directly to the shrine, so as to be there when it is cool and quiet and to see the sun rise. While the teacher prays for the novice, if he is not preoccupied with some extraneous matter or worry, his lightning will undoubtedly "speak." If everything is going well and the deceased calendar diviners are in accord with the proceedings on behalf of the novice, then the priest-shaman might receive a blood signal near the center of his left thigh (if the novice is female), or his right (if the novice is male).

The prayers on these permission days vary slightly according to which day it is on the divining calendar. In all cases, the diviner opens by asking pardon before Tiox and the Mundo, as well as the ancestors (Nantat); next, the particular shrine is greeted. For example, on 1 Quej, the "one-place" *(junabal)* is greeted: *Sa'j la k'ani mar saki mar, k'ani pila saki pila, ayin cho ayin plo* ("Come here yellow sea white sea, yellow spring white spring, all lakes all oceans"). Although the shrine is ordinarily called Paja' ("At the Water"), this name is not used in prayers; rather, the watery nature of the place is referred to. Next the particular day is greeted: *Sa'j la Ajaw Jun Quej* ("Come here Lord 1 Quej"). Then the petitioner announces, *Quinch'aj lak, quinch'aj taza chirij rakän, chirij ru-k'äb* [name of the novice] ("I am washing the plate, I am washing the cup before the arms, before the legs of [name of the novice]"). Here, "plate" and "cup" refer to the vessels that will be used at the time of initiation, while "arms" and "legs" are metonymies for the entire body. This is a particular moment at which the teacher is quite likely to experience a blood movement concerning the named novice. There are many possible messages besides the one on the thigh—for example, up the inside of the right thigh and into the left testicle, which would cause the teacher to ask the novice, in this case a female, whether she has had sexual relations with a man on this sacred day. The movement up the right, or male side of his body indicated that a male came up to her "taboo" *(awas)*, or vagina, represented in his left testicle.

At the end of his prayers, the teacher will hire a singer *(ajbix)*, a specialized type of calendar diviner who has both the most elegant prayers in Quiché and the knowledge of chanting Latin liturgy. This man is paid as much as twenty cents for his services, which take about ten minutes. The *ajbix* sings the name of the novice and reads off a long list of all the known names of his or her dead relatives—reckoned lineally, but with all the spouses of lineal relatives included—given to him on a piece of paper by the teacher. All of these singers possess body lightning and are constantly receiving messages concerning the named persons; the diviner who hires them expects that they might give a second opinion of how things are going with himself and the novice, and may discuss a recent dream with them (fig. 11).

Later that same day, the novice will visit his or her teacher, paying in advance for the offerings to be given on the next permission day—copal incense (twelve cents), candles (six cents), and sugar (five cents)—as well as for the teacher's time at the shrine (forty cents). Then the novice reports any dreams he or she had the previous week, and especially those of the previous night. The diviner will interpret these dreams in great detail and sometimes will tell the novice any of his own past dreams that may have had similar symbolism.

Besides discussing the week's dreams on each permission day, the teacher will also demonstrate the divining process with his own sacred paraphernalia: seeds of the *tz'ite* tree (*Erythrina coralloden-dron*, called *palo pito* in Spanish) and crystals. A permission day is convenient for this because it is a "kept day"—that is, neither the teacher nor the student have quarreled or had sexual intercourse—and the paraphernalia may be used only on days which have been "kept." At these times, the student observes, over and over again, the teacher's method of mixing, dividing, arranging, and counting the seeds. Since the teacher is not performing a formal divination for a client—although, in effect, he is asking whether or not the student is acceptable to the Day Lords, Tiox, the Mundo, and Nantat—he goes more slowly than he normally would, repeating himself over and over and setting aside divining seeds as mnemonic devices to help the student follow the complex summation of the

11. A one-day at Paja', the one-place shrine. All the people in the picture are calendar diviners of various ranks; the two men holding missals (left foreground and third from right in background) serve in the additional capacity of singer and are for hire to supplement and complete the rites performed by the others.

eight or more results in a given divination. Each seed the teacher sets aside represents a day resulting from a count, and the teacher repeats a simple phrase for each day, often with a sonic play on the day name—for example, for the day Aj, the phrase is *pa ri ja* ("in the house"), in which *ja* is a transposition or metathesis of the sounds in the day name Aj (see chapter 5). In this way, the student slowly builds a repertoire of phrases to go with each of the twenty day names.

During these demonstrations, the teacher tells the student whenever he experiences the movement of lightning, which can happen as often as four or five times per divination, and then explains precisely where in his body he felt it and what it means in the given context. If the student should experience what seems to be a movement of lightning, it must be described to the teacher. If the movement can be seen with the eyes or felt with the hand (as with a muscle spasm), it is a lie; the true lightning is totally interior, though felt near the surface. If the movement is a true one, the teacher will then explain the possible meanings.

After the "eight" days of the permissions are well under way, the novice is instructed to collect 150 ordinary dried beans or hard corn kernels (in either case, a substitute for the *tz'ite* seeds), and to begin a daily practice of mixing, arranging, and counting the days of the divinatory calendar. At this time, the novice is taught a simple divining prayer that is slowly elaborated as his or her knowledge of the calendar and divination grows. At first, the prayer does not include a divining question—for example, *La c'o rajaw, uwinakil wa' cäx?* ("Does this illness have a master [or owner]?")—since it is only for practice (see appendix B for a prayer of this type). But after initiation, the student will pose such questions and formally ask the Day Lords, Tiox, the Mundo, and Nantat to send the "clear light" (*sak k'alaj*) of divinatory knowledge, by way of the air, chilly wind, fog, and mist.

The Initiation and Practice of a Daykeeper

Finally, when 7 Tz'i' arrives, the teacher goes to the home of the novice. He asks the novice to present the dreams of the previous night for analysis. The teacher may present his own dreams as well, and then proceed to analyze them all together— *kuc'an rib ri wachic'* ("we put together our dreams")—as though they were closely related episodes, or parts, of the same narrative text. If the combined dream narrative is favorable, the teacher will then ask whether the novice is quite certain that he or she wishes to be initiated. Even the slightest uncertainty at this stage results in letting the matter drop for another 260-day period.

If everything seems favorable, the teacher and novice will drink an *atole* called *xchunaja'*, which is composed of corn, *zapote* seed, and *cuchun* root. Since drinking this traditional *atole* is considered "a signal that one has now accepted this custom, since one drank the water," the beverage is also referred to as "the water of the service" *(uja'l patan)*. After "drinking the water" with the novice, the teacher begins to pray at the altar that has been constructed on the floor before the household shrine. This temporary altar is made for the occasion from pine needles and boughs; the needles are first sprinkled on the floor and then the boughs are placed so that they delineate a space on the floor about three feet long and one foot wide. On the bed of pine needles, in the center of the altar, the priest-shaman places the small bundle of divining seeds and crystals, known as the *baraj*, that he has prepared for the novice. Next to this bundle, he places candles, a small container of sacred spring water from Paja', several packets of copal incense, and the money that will be used the next day to pay the singer at the public presentation of the novice.

He begins his prayers by announcing to the Day Lords, Tiox, the Mundo, and all the deceased members of his own patrilineage—as well as of the novice's patrilineage, if it is different from his own—that he is beginning the formal initiation of his novice. He then breaks a large unused cooking pot into pieces, which then become incense burners. Both he and the novice begin placing small black disks of copal and tallow candles into the potsherds, which they ignite with a pine-pitch torch while reciting special prayers for the occasion (see appendix B). During these prayers, the teacher sprinkles the novice's divining bundle with the sacred spring water.

After half the copal and candles have been burned, a ritual meal provided by the novice's family—consisting of large quantities of meat, tamales, beans, squash, and chili—is consumed by the participants and their families. After the final course, perhaps consisting of rolls and a chocolate beverage, the ceremony resumes.

When all the copal and candles have been burned, the ashes are scraped out of the potsherds and placed, together with the spring water, in a small gourd, pottery pitcher, or tin can (in any case referred to in Quiché as the *mulul* ["gourd"]), and the opening is closed with pine needles from the altar. This container, the potsherds, the bag of divining seeds and crystals, and the pine boughs are then carefully wrapped up in a square cloth. The bundle is placed where the altar was until the next day, when it will be carried to the "eight-place" shrine, Ch'uti Sabal (fig. 12). Once the bundle is ready, the participants and their families begin ritual toasts with *aguardiente* and set off fireworks. Now the novice pays the teacher for the weeks of prayer and instruction: two baskets of tamales, one large jar of meat stew, two water jars of *atole*, two quarts of *aguardiente*, fifty cents' worth of bread, plus twenty *quetzals* (dollars). Finally, the teacher and his family leave, and the novice (who must sleep separately from his or her spouse) will retire until the next day, which is 8 Batz'.

Before dawn on 8 Batz', the teacher and his wife arrive at the novice's home and take the novice and the bundle with them to Ch'uti Sabal. Here, the teacher unties the bundle and places the potsherds, water container, and pine boughs around the edge of the specific hearth where he himself (or both his wife and himself) were presented by his (their) own teacher. He then places his own and the novice's divining paraphernalia—along with heaps of copal, flowers, water, sugar, and candle offerings—before the semicircular pottery hearth (fig. 13). Now he prays much as he did when he visited this shrine each "eight" day before the initiation, when he was asking permission to present his novice. He speaks directly to the Day Lord 8 Batz', as well as to all the deceased members of his patrilineage who were presented at this particular hearth, lighting his offerings as he goes along. The ritual is completed by a singer (the same one the teacher employed during the permission period), who recites elegant Quiché prayers, the Latin liturgy, and a long list of all the known deceased and living daykeepers within the teacher's patrilineage (on no other occasion are living daykeepers mentioned in prayers). The teacher closes the ceremony at Ch'uti Sabal with the counter-clockwise twirling of first his own, then the novice's, divining bundles through the last puffs of copal smoke. He then kisses the bundles and places them together in his shoulder bag.

12. An eight-day at Ch'uti Sabal, the eight-place shrine.

13. A single hearth at Ch'uti Sabal, with a ten-foot-high accumulation of potsherds from past 8 Batz' celebrations.

Now the teacher and his wife, the student, and the singer all leave for the low shrine, Paja', which was the place visited each "one" day of the permission period before the initiation (fig. 14). There, the novice is presented at the teacher's lineage hearth with basically the same prayers and rituals as were used at Ch'uti Sabal except that no potsherds, water container, or pine boughs are involved. When the singer finishes, the teacher closes his final prayer with the words, *Jachtajic rech nuchak nupatan, nubaraj nupunto chiwäch la Mundo* ("My work my service, my mixing my pointing has been handed over before you World"). He then twirls his own divining bundle in the copal smoke, kisses it, and places it in his shoulder bag. Now, for the first time, the novice must take hold of his or her own divining bundle, saying, *Quinc'amo wa' nuchak nupatan, nubaraj nupunto* ("I receive this my work my service, my mixing my pointing"), then twirling the bundle in the copal smoke, kissing it, and placing it in his shoulder bag, or her cloth bundle.

Now the teacher and the student walk to the town center; outside the Roman Catholic church, they purchase three votive candles each. They then walk into the church and up the right side to the high altar, where they place the first candle on the railing. Praying aloud, they announce that the initiation has taken place: *Ximpechinaj cho ri Mundo Paja', Mundo Ch'uti Sabal* ("I came before Paja' Mountain, Ch'uti Sabal Mountain"). Next, they cross to the left side of the church, where they place one candle each for the patron saint Santiago and for San Antonio Pologuá, briefly informing them of the initiation. Finally, they enter a pew near the center of the nave, where the ancestors are buried beneath the floor, and formally notify them of the initiation.

Later that afternoon, after social drinking in the town center with other teachers and their initiates from near and far, the teacher and his student meet in order to divine together, using the initiate's official divining paraphernalia for the first time. Before beginning, they pray to the Day Lords, Tiox, the Mundo, and Nantat, formally thanking them for their blessings during the training and initiation. A request is then made that any mistakes in the language or performance of the teacher, novice, or singer during the 7 Tz'i and 8 Batz' rituals be forgiven. Finally, they ask that these deities return the financial expenses the initiate encountered during the training (see appendix B).

14. A single hearth at Paja', with smoking copal incense and flower offerings.

On the next day, 9 E, the initiate and his or her teacher meet again at dawn and visit Nima Sabal, the "nine-place" shrine, where the initiate is once again presented to the specific altar where he or she will make offerings in the future. In this case, he or she will visit Nima Sabal on four consecutive "nine" days: 9 E, 9 Can, 9 Tijax, and 9 Batz'. This 40-day period after 8 Batz' is considered "very delicate," since the spiritual "marriage"of the new daykeeper and his or her divining paraphernalia is not complete until the teacher and the novice arrive together at Nima Sabal on 9 Batz', indicating the completion of the training. In future 260-day periods, the initiate will end his or her visits to Nima Sabal on 9 Batz', since the rest of the "nine" days—from 9 C'at to 9 Toj—are reserved specifically for the visits of the priest-shamans or mother-fathers (fig. 15).

After 9 Batz', the initiate is considered a proper shaman-priest or daykeeper and may begin the practice of divination. From this time on, he or she cannot refuse when asked to divine the meaning of a dream for anyone who asks, without charge, or to take on patients and clients on a sliding scale of fees ranging from ten cents to five dollars for consultations concerning family problems, illnesses, deaths, marriages, or births. The new daykeeper must also visit and make offerings—for self, family, and divinatory clients—on each "one" and "eight" day, from 1 and 8 Quej to 1 and 8 Toj, at the specific altars at Paja' and Ch'uti Sabal where he or she was presented on 8 Batz', as well as on each "nine" day from 9 E to 9 Batz' at Nima Sabal.

During a following 260-day period, the daykeeper may be further trained concerning the "six-place" (*wakibal*) shrine. This is located on Paclom, a hill in the town center; it is the "heart" (*c'ux*) or center of the Momostecan world (fig. 16), spiritually connected to four inner hills of the four directions or corners, each located within a radius of about three kilometers. After presentation at Paclom and on these four inner hills, the ritual obligations of the daykeeper are enlarged to include offerings at Paclom on all "six" days from 6 Quej to 6 Toj, as well as at the altars of the inner corners: Paturas (east) on 8 Quej, Ch'uti Sabal (west) on 8 Junajpu, Chuwi Akan (south) on 8 Aj, and Cakbach'uy (north) on 8 Came (map 2).

Beyond the general knowledge of calendrical divination and the cycles of visits to shrines, the daykeeper may seek training in

15. Some hearths at Nima Sabal, the nine-place shrine.

16. Four hearths on Paclom, the six-place shrine at the center of the
world.

one or more of five specialized areas, those of the midwife *(iyom)*, bone-setter *(wikol bak)*, singer *(ajbix)*, marriage spokesman *(c'amal be*, "road guide"), and spiritualist *(ajnawal mesa*, "worker with the spiritual essence of the table"). Each of these specialties requires a further initiation by members of the specific peer group in question; in other words, midwives initiate midwives, and so on. Each of these five groups numbers between one and two hundred people; the only overlap in their respective memberships involves a few midwives and bone-setters who are also initiated spiritualists.

The status of midwife is held only by females; all bone-setters are male. The training and practice in both cases combines ritual and medical skills. The statuses of singer and marriage spokesman are held only by men, though there is no specific prohibition against women. Both these statuses require great proficiency in verbal skills. The singer must be able to remember hours of Latin liturgy and complex prayers in Quiché as well as lists of names of his clients' relatives. The marriage spokesman is able to recite hours of formal oratory for asking that a woman and her family accept a prospective bridegroom and for completing the marriage ceremony in case of success. These two specialties are highly enough paid to enable an especially successful practitioner to support himself and his family on the proceeds (fig. 17).

The status of spiritualist *(ajnawal mesa)*, unlike the other specialties, is considered very dangerous. These men and women conduct séances at midnight in totally darkened rooms, during which the ancestors and sacred mountains *(mundos)* arrive and speak through them. They are widely believed to send illness and even death to their enemies and their clients' enemies and are thus felt by many Momostecans to be witches *(ajitz)*. At the same time, they are highly respected and often chosen as lineage or canton priest-shamans as well as civil leaders. The office of head *(ilol katinimit)* of the Auxiliary Organization tends to be given to a spiritualist during every other term.

Recruitment, Training, Initiation, and Practice of a Mother-Father

A daykeeper becomes the head "mother-father" or priest-shaman of his own patrilineage as the result of a divination performed

17. Five Momostecan calendar diviners, from left to right: a midwife; her husband, the head of the Auxiliary Organization (as of 1979); the previous head (who is a lineage priest-shaman and a bone-setter) bending over in front of him; a marriage spokesman (wearing hat); and a singer.

at least a year, or perhaps two years, after the death of his predecessor. By this time, a series of disturbing dreams, illnesses, and
other misfortunes may have taken place in the lineage. Further,
one of the male daykeepers of the lineage may have had a recruitment dream such as the following:

> Two women were across from me, but there was a deep
> canyon between us. I was on one side, they were on the
> other, and they were laughing at me. I wanted to pass
> over but I couldn't because of the canyon. It was a few
> days later when the patrilineage met. "What'll we do?
> We're getting done in by the foundation shrine." "Very
> well, let's look for someone to be put in charge of this."
> And when the time came, I had to do it. The announce-
> ment had already come, I already knew, but I didn't
> know what it was. I had said it would be some service: a
> woman means the foundation shrine, or the divining
> seeds, or service in the army or the government.

In this particular case, three priest-shamans from the neighboring
lineages immediately agreed that they had the right person, and
they accepted him as a novice. But if no one in the lineage had had
such a clear indication, the priest-shamans would have divined
simultaneously, naming each male daykeeper in the lineage in
order of seniority until their counting of the divining seeds con-
verged on some of the days on which the main lineage rituals are
performed: Ak'abal, Came, Quej, K'anil, E, Aj, Ix, Tz'iquin, or
Ajmac. They would have then agreed on the candidate thus indicated, if their blood lightning had unanimously confirmed the
choice.

A priest-shaman from one of the neighboring lineages will then
begin the permissions and training of the novice priest-shaman, the
"burden of the taboo" (ëkomal rech awas). The permissions, called
"washing the taboo" (ch'ajbal awas), involve the removal of all
previous copal ashes from the lineage shrine and the washing off of
the potsherds, as well as hours of prayers and heaps of offerings.
The specific permission days are the same as those used for the
training of a daykeeper, with "one" days for the "water-place" (uja'l)
lineage shrines, located on lineage lands near seeps and springs,
and "eight" days for the "mountain-place" (ujuyubal) lineage

shrines, located on steep slopes. Analogous patterns are followed
for a new canton priest-shaman, who is selected and trained by a
canton priest-shaman from a neighboring canton, and for the town
priest-shaman, who is selected after the death of his predecessor
by the canton priest-shamans and then trained by one of them.

The religious duties of the lineage priest-shaman include an
obligation to make periodic visits to the shrines where they first
received the offices of *chac patan* and *baraj punto*. The obligatory
visits to Paja' stretch in a series from 1 Quej to 1 Toj, those to Ch'uti
Sabal from 8 Quej to 8 Toj, and those to Nima Sabal from 9 Quej to
9 Toj (fig. 18). In addition, some of them visit the shrine on Paclom
on a series of days bearing the number six. Each visit follows the
same general scheme as that described earlier for permissions:
prayers are said and offerings are given on behalf of the priest-
shaman, his household, and any patients or clients who may have
asked him to pray for their health and business.

The priest-shamans also visit both public and special lineage
shrines on specific days in order to commemorate births, marriages,
deaths, planting, and harvesting within the lineage. The lineage
shrines ideally consist of nine "sowing places, planting places"
(*awexibal ticbal*). They are divided into three different groups: the
warabalja ("sleeping place [bed or foundation] of the house"), consisting of four separate shrines devoted to human and animal in-
crease, health, and prosperity; the *winel*, with three shrines for
agricultural success; and the *mebil*, with two shrines for financial
and business success.

The four foundation shrines are divided into two pairs. One
pair is called "foundation of the people" (*warabalja rech winak*) and
may also be referred to as 6 E, 7 Aj, 8 Ix (because these are the
most important days for making offerings there); it is dedicated to
the health and prosperity of the human members of the lineage (fig.
19). One of the pair, the water-place, is next to a seep or spring in
a hollow or valley, and the other, the mountain-place, is located on
a hill or mountaintop. In the same two locations is the pair of
shrines known as "foundation of the animals" (*warabalja rech awaj*),
also called 4 E, 5 Aj, 6 Ix (after the main days of its ceremonial use).
It is dedicated to the health of all the pigs, chickens, turkeys,
ducks, cows, horses, and other livestock a lineage may own.

Each 260 days, when the lineage priest-shaman opens these
foundation shrines, he specifically asks that nothing happen to the

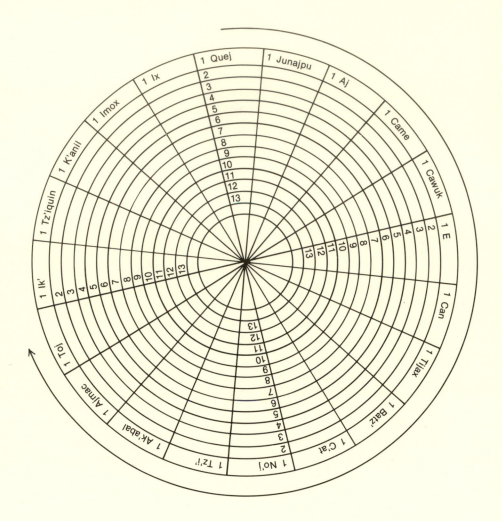

18. The 260-day calendar arranged by number.

19. A lineage foundation shrine.

houses, and thus to the inhabitants and the animals, of his lineage. During his prayer, he enumerates a list of possible disasters, asking that they not come: *mä c'o ta rayo, mä c'o ta ja', mä c'o ta jul, mä c'o ta siwan, mä c'o ta k'ak'* ("that there not be lightning, not be water [flood], not be hole, not be ravine [a landslide causing the house to fall into a ravine], not be fire"). He also gives thanks that none of the houses, family members, and animals in his patrilineage were harmed during the last nine months. If something bad did happen, he will report that fact and ask that nothing else happen. As one priest-shaman explained it, "These shrines are like a book where everything—all births, marriages, deaths, successes, and failures—is written down."

When a woman of the patrilineage is pregnant, the priest-shaman of the lineage goes on a low-numbered Quej day, first to the low foundation shrine of the people and then to the high one, in order to notify the ancestors of this event and to metaphorically sow *(awex)* or plant *(ticon)* the child within the family. Later, when the child is born, he goes again in order to give thanks for this new member of the lineage. On the main days of the foundation of the people—6 E, 7 Aj, 8 Ix—he gives thanks collectively for all the babies born into his lineage during the last 260 days.

The three *winel* shrines of a patrilineage, also called 7 Quej, 8 K'anil, are all located in or at the edges of milpas. They consist of a low "water-place" *(uja'l)*, a high "mountain-place" *(ujuyubal)*, and a "middle" or "center" *(uc'ux)*, also known in Spanish as the *sacramenta*. At these places, the priest-shaman asks for (and later acknowledges) abundance of all the crops and fruit trees of the milpa. This is done on each 7 Quej, 8 K'anil, as well as on the nearest Quej and K'anil before each planting and after each harvest, except that the *uc'ux* or *sacramenta* is used only at harvest. On a Quej day just after harvest, the priest-shaman carries an armload of cornstalks from each of the houses of his patrilineage, as well as a collection of corn smut, insects, and other corn pests, and arranges these around the shrine to show Tiox, the Mundo, and Nantat that the lineage has now harvested and that there were problems with the crop. From each household he also takes four corn ears—one each of "yellow face" *(k'an wäch)*, "white face" *(sak wäch)*, "blue face" *(rax wäch)*, and "speckled" *(xolob)*—and holds them over his offering fire in order to bless them. After this is done, each household places its four corn ears in the center of its own harvest in order to encourage the harvest to abound even while in the storage bin.

The lineage *mebil*, also called 7 Ix, 8 Tz'iquin, and "heart of money" *(uc'ux pwak)*, consists of two parts. The high part is inside the house of the lineage priest-shaman, and the low part is outside, near the low foundation shrines. The priest-shaman first burns copal at the high shrine, later taking it outside to deposit in the low shrine; he asks for an abundance of silver or money *(pwak)* for his lineage. On a table at the high place, he keeps a small wooden box full of objects that he and other members of his patrilineage have come across while working in the milpa or walking somewhere: potsherds, stone figurines, axe heads, old or foreign coins, and stone concretions in the shape of animals, vegetables, and fruits. These objects are removed only once every 260 days, on 7 Ix, and left out on the table overnight. As more articles are added, the box is replaced with a larger one, ideally just large enough to hold everything so far accumulated. In contrast with the cases of the foundation and *winel* shrines, individual households within a patrilineage may have their own private *mebil*, but only the indoor part.

Sometimes the lineage shrines are located on currently owned lineage lands, but at other times they may be on land now claimed by another lineage or else on abandoned land. Shrines may be as far away from the particular lineage segment as six to nine kilometers, perhaps even in a different canton from the one in which the members are currently living. Usually, however, the shrines are closer than two kilometers and are located on or near the particular lineage land holdings. Some lineages lack the full complement of nine shrines; others have more than nine through having acquired lands that were previously owned by other lineages or through the discovery of forgotten shrines of unknown antiquity. If a lineage neglects or forgets any of the shrines on its lands, such shrines may become hungry for offerings and cause sickness and death or invasions of the milpas and homes by animals of the Mundo (such as the coyote). Three or four priest-shamans from neighboring lineages may be called in to help find any neglected shrines. They do this by means of divining crystals, looking at a small yellow flicker of light inside a crystal while standing in the area of a suspected shrine. When this light suddenly moves upward and to the right or left, it is pointing out the exact location of the untended shrine (fig. 20).

The patrilineage shrines are partially duplicated on both the canton and the town levels, so that the fourteen canton priest-shamans and the two town priest-shamans perform similar rituals and prayers on many of the same days. For example, on 6 E, 7 Aj, 8 Ix, the town priest-shaman from Los Cipréses burns copal and prays both at the town's low foundation shrine, located on the plaza next to the offices of the Auxiliary Organization (inside a locked room that only he can enter), and at the high shrine, located on Paclom, a hill in the center of town. At both places, he dedicates his offerings specifically to the ancestors who were political and religious leaders of Momostenango during the colonial period, as well as more recently deceased mayors and city managers of the municipality. On the same days, the town priest-shaman from Pueblo Viejo performs the same rituals at the foundation shrines located behind the church and on a little hill nearby, in Pueblo Viejo, the old center of the town. Both of them pray for the well-being, health, and prosperity of all Momostecans.

There is no *winel* for the town, but there is a *mebil*, located in the Sierra de los Cuchumatanes (forty kilometers to the north). The town priest-shaman from Pueblo Viejo visits this shrine each 8 Quej and 9 K'anil. The upper part is located in the basilica in Chiantla and the lower part on Minas, a foothill of the Cuchumatanes.

The town priest-shaman from Los Cipréses makes a four-part pilgrimage, stretching over a 40-day period, that takes him to each of the mountains of the four directions, located at or near the boundaries of the municipality (see map 2). First, on 11 Quej, he visits Quilaja, mountain of the east; thirteen days later, on 11 Junajpu, he visits Socop, mountain of the west; after another thirteen days, on 11 Aj, he visits Tamancu, mountain of the "four corners of sky" *(cajxucut caj)*, or south; finally, thirteen days later, on 11 Came, he visits Pipil, mountain of the "four corners of the earth" *(cajxucut ulew)*, or north. This sacred circuit is called both the "sowing and planting" *(awexibal ticbal)* of the town and the "stabilization" *(chac'alic)* of the town. The Quiché term *chac'alic*, which in everyday usage refers to the firm placement of a table on its four legs, here refers to the firm placement of the town within its four mountains, so that it will not wobble or tip over during a revolution, earthquake, landslide, or other catastrophe. During his visits to the mountains, the town priest-shaman addresses the Day Lords, Ancestors, Tiox, and the Mundo, asking for health, adequate rainfall, and protection from lightning, flood, hail, earthquakes, landslides, and fires.

20. An abandoned lineage foundation shrine.

The Wider Quichean Context

The literature on other Quiché towns leaves it unclear as to what extent the priest-shaman hierarchy of Momostenango represents a larger Quichean pattern. Specialists who are variously called *chuchkajaw* or *ajk'ij* and who do calendrical divination with *tz'ite* seeds have been widely reported, but there is disagreement as to their shamanic or priestly nature. Bunzel asserts that the *chuchkajawib* of Chichicastenango neither have a "special gift" nor provide a "necessary link" between man and the supernatural, in effect saying (in cultural terms) that they are neither shamans nor priests. But elsewhere in this same work, she describes them as having the same shamanic gift as the diviners of Momostenango: they are "masters of the blood" and have "indescribable sensations in the veins of their arms."[30] In Tax's Chichicastenango notes, these same practitioners are referred to as shamans, but the closest he comes to describing their priestly role is to say that their "duties" include "praying."[31] On the other hand, Flavio Rodas N., Ovidio Rodas C., and Lawrence F. Hawkins call them priests on the basis of their employment as mediators between lay people and the supernatural.[32] Leonhard Schultze Jena describes various mediating roles, but he avoids the priest/shaman problem by consistently using the term "diviner."[33] Since he worked in both Chichicastenango and Momostenango but reported the existence of a "family" shrine (*guarabaljá* in his transcription) only for the latter, it may be that he looked for similar shrines in Chichicastenango and failed to find them. Though he discovered neither the patrilineage nor the term *alaxic* at Momostenango, he did report the use of this word (*alxik* in his transcription) at Chichicastenango, where he was told that it referred to stone figurines kept in the divining bundles of that town. It remains a mystery as to whether these figurines (or their owners) have any connections with lineage rituals, but Carmack does report that lineage organization is an important part of rural culture at Chichicastenango.[34]

Whether or not there are priest-shamans at Chichicastenengo who act on behalf of lineage, canton, or town, there are diviners who are employed as mediators and are priestly in that sense. In the company of a priest-shaman from Momostenango, I visited Turucaj, the best-known shrine at Chichicastenango, and I can report that only those locals who have the *baraj* may present offerings there, acting on behalf of those who do not (fig. 21).

In San Cristóbal Totonicapán, a Quiché community south of Momostenango, there are households with the indoor *mebil*. In addition, I have seen examples of the *uc'ux* or *sacramenta*, the middle portion of the *winel*, in the cornfields there. Whether or not the diviners of this town are organized into a full hierarchy, the existence of these shrines does suggest priestly activities at the lineage level. In Chinique, to the east of Chichicastenango, there is no formal hierarchy, but the most prominent local daykeeper has paired "water-place" and "mountain-place" shrines, on his own land, where he prays and makes offerings not only for his own household but for the households of all his brothers as well. Once a year, at these same shrines, he gives offerings on behalf of visitors from all over the municipality; local ladinos are among those who contribute to these offerings (fig. 22).

In the *Popol Vuh*, calendrical divination with *tz'ite* seeds is performed by the deities Xpiacoc and Xmucane, who are called, among other things, "daykeepers" (*ah quih* in the manuscript), just as contemporary diviners are.[35] They call their seeds both by the species name, *tz'ite*, and by the metaphor *ixim* ("corn kernels"), just as Momostecan diviners do. Furthermore, they are husband and wife, which recalls the Momostecan ideal that both members of a couple should be diviners.[36] One of their epithets is *ah raxa lac, ah raxa tzel* ("person of the blue-green plate, person of the blue-green bowl"),[37] which suggests the "plate" (*lak*) and the "cup" (*taza*) that are "washed" for novice Momostecan diviners by lineage priest-shamans. The connection of Xpiacoc and Xmucane with lineage rites is confirmed by the story of their two sons, who become the first patrilineal ancestors to be venerated in the *Popol Vuh*.[38]

21. The shrine on Turucaj in Chichicastenango; note the stone image between the flower stalks.

22. A priest-shaman at a lineage water-place shrine in Chinique.

4.

The Calendar

During Precolumbian times, the civilizations of Mesoamerica kept an intricate calendar consisting of both civil, or solar, and sacred, or divinatory, cycles; these combined to produce what is called the "Calendar Round" in the literature on the Maya. The civil year, called *haab* by the Yucatec Maya and *macewal k'ij* ("common days") by the Quiché Maya,[1] was a 365-day solar calendar containing eighteen months of 20 days with 5 remaining days. The sacred or divinatory calendar, generally referred to in the literature by the invented Yucatec word *tzolkin*,[2] was not marked off into months but was a succession of day designations created by the combination of a number from 1 to 13 with one of twenty possible names. The twenty names to which consecutive numbers were prefixed are shown in two Mayan languages, Yucatec and Quiché, in table 2. Since 13 and 20 have no common factor, this process creates 260 different combinations of number and name (fig. 23).

The two cycles, one lasting 365 days and the other 260 days, mesh to produce the Calendar Round. On this combined calendar, the first day of the first month on the solar calendar, called the Mam in Highland Mayan languages and generally referred to as the

Table 2. The Twenty Days

Numbers	Names	
	Yucatec Maya	**Quiché Maya**
1	Ik	Ik'
2	Akbal	Ak'abal
3	Kan	C'at
4	Chicchan	Can
5	Cimi	Came
6	Manik	Quej
7	Lamat	K'anil
8	Muluc	Toj
9	Oc	Tz'i'
10	Chuen	Batz'
11	Eb	E
12	Ben	Aj
13	Ix	Ix
1	Men	Tz'iquin
2	Cib	Ajmac
3	Caban	No'j
4	Eznab	Tijax
5	Cauac	Cawuk
6	Ahau	Junajpu
7	Imix	Imöx

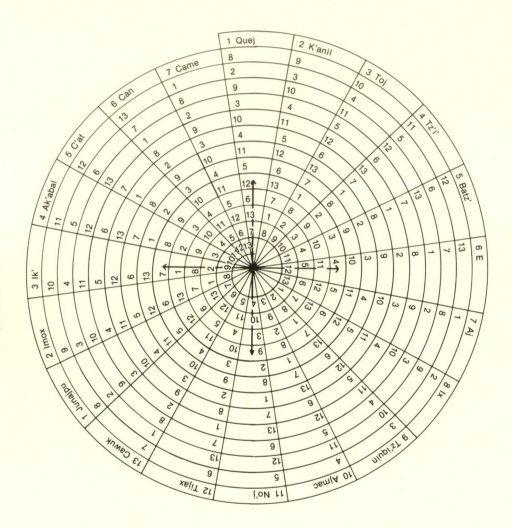

23. The 260-day calendar.

"Year-bearer" in the literature on the Lowland Maya, can only occur on 52 (4 x 13) possible days from the 260-day calendar. The mathematical reasons for this are as follows: a given 365-day cycle will accommodate twenty-eight complete cycles of 13 days each, but 13 x 28 = 364, leaving one extra day; this means that the *number* of the day that ends the solar year will be the same as the number of the day that began it, and that the day number that begins the new solar year will advance one place in the cycle of 13 day numbers each year, returning to 1 after 13 has been passed. As for the day name, the solar year accommodates eighteen cycles of 20 days each; 18 x 20 = 360, leaving 5 extra days. The result is that the *name* of the day that begins the next solar cycle will advance five places in the cycle of 20 day names each year. Since five divides into twenty evenly, giving four, this means that only four of the day names, evenly spaced in the cycle of 20, can ever begin a solar year. In Yucatán, during the Classic Period, the 4 days were Ik, Manik, Eb, and Caban, while among the Quiché, the same positions were occupied by Ik', Quej, E, and No'j. However, at some point in the Postclassic, the Yucatec Year-bearers shifted forward two positions, so that instead of beginning with Ik, Manik, Eb, or Caban, the year began with Kan, Muluc, Ix, or Cauac.[3]

The oldest record of a calendar day sign with a numerical coefficient, probably part of a 260-day cycle, comes from the Monte Albán I period in highland Oaxaca and dates from about 600 B.C.[4] The geographic location of the original calendar is debated, with evidence for both a highland and a lowland origin.[5] But it has been argued, from the fact that several of the day names known from the fully documented calendars refer to fauna not found in the highlands of Mexico or Guatemala, that the calendar must have had a lowland origin. It is undeniable that monkeys, crocodiles, and jaguars (the most common linguistic and iconographic interpretations of three of the twenty day names) do not currently live in the highlands of either Mexico or Guatemala. However, in the case of jaguars, at least, this is a relatively new situation caused by the massive human occupation of the highlands. Further, there is no particular reason why the faunal knowledge of the originators of the calendar need have been exclusively highland or exclusively lowland; a number of modern linguistic groups centered in highland areas, including the Quiché, occupy territories that overlap the lowland environment, even within the space of a single municipality.

After the Spanish conquest, much of the aboriginal calendar system was clandestinely maintained throughout the colonial period. In some areas, calendrical knowledge was apparently maintained on a strictly oral basis while in others, it was maintained with the aid of written calendar wheels, perhaps modeled after Precolumbian calendar wheels found in the codices or perhaps after the pecked cross and circle symbols found in many archaeological sites in Mesoamerica.[6] Today, this intricate calendar system, or parts of the system, exist in many communities in Veracruz, Oaxaca, and Chiapas, as well as throughout the Guatemalan highlands. Suzanna W. Miles reported on eighty-seven communities in these areas that were known to retain native calendars; of these, eighty-two were described in enough detail for the purposes of her analysis.[7] She was able to divide seventy-eight of the eighty-two into three structural types: those having only the 260-day cycle, those having only the 365-day cycle, and those combining both cycles.

In the Guatemalan highlands, there are thirty-four Ixil, Mam, and Pokomchí towns that have preserved the 365-day cycle with eighteen months of 20 named days and a 5-day terminal period, the 260-day cycle with its 20 day names and 13 numbers, and the system of Year-bearers that links these two cycles. Miles noted, however, that seven of these towns have neither public nor private ceremonies for the Year-bearer; instead, their calendars simply have automatic structural Year-bearers unmarked by observances. Also, thirty-one of these calendars have lost the month names. A second type of calendar, found in twenty-one communities of Oaxaca, Veracruz, and Chiapas, retains the 365-day year with eighteen named months and the 5-day terminal period, but it has lost the 20 day names and 13 numbers of the divinatory counts. In 1969, Gary H. Gossen made the important discovery of a graphic representation of this type of calendar in the form of a marked rectangular board in use in the Tzotzil-speaking community of Chamula.[8] The third type of calendar, occurring in twenty-three communities of the midwestern Guatemalan highlands, includes only the 260-day count, reckoned without regard to the solar year. Miles listed Momostenango, as well as other Quiché communities that are known to have the divinatory calendar, under this last type, but she was in error. Both Momostenango and Santa María Chiquimula share with Ixil, Mam, and Pokomchí communities the Classic Maya Year-bearers of the solar calendar: Quej, E, No'j, and Ik'.[9]

Future research will probably add to the list of Quiché communities known to have this feature in their calendars.

The Divinatory Calendar

The question of how and why a period of 260 days was chosen for the divinatory cycle is much contested. Common answers include: (1) that this cycle was simply created by a permutation of its subcycles 13 and 20, both of which are important numbers in Mesoamerican thought;[10] (2) that the 260-day period is the interval between zenithal transits of the sun near the latitude 15° North;[11] (3) that a double *tzolkin* (520 days) equaled three eclipse half-years;[12] and (4) that 260 days equaled nine lunations, each consisting of slightly less than 29 days—or the same number of months a woman is pregnant.[13] J. Eric S. Thompson specifically attacked this last view, finding it "not a very happy explanation because there is no logical reason why the period of pregnancy should be considered in establishing a divinatory almanac."[14] Nevertheless, Momostecans as well as Maxeños (the people of Chichicastenango) explicitly offer the period of human gestation as an explanation for the 260-day cycle, while the numerological and astronomical explanations for the cycle are speculations without direct support from archaeological, ethnohistorical, or ethnographic evidence. Furthermore, as the next chapter clearly shows, a human model for the divinatory calendar is quite consistent with the explicit connection, in the larger divinatory system, between the external cosmos and the internal human microcosm.

A second major controversy about the 260-day calendar concerns the beginning day of the cycle. Central Mexican lists of the twenty day names usually begin with Cipactli (equivalent to Imöx in Quiché and Imix in Yucatec), but the Mayan picture is less clear.[15] Morley noted that "since the sequence of twenty day names was continuous, it is obvious that it had no beginning or ending, like a rim of a wheel: consequently, any day name may be chosen arbitrarily as the starting point."[16] In contrast, Thompson claimed that "there are no grounds for doubting that the cycle started with the day Imix, and small reason for not supposing that the accompanying number was one."[17] He based his assertions on the following evidence:

> The incomplete cycle of 260 days which stretches across
> Madrid [Codex pages] 13–18 starts with the day Imix,
> but no numbers are given; Nuñez de la Vega says that
> Imox was the head of the count, and Ximénez opens his
> 20 days with Imox, and compares it to New Year's day;
> La Farge . . . notes that at Santa Eulalia he received a
> very strong impression that Imox led the list. (Thompson
> 1950:102)

But there are problems with Thompson's two Guatemalan sources,
Ximénez and La Farge. What Ximénez actually said was that "their
year began on February 21, and this was like new year's day. This
day has the sign Imox."[18] His subsequent discussion makes it quite
clear that he thought he was talking about the solar year, not the
260-day calendar; the latter could not possibly have a fixed "new
year's day" corresponding to February 21 or any other solar date.
After giving the rest of the twenty day names, he goes on to state
that after 360 days, the next 5 days were not counted. If this were
the case, then each solar year could indeed begin with Imöx, since
360 is divisible by 20, but in fact it is the counting of the eighteen
20-day months that stops for 5 days at the end of the solar year, not
the counting of the twenty day names and thirteen day numbers.
Ximénez, who drew rather freely on non-Guatemalan sources, was
apparently confusing the 365-day year with the 360-day cycle of the
Lowland Maya *tun*, which always began on the Lowland equivalent
of Imöx. A 400-day cycle is known from the Guatemalan highlands,
specifically documented for the Cakchiquel, but that began on Aj,
not Imöx.[19] In summary, Ximénez mixed both his cycles and his
sources, and an argument that the Guatemalan 260-day calendar
began on Imöx cannot rest on his confused testimony.

La Farge seems to have based his "strong impression that imŭc
[Imöx] led the list" on written sources rather than on his own
excellent ethnographic research:

> I believe that there is some reason for conceiving the
> lords of the days as arranged in a single sequence begin-
> ning with imŭc and that it is not by pure chance that the
> custom of listing these names with imŭc (Imix) at the
> head has been conveyed to us from early sources. A
> soothsayer listing the days will always begin with the

current one, but I received a very strong impression that imŭc led the list and that ahau came climactically at the end. (La Farge 1947:179)

Like so many ethnographers, La Farge seems to have felt that he had failed to find something that the weight of previous scholarship told him should be there. Even though his own consultants began listing the days with the day they were currently sharing with him, he chose to begin his discussion of the twenty day names with Imŭc. He thus took an "objectivist" rather than an "intersubjective" position and gave a "constructed object" priority over actual native practice.[20] By way of contrast, note the manner in which Lincoln dealt with similar information: "So far as I have been able to gather, the Ixil do not recognize a starting point for this 260-day count, but among the Maya of Yucatán and among the people of central Mexico, the starting points were the equivalents of 1 Imux." Perhaps the Ixil have "lost" the sense of a beginning day for the divinatory calendar, or perhaps they are simply different from the Maya of Yucatán and the people of central Mexico. In any case, Lincoln chose not to follow an objectivist path. As he himself explained, since the Ixil 260-day calendar does not have a fixed first day, he chose to begin his discussion of the days on E because in 1939 the solar calendar happened to begin on 5 E.[21]

Some modern ethnographers claim to have found a beginning day for the 260-day cycle that is not Imöx or its equivalent. Oakes reports that in Todos Santos, "the chimanes recognize a starting day in the use of their calendar; this is always k'máne," which, she noted, was the same as Ee of the Ixil and which Lincoln used as his first day.[22] Bunzel also claims to have found an opening day in Chichicastenango: "Although the days run in endless cycles, all the ancient calendars begin on the day 1 imux (Aztec 1 cipactli). However, Quiché diviners all began with 1 bats, and the manuscripts of calendars that were shown me began with this day." She thus began her list of 260 days, which she labeled "Quiché Tonalamatl," with "1 bats."[23] Schultze Jena reports that the 260-day calendar began with "One Monkey" (1 Batz') in Chichicastenango and with "Eight Monkey" in Momostenango. Yet he starts his own list of twenty day names with Imöx.[24] Goubaud, in his article on Momostenango, also claims that 8 Batz' was the first day of the calendar, but he likewise begins his calendric discussion with Imöx.[25] Saler, on the other hand, who worked in El Palmar (a community settled by Momostecans), begins his list of the twenty day names with Batz', though he does not state why.[26]

From the evidence so far, it would seem that although the Lowland Maya and Aztec 260-day counts may have begun with Imöx, there is no reason to think that the Highland Maya count did. Girard's Highland data further complicate the picture, since he asserts that there are different first days in different Quiché communities. He lists 8 Batz' as the first day for Momostenango, 8 Quej for Santa María Chiquimula, and 1 Batz' for Chichicastenango.[27] If we add the fact that the 1722 "Calendario de los Indios de Guatemala," collected in the Quezaltenango area, begins with 1 Quej,[28] it begins to look as though each Quiché community might have its own pattern. On the other hand, we might hypothesize that there are only 4 possible first days—1 or 8 Quej, or 1 or 8 Batz'—for all Quiché communities. However, my own experience in eliciting various day lists and then being formally taught the calendar causes me to doubt seriously that any of these 4 days might decisively be called the "first" day of the 260-day calendar, even in a particular community.

When I elicited descriptions of the calendar from several different diviners early in my studies, they began in three different ways. The first method was to start with whatever day it actually was and then count through, discussing the next twenty days. The second method was to begin with the first day or Mam of the current solar year, for example 4 Ik' in 1977–78, and count forward so as to include all twenty day names (and thus all four possible Mam names). The third method was to begin with the most recent day bearing the number one (which was arrived at by counting backwards) and then count forward from that day, running through three complete series of thirteen days each and then adding a fortieth day to end on the number one. Rodríguez, who also elicited the day names in Momostenango, seems to have experienced this third method, since his presentation of the calendar began with 1 E and continued with three groups of 13 day numbers and names.[29] This method of presenting the calendar is quite effective as each of the twenty day names is repeated twice.

None of my consultants felt that 8 Batz' was the "first" day, though it was admittedly a very important day on the calendar. When pushed for the first day, one person said, "This year began with 3 No'j"—that is, with the Mam—by which he meant that the 365-day solar calendar touched the ritual 260-day calendar on this day in 1976. Later, when I was being trained to count the numbers and days (both forward and backward) in their proper sequences, I often asked what the first day was and was always laughed at and told that there was no "first day," though perhaps there was a "middle day." The middle day that was mentioned by my teacher varied: sometimes it was 8 Batz', while at other times it was 8 Quej. Actually, 8 Quej is nearly as important a day in Momostenango as 8 Batz', since a priest-shaman must arrive on 8 Quej at the shrine where he will be presenting a novice on the following 8 Batz'. If he does not live too far away, he should also arrive on 1 Quej, but this day is not absolutely obligatory the way 8 Quej is. I observed that on 8 Quej, unlike any other day except 8 Batz', there are so many pilgrims from other Quiché communities that dozens of food stands are set up to take care of the travelers.

The period stretching from 1 Quej and 8 Quej (which are 20 days apart) to 1 Batz' and 8 Batz' (also 20 days apart) is an intensive "permission" period for personal and patrilineage rituals in Momostenango (see the previous chapter). Bunzel noted that 8 Quej was "a great day of obligation" in Chichicastenango, similar to 8 Batz' in Momostenango.[30] Although it is clear that 1 and 8 Quej and 1 and 8 Batz' are important religious days in several if not all Quiché communities, there is no reason to conclude that one of them rather than another is actually the "first day" of the 260-day calendar. Among the Quiché, and probably among the Highland Maya in general, the question of a beginning day for this cycle remains an academic one. When pressed for such a day, a consultant will simply provide the name of an important day within the 260-day cycle, or else beg the question by appealing to a cycle that does have a beginning day, as when a Mam is given as an answer. Similarly, when Aztec and Lowland Maya codices begin lists of days with Imöx, that may not be because the 260-day cycle ever contained its own beginning day, but because the necessity of beginning a written account somewhere has caused an appeal to a different cycle. In the Lowland Maya case, that would be the 360-day *tun* mentioned earlier, which always began on Imöx. Thus Morley's general sense of the divinatory cycle as a continuous, unbroken one remains quite plausible.

A third problem area in discussing the 260-day divinatory

calendar is the characterization, in the past anthropological literature, of each of the 20 days as having either a "good" or "bad"
augury. Thompson, asserting that "the Maya calendar of today is a
pitiful survival," with only its bare structure remaining and all
"embellishments" gone, based this appraisal on today's "striking
disagreement as to the values of the days in terms of benevolence
and malevolence." His main example was the lack of agreement he
perceived between Sapper's and Schultze Jena's presentations of
the Quiché divinatory calendar, in which "a day is lucky in one
Quiché town and unlucky in another town of the same speech."[31]
However, in abstracting these data from the primary sources,
Thompson misrecorded and misinterpreted some of them, adding
to the chaos and apparent disagreements. For example, he shows
Sapper's Quezaltenango and Momostenango data to be in conflict
with Schultze Jena's Chichicastenango and Momostenango data on
the auguries of the days K'anil and Toj: in the former case, these
two days contrast, being "good" and "bad" respectively, while in the
latter, they are the same, belonging to a third category of days
Thompson describes as "favorable for prayers for some special
matter, usually of secondary nature." But an examination of the
sources shows that K'anil is just as "good" and Toj is just as "bad" in
Schultze Jena's data as they are in Sapper's, the only difference
being that Schultze Jena explained the proper rituals done on these
days while Sapper did not.[32]

More fundamental than the question as to how Thompson
interpreted ethnographic data is the question as to whether it is
worthwhile to think in terms of "good" or "bad" days in the first
place. As I myself have learned, consultants in the same community, when asked to separate the days as "good" or "bad," often
contradict one another and even themselves. My own early data
are full of conflicting statements as to whether or not a given day is
good or bad, together with cases in which the consultant gives a
description of a good ritual as being performed on a day that is
otherwise characterized as bad. Rodríguez ran into this same problem in Momostenango where he was told that 3 Ix was bad even
though the consultant described this day as simply one "to ask for
good harvests and good crops from Dios Mundo."[33] Both because
of this kind of problem and for other reasons that will emerge in
the discussion of the individual days in the next chapter, I have

chosen not to impose a good/bad analytical opposition on my own data but to allow each day its full complexity.

The Solar Calendar

Rafael Girard, during his two seasons of fieldwork in Momostenango (July of 1959 and May of 1960), recorded the following Quiché day names for the Year-bearers, or Mam: 11 Quej (1958–59), 12 E (1959–60), and 13 No'j (1960–61).[34] He reported that his consultants were able to tell him the complete day name, both the number and the proper name, for two previous years (1958 and 1959), but that when it came to projecting the solar calendar forward they knew only the proper order of the nonnumerical half of the day name: Ik' (1961), Quej (1962), and so on. In other words, they did not know that in 1961 the Mam would fall on 1 Ik' and that in 1962 it would be 2 Quej. This was not the case with my own consultants, who could project both forward and backward indefinitely. For example, in 1976 the Mam was 3 No'j, and all the calendar diviners I talked with knew that in 1977 the Year-bearer would fall on 4 Ik', then in 1978 on 5 Quej, in 1979 on 6 E, and so on, going through the 13 numbers one by one and always keeping the same order in the four possible day names: Quej, E, No'j, Ik'.

The four Mam are ranked, with Quej considered the first and most important of the Year-bearers, followed by E, No'j, Ik'. Table 3 shows that the Year-bearer 1 Quej is followed thirteen years later by the Year-bearer 1 E, who is followed thirteen years later by 1 No'j and then finally 1 Ik'. These four thirteen-year periods make up one fifty-two-year cycle, after which 1 Quej returns as the Year-bearer. I have not yet been able to learn whether or not there are additional prayers or ceremonies during the annual celebration of a Mam that specifically commemorate the thirteen-year period or the fifty-two-year cycle.

The first-ranking Mam, Quej, is received (or greeted) on Qui-

Table 3. The Year-bearers

Quej	①	5	9	13	4	8	12	3	7	11	2	6	10
E	2	6	10	①	5	9	13	4	8	12	3	7	11
No'j	3	7	11	2	6	10	①	5	9	13	4	8	12
Ik'	4	8	12	3	7	11	2	6	10	①	5	9	13

laja, the mountain of the east. The other sacred mountains, for purposes of the solar calendar, are Tamancu, Joyan, Socop, Paclom, and Pipil (fig. 24). After Quej finishes his year of service, E, the second most important Mam, enters and is received on Tamancu, to be followed on the third year by the Mam No'j on Joyan (fig. 25), to the south southwest; finally, the Mam Ik' is received on Socop, the mountain of the west. As can be seen in figure 24, these Mam move, during a four-year period, along a clockwise arc stretching from east to west.

The four Mam, also called *alcaldes*, are assisted by two secretaries *(ajtzib)*, C'at and Tz'iquin. Secretary C'at enters on Joyan and serves No'j and E, while secretary Tz'iquin enters on Pipil and serves Ik' and Quej. For example, on March 2, 1977, the Mam 4 Ik' entered on Socop and was served by Secretary 4 Tz'iquin, who, on March 15, entered at Pipil. Now, to further complicate the picture in characteristic Quiché fashion, both a Mam and his Secretary are doubled, giving four days as leaders each solar year. The first Mam and Secretary are the first occurrences of the appropriate day names during the solar year, and the second Mam and Secretary are the second occurrences (table 4). During 1977, the first Mam or Nabe Mam (4 Ik') arrived on March 2, while the second Mam or Ucab Mam (11 Ik') arrived twenty days later on March 22; the first Secretary (4 Tz'iquin) arrived on March 15 and the second (11 Tz'iquin) arrived twenty days later on April 4.

Each of the four Mam affects the year that it rules. Mam Quej, who entered during 1974 and again in 1978, is a wild Year-bearer who likes "to throw off his cargo," "to mount," and also "to trample" people underfoot. There are many business losses and many illnesses during a Quej year. Mam E, who entered in 1975 and in 1979, is quiet, calm, and enduring. An E year is good for business and health. Mam No'j (1976 and 1980), who "has a good head, and many thoughts," is a creative year, both for good and for evil. Finally, Mam Ik' (1977 and 1981) is very *bravo*, bringing violent rainstorms or else no rain at all. Many people die from being struck by lightning, from drowning, or else from hunger.

Within each solar year, the five days between the last occurrence of the old Mam and the entrance of the new Mam are a dangerous time; people curtail social and business activity. Then, at noon on the day before *(mixprix)* the day on which the midnight arrival of the first Mam will be awaited, the observances begin with

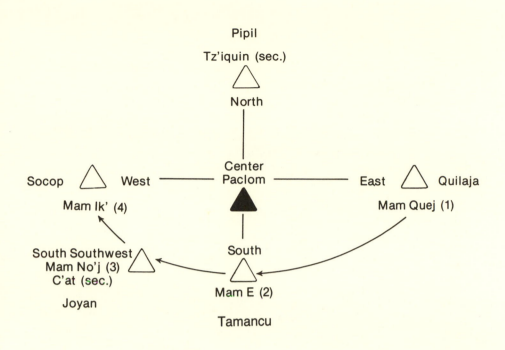

24. The sacred mountains.

the tying of red thread around the left wrist and right ankle. This thread is left on until the second Mam arrives twenty days later. It is a protection from the Mam, who is thought of (to varying degrees) as domineering, bewitching, and dangerous. Without the thread, one does not remember things, wakes up late, and is extremely weak. During this same twenty-day period, everyone should abstain from sexual intercourse and green vegetables, both of which weaken the person. Green vegetables are also taboo because they are full of cold water, which is displeasing to the fiery heat of the Mam, who live near the sun. Meals include a special tamale, called *uben* in Quiché and *tayuya* in Spanish, that includes equal parts of black beans and corn dough; this gives people the strength to withstand the power of the Mam.

When the day following the *mixprix* reaches its end, at midnight, the first Mam enters. Celebrations involving the burning of copal and the setting off of fireworks take place on the appropriate mountain, as well as in each canton, on Nima Sabal, and in the town center on Paclom. The celebration in the center includes the important act, performed by the town priest-shaman from Los

25. Mountain-top shrines at Joyan, for rites pertaining to the solar calendar.

Table 4. The arrival of the Mam in 1977

4 Ik' (Mam)	March 2	8 Cawuk	March 19
5 Ak'abal	March 3	9 Junajpu	March 20
6 C'at	March 4	10 Imöx	March 21
7 Can	March 5	11 Ik' (Mam)	March 22
8 Came	March 6	12 Ak'abal	March 23
9 Quej	March 7	13 C'at	March 24
10 K'anil	March 8	1 Can	March 25
11 Toj	March 9	2 Came	March 26
12 Tz'i'	March 10	3 Quej	March 27
13 Batz'	March 11	4 K'anil	March 28
1 E	March 12	5 Toj	March 29
2 Aj	March 13	6 Tz'i'	March 30
3 Ix	March 14	7 Batz'	March 31
4 Tz'iquin (Sec.)	March 15	8 E	April 1
5 Ajmac	March 16	9 Aj	April 2
6 No'j	March 17	10 Ix	April 3
7 Tijax	March 18	11 Tz'iquin (Sec.)	April 4

Cipréses, of passing the wooden staff of office *(vara)* of all indigenous civil authorities through the copal smoke. Although the *alcaldes* of each of the fourteen cantons enter office, following the Gregorian calendar, on January 1, their spiritual investiture awaits the entrance of the Mam at the beginning of the Quiché solar year.

Throughout the year, the Mam is commemorated, both in the center and in the cantons, on each occurrence of his day with firecrackers, copal, and special prayers. In this sense, the eighteen twenty-day months are still celebrated, although only the first two month names—Nabe Mam and Ucab Mam—are clearly retained, so far as I have been able to determine. There is an exception to the monthly celebration of the Mam: the Mam Ik', who is so powerfully connected to the western direction and death, is only commemorated on the commonest day numbers for religious ceremony, namely 1, 6, and 8.

The current Mam has an influence on divinations that utilize the 260-day calendar. For example, a partly negative diagnosis during an Ik' year, because of the strength of this Year-bearer, becomes extremely negative. If the question concerns a client's life in general outline, the diviner may ask each of the four Mam and the two Secretaries, one by one, the question of his or her destiny, starting with the current Mam and Secretary and going forward four years.

By now it should be clear that Momostenango, far from lacking the solar calendar, as previously reported, has elaborate solar observances. There remains the question as to why the solar elements of the calendar should be differentially present among Highland Maya communities. Manning Nash has suggested that the solar elements are perpetuated wherever "the social structure institutionalizes the role of calendar expert." He apparently means that towns having an expert in the service of the community as a whole will keep the solar calendar, whereas communities lacking such an expert will retain only the divinatory calendar.[35] This seems consistent with the situation depicted in the myth of the origin of the customs of Momostenango (see appendix A). According to this myth, the burden of instituting the customs of the Mam (and therefore of the solar calendar) was charged directly to the civil officials of the town and to the town priest-shamans, whereas customs regulated solely by the divinatory calendar were charged to priest-shamans acting on behalf of lineages. But this hardly constitutes the polar opposition, as seen by Nash, between the "chronological" or solar calendar of the "priest" and the "divinatory" calendar of the "shaman." Rather, as detailed in the previous chapter, there is a hierarchy of priestly roles among Momostecan calendar diviners, but those who take these roles are also shamans. As for the calendar they all share, the "solar" years take their names from the "divinatory" calendar, and divinatory interpretation takes account of the current solar year.

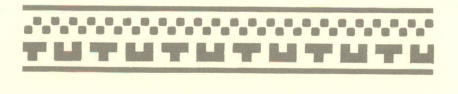

5.

The Day Lords

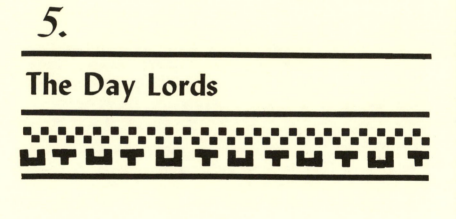

The twenty Quiché day names are not only proper names but divine ones. When a given day is addressed directly, the name is prefixed with the respectful title *ajaw*, as in *Sa'j la, Ajaw Wajxaquib Batz'* ("Greetings sir, Lord 8 Batz'"). In the *Popol Vuh*, 1 Batz', 1 and 7 Junajpu, and 1 and 7 Came all figure as divine characters,[1] but among the modern Quiché, only the Day Lords who serve as a Mam or Secretary to a Mam play roles in myths (see previous chapter and appendix A).

The day names have been "translated" into German, Spanish, and English common nouns by previous researchers, but they cannot be properly glossed except as day names. Even apparently translatable names such as Batz' ("monkey"), Tz'iquin ("bird"), Ix ("jaguar"), and C'at ("net") are taken by Quiché diviners to be untranslatable proper names within the context of calendrical divination. The day names as understood and used in Quiché communities are not interpreted by linking them to a fixed inventory of static symbols through glosses or etymologies; rather, a given day name is interpreted by means of mnemonic phrases that map the meanings of the days in terms of the social actions that characterize them. These phrases often include the sounds of the day name but not necessarily the name as such. Previous attempts to interpret the 260-day ritual cycle according to the supposed symbolic and metaphoric associations of each day name have treated the names as if they were, in effect, pictographs in a writing system lacking a phonetic dimension. Instead, in actual practice the names are "read" not as words in themselves but as a kind of oral rebus for quite other words; these other words are linked to the day name by means of paronomasia—that is, by means of poetic sound play.

Before discussing each of the twenty day names, a general word is needed concerning the day numbers. Although it is true that the day number affects the meaning of a given day name, Thompson's statement that "the combination of the number and day [is] a unit, and the one part [is] as meaningless without the other as a telephone number is without the name of the exchange"[2] does not apply to the Quiché. Bunzel noted in Chichicastenango (and it is equally true in Momostenango) that low numbers—1, 2, and 3—are "gentle," while the high numbers—11, 12, and 13— are "violent"; the middle numbers—7, 8, and 9—are "indifferent," neither gentle nor violent. The latter form "the days of measured strength," which are used for "the regularly recurring ceremonies to ensure tranquil life."[3] In Momostenango, and perhaps in Chichicastenango as well, low numbers are considered gentle or weak because they indicate something young or new, while higher numbers are powerful and even violent, since they indicate older, riper, more serious matters. Further, the number designates a specific shrine to be visited on day names bearing that number. For example, at the level of rites performed by diviners on behalf of their own immediate families or their private clients, the day 1 Ak'abal indicates a visit to the *junabal* or "one-place" shrine, which is Paja'; 6 Ak'abal indicates the *wakibal* or "six-place" shrine on Paclom as the place to visit; 8 Ak'abal indicates the *wajxakibal* or "eight-place" shrine, known as Ch'uti Sabal; and 9 Ak'abal corresponds to the *belejebal* or "nine-place" shrine, or Nima Sabal (see chapter 3).

Long before I began formal training in calendrical divination, I elicited the twenty days and their meanings from several different calendar diviners. The first time I did this, the list began with Ak'abal, since it was June 22, 1975, which was 9 Ak'abal. Because (as I have argued in the previous chapter) there is no fixed "first" day for the 260-day divinatory calendar, I shall simply begin my discussion of the twenty day names with Ak'abal. For each day, I shall first quote the mnemonic phrase or phrases for that day. Then I shall list the rituals performed either regularly or occasionally on that day, according to the accompanying number and place. Next, I shall enlarge this cognitive and behavorial map of the days by displaying some of the possible meanings of the day within the most frequent divinatory occasions: during an illness or after a death, or before a marriage, a business deal, or the selection of a religious leader. Finally, I shall explain the "face of his [her] day" (*uwäch uk'ij*) or the "character" of a child born on that day. Having presented the twenty day names, I shall compare the Momostecan data with other Quiché communities and discuss the significance of my findings for the field of Mayan hieroglyphic decipherment.

The Twenty Days

Ak'abal.—The mnemonics for Ak'abal are *ak'abil* ("at dawn"), *c'abal* ("opening"), and *chak'abaj!* (*ch*-imperative, *a*-you [intimate], *k'abaj* from *k'abanic*, "to blame, conceal," meaning "you blame!"— or, more broadly, a lie, trick, slander).

On 1, 8, and 9 Ak'abal, the teacher of a new priest-shaman performs an opening ritual *(c'abal)* for the shrines of his student's patrilineage; he cleans out all the ashes accumulated by the student's predecessor. During the days on which lineage rituals were performed at these shrines, any ill feelings voiced within the patrilineage entered the shrine, which as a "little volcano" connected with all other volcanoes and mountains, placed these words directly before the Mundo. This is the source of the mnemonic *chak'abaj* ("tricks, lies, slander, and blame"); the removal of the ashes starts the initiate out with a clean slate—or rather, a clean hearth. Also on Ak'abal, a young man and his family plan his marriage, first approaching the Mundo through the agency of his lineage priest-shaman, who will open *(c'abal)* the lineage shrines on 1 Ak'abal, and then—on 2, 3, 4, 5, 6, 7, 8, or 9 Ak'abal—approaching the girl's family. This approach is usually made in early dawn, hence the mnemonic *ak'abil* ("at dawn"). An Ak'abal day is also chosen to introduce (through prayer) a new baby to the ancestors at the lineage shrine.

When the day Ak'abal appears in a divination, the diviner must select from the three mnemonics and their ritual associations a coherent but inspired answer to the client's question. For example, if 1, 8, or 9 Ak'abal should appear in divining why a person is ill, the diviner will explore with the client (if the client is a member of his own patrilineage) the possibility that a family member fought with him or spoke ill of him behind his back on one of the days of the lineage rituals. If, however, the diviner is from another patrilineage, he will explore whether or not the priest-shaman of the client's own patrilineage—who might even be the client's own father, brother, or uncle—had reason to complain about him before the Mundo. Was the client not giving money to this priest-shaman? Or did he drunkenly abuse the priest-shaman or his wife, sister, or daughter?, and so forth.

If the question concerns whether or not a specific woman will marry the client, and an Ak'abal of any number 1 through 9 appears first, then the answer is yes. If the assembled priest-shamans of a patrilineage, a canton, or the entire town are divining whether a particular person should fill a vacancy in their ranks and if a great majority, if not all of them, arrive at Ak'abal on the first round, then the answer is yes. If the question concerns whether a particular journey should be undertaken and the first answer is either a low or middle-numbered Ak'abal, then the answer is yes, the road is open. But if the result is 10, 11, 12, or 13 Ak'abal, the answer is no: there is something hidden in the road. The high number calls attention to the negative aspect of Ak'abal.

Ak'abal, like any day, imparts its *nawal*,[4] also called *uwäch uk'ij* ("face of his day" or "his character"), to a child born on that day. In the case of Ak'abal, because of the various associations mentioned, the child (of either sex) will be feminine, wealthy, verbally skillful, and possibly a liar, cheat, or complainer. Ak'abal is one of ten days that also give a child the extra body-soul called "lightning" *(coyopa)*. This soul specifically enables the child to communicate directly with both the natural and supernatural worlds, as will be discussed at greater length in the next chapter. As a result, a child born on Ak'abal might become either a lineage (or higher) priest-shaman or else a "road guide" *(c'amal be)* or marriage spokesman, both of whom perform important rituals on Ak'abal days.

C'at.—The mnemonics for C'at are *c'atic* ("to burn"), *pa c'at, pa chim* ("in nets, in heaps"), and *c'asaj c'olic* ("to be in debt"). C'at serves as the Secretary (and Treasurer) for Mam E and Mam No'j. As such, it is the day for paying one's debts *(c'asaj)* to the Mundo and to Nantat (ancestors). One pays these debts by offering netsfull or great heaps *(pa c'at, pa chim)* of copal, which are burned *(c'atic)*.

During the two consecutive years when C'at is Secretary— for example, in 1975 and 1976—great stacks of offerings are given on 1, 6, 8, and 9 C'at in order to make up for any neglect of duties to the Mundo or the ancestors. At this time, people also take care of monetary, work, or other debts, both within the immediate family and at the local stores. The verb *c'atic*, besides meaning "to burn," carries the metaphorical meaning that a married person is committing adultery with a virgin of either sex, expressed in full by the idiom *c'atic rakan*, "to burn his or her leg." This sort of sexual misconduct is a serious offense before the Mundo, who places the person "in debt" *(c'asaj)*; if the debt is not cancelled, it will bring illness and even death to the offender.

When the day C'at appears in divination, the diviner has a pretty good idea that, regardless of the question, the client is somehow lacking in his duties to the Mundo or ancestors, or else in the everyday social world. The number that preceeds C'at then indicates how recent this debt is and (consequently) how serious.

For example, 3 C'at indicates a fairly recent and inconsequential debt, while 10 C'at indicates *nimalaj c'asaj* (a large, old, serious debt or quantity of debts). As the diviner says, the client "is carrying a heavy net bag or suitcase." In order to cancel these debts, the client must give the priest-shaman netsfull or heaps *(pa c'at, pa chim)* of copal, which will then be offered in his or her name to the Mundo and the ancestors.

A person whose birthday is C'at, because of the associations of this day, will be a fornicator or debtor or both. Such a person would not be trained as a diviner and is considered unfit for any sort of civil, political, military, or religious office.

Can.—The mnemonics for Can are *caban ri mesa* ("it is the mesa"), *caban mes* ("he is sweeping"), and *ri c'ulel* ("the enemy").

Can is associated with the actions of a calendar diviner who has been trained as an *ajmesa*, or *ajnawal mesa*. These practitioners are simultaneously the most successful curers and a source of serious illness and death. Because of their power, some patrilineages in Momostenango have even selected an *ajmesa* as their patrilineage priest-shaman. On Can days with high numbers—11, 12, 13—these powerful diviners visit the sacred mountains of Momostenango and even distant volcanoes, speaking directly to the Mundo in order to cause or cure specific illnesses according to the desires of their patrilineage members or private clients. On low-numbered Can days—for example, 1, 6, and 8—diviners who are not *ajmesa* petition the Mundo not to allow the latter to send illnesses to their lineage, their clients, or themselves. On 9 Can, *ajmesa* come from several Quiché municipalities to the foot of a high waterfall near San Cristóbal Totonicapán, known as "Nine Chairs Nine Tables" (Belejeb Silla Belejeb Mesa). There they first sweep *(caban mes)* the shrines ("chair" shrines are small individual shrines and "table" shrines are large public shrines) and then sacrifice chickens in order to cure illnesses sent to their clients by witches from the coast and from the municipality of Cobán. The *ajmesa* may use both middle and high-numbered Can days in order to conduct séances, during which the Mundo speaks directly through him or her to the client.

When Can appears in a divination, the diviner immediately asks the client who his enemy *(ri c'ulel)* could be. He may then explore the possibility that an *ajmesa* might have been hired by this enemy to send illness or death. If the client is already ill, the diviner will help the client to determine which *ajmesa* was hired to work against him; then he will help him choose a different, but equally powerful, *ajmesa* to defend him before the Mundo. If the divination concerns marriage, a business deal, or the selection of a religious leader, the day Can means that the woman, business associate, or priest-shaman in question is an enemy *(ri c'ulel)* or may become one, and all plans should be dropped immediately.

A person whose birthday is Can will be a strong, powerful, evil person; the higher the number, the more extreme the character. Also, since Can is one of the ten days that gives the child body lightning, he or she should tame and direct his or her power by becoming an *ajnawal mesa*.

Came.—The mnemonics for Came are *camej lal rutz'il* ("asking for good"), *camical* ("the deceased"), and *c'ulanem* ("marriage"). The day Came is primarily associated with *camej lal rutz'il* ("asking for good") for oneself as well as for one's family and clients.

On 1 and 8 Came, permission days for the divining seeds, a priest-shaman who has a student burns copal at the earth shrines. He requests tranquility among his students, himself, and all deceased diviners, as well as between himself and his own divining equipment, and between himself and all other members, both living and dead, of his own patrilineage. Low-numbered Came days are also used for marriage proposals, as well as for the indigenous marriage ceremony itself. Since marriage *(c'ulanem)*, which is an important alliance between the living members of different patrilineages, is also an alliance between dead *(camical)* family members of both patrilineages, these dead kin must be in accord or else they will send trouble, illness, and even death into the new home. On 11 Came, the town priest-shaman from Los Cipréses visits Pipil, the sacred mountain of the north, in order to ask for tranquility between women and men, indigenes and ladinos, the people of Guatemala and the government of Guatemala, and between the nation of Guatemala and all other nations of the world.

When a divination concerns whether or not a particular woman will make a good wife for the client, a high-numbered Came means an emphatic yes, while a low number is less clearly affirmative. Since money, business, and travel are considered analogous to spouses, the question as to whether or not to take a particular trip or make a particular business deal is answered affirmatively when Came appears. At this moment, the diviner might say, *Camej lal mayij tok'ob* ("There is a favor"). The amount of the favor depends upon the size of the number, with 13 Came representing a tremendous success or a great fortune. However, if the divination concerns the cause of an illness, 13 Came could mean that a very long dead (*camical*) member of the client's own patrilineage sent the illness, and that the client probably will not recover.

A child born on Came (because of the associations with the patrilineage and specifically with marriage alliances), like a child born on Ak'abal, will be wealthy, somewhat feminine, and verbally skillful. Since a person born on this day also receives body lightning, he might become a lineage priest-shaman or a marriage spokesman, in the latter case petitioning the living and dead members of a patrilineage for their living women in marriage.

Quej.—The mnemonics for Quej are *quejaj* ("mounting"), *ch'awanel* ("talker"), and *chuchkajaw* ("mother-father"[priest-shaman]). Quej, one of the four Mam, is a strong, domineering day that can easily mount *(quejaj)* a person who is weak, immoral, or ill.

Because of the strength of Quej, there are many individual, clan, canton, and town rituals performed by *ch'awanel* ("talkers"[meaning the priest-shamans]), on this day. A Quej day is always selected for the October and January meetings of the town elders. On 1 and 8 Quej, which are the most important permission days for new calendar diviners, the priest-shaman goes to the shrines and informs the Mundo of the name of any novice he is going to present on the upcoming 8 Batz'. On 6 and 7 Quej, the "broom" *(mesebal)* ritual is performed at the lineage shrine called the *winel*. At this time, the lineage priest-shaman cleans the three parts of the *winel*, first the low part, then the high part, and finally the center *(c'ux,* literally "heart"), also called *sacramenta*. Then, depending on whether it is planting or harvest time, he symbolically "plants" and prays for a good crop, or else he symbolically "cuts" and gives thanks for the harvest. If 8 Quej falls soon after planting, then the town priest-shaman visits Quilaja, the sacred mountain of the east, to ask for rain for the new crop; on 11 Quej, he begins his regular circuit of all four sacred mountains by going to Quilaja. On 1, 2, 3, or 4 Quej, the unborn children of the currently pregnant wives of the patrilineage are "sown" and "planted" *(awexibal ticbal)* in the "foundation shrine" *(warabalja)* by the lineage priest-shaman (see chapter 3).

In divination, the day Quej points to a calendar diviner of

some type. For example, if a group of priest-shamans of a patrilineage, a canton, or the entire town are divining in order to fill a vacancy in their ranks, and a middle or high-numbered Quej arrives on the first round, then they have found the proper candidate. If the question concerns the cause of an illness and the day Quej appears, the diviner has "mounted" the patient by sending the illness into him. If the illness is a serious one, the diviner who was hired by the patient (or by his family) may begin a series of 9 or 13 consecutive rituals (one each day) in which he will "mount" the evil diviner in order to return the illness to its source.

A baby born on Quej will be physically, psychically, and verbally strong, domineering, and masculine. Such a child, after his or her initiation as a shaman-priest, will either become a leader in both worldly and religious matters, or else an evil witch who will go through life mounting *(quejaj)* others, causing trouble and sorrow to all who know her or him. Finally, after enough calendar diviners have returned these troubles and illnesses, he or she weakens and dies.

K'anil.—The mnemonics for K'anil are *k'anal* ("it ripens, to have corn and money"–literally "yellowness"), *cak'anaric uwäch ulew* ("harvest"–literally, "the face of the earth becomes yellow"), *awexibal ticbal* ("sowing [and] planting"), *tzukunel* ("feeder"), and *ixk'anil* ("sunset").

The lineage rituals called "sowing and planting" begun on 6 and 7 Quej in the *winel*, have their final or "big day" *(nima k'ij)* on 7 and 8 K'anil, respectively. On these days, the lineage priest-shaman, depending on whether planting or harvest time is closer, passes seeds saved from the previous year, or else fresh corn ears that have been chosen as seed ears for the next year, through the copal smoke. In so doing, he is symbolically feeding *(tzukunic)* both the Mundo and his own ancestors. Thus, one name for the priest-shaman is feeder *(tzukunel)*.

If a divinatory question concerns whether a woman will marry a man and K'anil appears, it means she is now ripe or mature *(k'anaric)*, ready to marry him. If the question is for a merchant and the day Tz'iquin (which indicates silver) appears in combination with K'anil, it means that the business deal is ripe, ready for picking. If the question concerns why an illness came to the client, K'anil means that he was not feeding *(tzukunic)* the Mundo or ancestors, who then sent the illness to him. If the question concerns whether the sick person will recover, K'anil means "sunset" (*ixk'anil*). Just as the clouds become yellowish-red or orange and then darkness sets in, so the patient's illness is now well ripened, and he or she will soon die.

A baby born on K'anil should become a daykeeper (calendar diviner), a "feeder" (*tzukunel*) of the Mundo and the dead. If a male takes on these duties, he might eventually become a priest-shaman, looking after the harvest rituals for his patrilineage.

Toj.—The mnemonics for Toj are *tojonic* ("to pay"), and *c'äx* ("illness," "pain"— *pena* in Spanish). Like C'at, Toj is a treasurer for the Mundo.

On 1, 6, and 8 Toj, individual diviners visit the community shrines Paja' (on 1), Paclom (6), and Ch'uti Sabal (8), in order to make up for any one, six, or eight days missed since the opening of the cycle of obligatory shrine visits on 1, 6, and 8 Quej. At this time, they burn all the copal and candles they have omitted plus a penalty for having not made the offerings on the proper days. Since these Toj days are each the thirteenth occurrence of an obligatory day of a given number, they are extremely powerful days for both evil and good. At Nima Sabal, 9 Toj is reserved for lineage priest-shamans. If a lineage priest-shaman should neglect his duties on these Toj days, particularly on 9 Toj, someone in his patrilineage would suffer serious punishment in the form of an illness or injury (*c'äx*) from the Mundo.

In divination, a low-numbered Toj indicates that one owes (*tojonic*) in the customs of the Mundo or the ancestors, and by extension one may owe a favor, work, or money to another person. If the client is ill, this means that the pain (*c'äx*) is a punishment for this debt; the only way to cure it is to pay (*tojonic*) the Mundo, ancestors, or creditor what is owed, plus a penalty for the neglect. Since the number is low, the person will recover after paying. A middle-numbered Toj—such as 7, 8, or 9 Toj—indicates that someone in the client's family will die, and, as a consequence, the client will have to borrow money to hold the proper sort of wake. The day 13 Toj indicates that an *ajmesa lok'ej ri camical, lok'ej ri sachical, lok'ej ri mac* ("cries for death, cries for disappearance, cries for sin") for the client. This is a serious matter that the diviner will turn over to an *ajmesa*, who will begin counter-witchcraft rites for the patient.

A child born on Toj will be chronically ill and in debt much of his or her life. Such a person should be a constant client of diviners, including *ajmesa*, who could help him or her live out a normal life-span despite the indebtedness with which he or she was born.

Tz'i'.—The mnemonics for Tz'i' are *tz'ilonic* ("to be dirty, soiled, stained, impure"—with the connotation of making love either to the wrong person or at the wrong time or place), *tz'iyalaj tzij* ("jealous words" between husband and wife), and *catz'iyaric* ("it isn't certain").

The only Tz'i' day used for ritual purposes is 7 Tz'i', which is the *mixprix* or eve of 8 Batz'. On this crucial day, the novice is formally quizzed about his or her recent dreams, and the teacher tells any of his own; the latter will then make his final decision as to whether or not to go ahead with the initiation. He asks if the novice has lost confidence *(catz'iyaric)*, or is willing to go through with the initiation. When he has assured himself that the novice is decisive, he immediately begins the initiation ritual, which will be publicly completed on the next two days, 8 Batz' and 9 E.

In divination, a low-numbered Tz'i' indicates *catz'iyari chi, catz'iyari wäch* ("one loses confidence"—literally "the mouth is uncertain, the face is uncertain"). This indicates that the person wants to do something one minute and does not want to do it the next. The person is uncertain and discouraged. A middle-numbered Tz'i' indicates that the novice has dirtied *(tz'ilonic)* him or herself by making love on one of the permission days, or else that a man and woman are exchanging jealous words *(tz'iyalaj tzij)* because of a lack of faithfulness on one or the other's part. A high-numbered Tz'i' indicates that the person has committed a serious sexual sin *(tz'ilonic)* such as incest, adultery, or sodomy. In a divination for a marriage, Tz'i' indicates that the woman already has a lover; consequently, all plans for marriage are stopped. No business deal or journey would be initiated on Tz'i', which is a weak, indifferent day.

A child born on Tz'i' will be a confused, weak, unlucky person who will always be looking for someone to have sexual relations with. Such a person could easily become a homosexual, fornicator, or prostitute. Because of the impurity and weakness indiscriminate sex brings, such a person would not be trained as a diviner.

Batz'.—The mnemonics for Batz' are *cabätz'inic* ("to spin," as in spinning thread), *cabotz'ic* ("to roll up"), *botz'oj* ("winding"), and *tz'onoj* ("asking").

Two rituals performed on Batz' are the asking *(tz'onoj)* part of the native marriage ceremony and the initiation of a daykeeper or diviner. Forty days before marriage *(c'ulanem)*, the groom, his "road guide" *(c'amal be)*, and his family all go to the house of the prospective bride, carrying sticks, called *botz'oj*, that are elaborately wound with flowers. This ritual, which involves hours of formal oratory called *tz'onoj*, is most frequently performed on a low-numbered Batz', although Came, Ak'abal, and Aj are also possible. The marriage itself will be performed on a day of the same name, but with the next higher number; thus a successful *tz'onoj* falling on 1 Batz' will be followed by a wedding forty days later, on 2 Batz'. On 8 Batz', a novice diviner is publicly presented with his divining seeds, first at Ch'uti Sabal and then at Paja', at the particular hearths where the teacher and his wife received their own divining paraphernalia. This is parallel to the matrimonial "asking" in that the new diviner and his or her divining paraphernalia are thereafter considered to be husband and wife. Forty days later, on 9 Batz', the "marriage" of the diviner and the divining seeds is completed with a formal giving of thanks at Nima Sabal.

In divination, if the question concerns whether to make a particular trip, business deal, or ask for a woman, Batz' of any number is affirmative: one will spin *(cabätz'inic)* or roll up *(cabotz'ic)* luck, business, or a marriage arrangement. The higher the number, the luckier and better the situation. If the question concerns why a person is ill, Batz' means, *At falta cho ri chac patan, at falta cho wa Mundo*, "You [familiar] lack before the divining seeds, you lack before the Mundo." The higher the number, the greater the lack of proper offerings and prayers.

A child born on Batz' will be lucky in business, marriage, and life. He or she will easily roll up *(cabotz'ic)* everything: money, animals, harvest, children. Such a person will automatically be rich and respected without needing to be formally initiated as a diviner.

E.—The mnemonics for E are *ri E* ("the E" referring to the foundation shrine, *warabalja*), *ri be* ("the road"), *ri utzilaj be, ri calominaj be, ri nimalaj be* ("the good road, the straight road, the long road"), *c'ama la kabe* ("that we be guided on our road"), and *xasachom ube* ("he has lost his road"). E, as one of the four Mam, indicates a quiet, calm, good year for people and animals.

In an E year, each of the eighteen occurrences of the day E is celebrated with firecrackers, copal, and feasting at many locations in the municipality. The days 4 and 6 E are the eve *(mixprix)* of the ceremonies in the foundation shrine *(warabalja)* of both the canton and the patrilineage. The ceremony at the foundation shrine for people begins on 6 E, while that at the foundation for animals begins on 4 E. On these days, the patrilineage priest-shaman goes first to Paja', the low, watery public shrine, and then to the low part of his own lineage's foundation shrine. The day 9 E is the final day or "big day" *(nima k'ij)* for the initiation of a novice daykeeper, which takes place at Nima Sabal. On this day, the novice formally begins *ri utzilaj be, ri calominaj be, ri nimalaj be* ("the good road, the straight road, the long road") of his or her service to the people.

In divination, E generally indicates the road *(ri be)*, which, as my teacher explained, means more than "the road you can see with your eyes," for it is the road of life. In a destiny divination, the meaning of E depends on the other days appearing with it. For example, if Imöx—which indicates a confused, crazy, possessed condition—immediately preceeds E in the results, it means "he has lost his road" *(xasachom ube)*. On the other hand, a combination of E and Quej would indicate either that "we be guided on our road" *(c'ama la kabe)* by the lineage priest-shaman, or that the client's destiny is to become a priest-shaman. However, if the person is ill and the question concerns who caused the illness, then the combination of Quej and E would indicate that a lineage priest-shaman placed a trap in the client's road.

A male child born on E, especially if it happens to be an E year as well, might become a lineage priest-shaman, performing rituals at the nine family shrines. A female child born on E, especially in an E year, might become a midwife *(iyom)*, helping women and their babies on the road of life. In any case, a child of either sex born on E will have a good, long, healthy life.

Aj.—The mnemonics for Aj are *pa ri ja, pa ri c'olibal* ("in the house, in the place"), *pa ri alaxic* ("in the patrilineage"), and *baraj* ("mixing"), this last referring to the divining seeds.

On 1 and 8 Aj—as on 1 and 8 Quej, Ajpu, and Came, all of which are permission days specifically for the divination parapher-nalia— the priest-shaman visits the public shrines in order to ask the ancestors to help his student learn to divine properly. 5 and 7 Aj are the second or "broom" *(mesebal)* days following 4 and 6 E in the respective ceremonies of the foundations of the animals and of the people. On 7 Aj, in the ceremony for the people, the lineage priest-shaman first visits Ch'uti Sabal, where he leaves paraffin candles for all known deceased priest-shamans of his patrilineage; then he goes and leaves vigil lights in the church for these same dead. On 8 and 9 Aj (and 8 and 9 Ajmac) the confraternities do the "washing of clothes" *(ch'ajbal atz'iak)* for the saints in the parish church and cemetery chapel. On 11 Aj, the town priest-shaman from Los Cipréses visits Tamancu, the sacred mountain of the south, and then returns to offer paraffin candles on Paclom (in the center) to all dead lineage, canton, and town priest-shamans.

In divination, Aj usually indicates that the answer lies "in the house, in the place" *(pa ri ja, pa ri c'olibal)*. For example, if the question concerns the cause of an illness, a low-numbered Aj would indicate that a recent fight within the patrilineage *(pa ri alaxic)* was the cause, while a high number would indicate a fight in the distant past, perhaps before the sick person was even born. If 7 Aj appears, it specifically means that a dead priest-shaman of the client's own lineage has been neglected or offended and has sent illness to the sufferer.

Any child born on Aj will be lucky in love, business, and family life. A male child born on this day should make a good lineage, canton, or town priest-shaman, dutifully looking after the appropriate foundation shrines. A female child born on Aj will be a responsible mother and wife, especially lucky with the raising of animals and children.

Ix.—The mnemonics for Ix are *jix* ("to withdraw, remove, to be free") and *chu wa Mundo* ("before the Earth").

6 and 8 Ix are the third and final or "big days" *(nima k'ij)* following 4 and 6 E *(mixprix)* and 5 and 7 Aj *(mesebal)* in the ceremonies of the foundation shrines. On this final day, the lineage priest-shaman first goes to Ch'uti Sabal, which is considered the mother and father of all the foundation shrines. There, he prays and offers copal to the Mundo, since Ix is the day specifically dedicated to the Mundo. After this, he goes to the high part of his own lineage's foundation shrine and gives thanks *(c'amowa)* to the Mundo that the animals (6 Ix) or people (8 Ix) of his patrilineage are healthy. 6 and 7 Ix are the "broom days" for the *mebil* ceremony. On these days, the lineage priest-shaman opens both the lower and upper *mebil* shrines, where he asks the Mundo for money to buy

the land and materials necessary to build a house. If a house is currently being built somewhere within his patrilineage, he then goes to the site to perform the house "planting" rituals, which protect the house from being hit by lightning, dissolved in a rainstorm, collapsed by an earthquake, or washed away in a flood.

In a divination concerning a sick client, a low-numbered Ix indicates that the Mundo will withdraw (*jix*) the illness or financial trouble he has inflicted upon the person. A middle or high-numbered Ix, however, indicates that the trouble was sent by the Mundo, that the Mundo is the enemy. In this case, the only way to withdraw the illness is to change one's relationship with the Mundo. Since Ix is a secretary to the Mundo, the best way to do this is to pay a fine to the secretary, who will give the money—in the form of copal, candles, sugar, and flowers—to the two secretary-treasurers, C'at and Tz'iquin. Only in this way can the patient free himself (*jix*) from the jail of the Mundo. In divining whether a person should become a daykeeper, Ix in combination with Quej indicates that the Mundo is in agreement, while Ix in combination with Ik' indicates that the candidate is an enemy of the Mundo.

A child born on Ix will have a close relationship with the Mundo. As a result of this, he or she will be wealthy, since all gold, silver, and precious stones belong to the Mundo. However, this child will also suffer many physical ailments, which the Mundo inflicts quite suddenly with only slight cause. As a result of these ailments, he or she will eventually become a daykeeper or else die. A male child born on this day might go on to become a lineage priest-shaman, looking after the *mebil* as well as other shrines for his patrilineage, canton, or even for the entire town.

Tz'iquin.—The mnemonics for Tz'iquin are *ok'etalic siqu'italic* ("to cry for, to ask for") and *pwak* ("money, silver").

7 and 8 Tz'iquin are the "big days" for the *mebil* shrines. On these days, the lineage priest-shaman crys for, asks for (*ok'etalic siqu'italic*) material blessings in the form of money (*pwak*) for buying the necessities of life for all members of his patrilineage. Tz'iquin, like C'at, is a secretary-treasurer for the Mundo, but Tz'iquin consecutively serves as secretary to the two most powerful and violent Mam, namely Quej and Ik', who are just as likely to destroy material well-being as to create it. The crying and asking (*ok'etalic siqu'italic*) at the shrines on 1, 6, and 8 Tz'iquin during a

Quej or Ik' year is for protection from these powerful, cruel Mam.

In divination concerning the cause of an illness, Tz'iquin would indicate that the person had an enemy who cried or asked for (*xasiqu'italic, xatz'onotalic*) the financial ruin of the client, ruin that the illness could cause if not quickly cured. A low-numbered Tz'iquin would indicate that the client had a recent enemy, while a high-numbered Tz'iquin would indicate an enemy of some years. If the divination concerns a business trip, Tz'iquin would indicate a financial success; the higher the number the greater the success. In divining during the training of a novice daykeeper, Tz'iquin means that this person desires and cries for (*ok'etalic siqu'italic*) knowledge.

A child born on Tz'iquin will cry for, desire (*rok'em usiqu'in*) everything necessary for a good life, both material and spiritual. Such a child, if called by the Mundo, will be trained as a daykeeper. As a daykeeper, he or she will be an elegant prayermaker and much in demand for both good and evil desires. If the child is male, he might be selected by his patrilineage as their priest-shaman to look after the *mebil* and other shrines. Later, he might become a priest-shaman at a higher level, helping the people to prosper.

Ajmac.—The mnemonics for Ajmac are *pa ri alaxic* ("in the patrilineage") and *sachbal ajmac, chila' chi kaj, chuwäch ri Tiox, chuwäch ri Mundo, chiquiwäch ri Nantat* ("pardoning your sins there before the sky, before God, before Earth, before the Ancestors").

1, 6, 8, and 9 Ajmac are days when priest-shamans visit the community shrines to ask pardon (*sachbal ajmac*) before Tiox, Mundo, and Nantat for fighting within the patrilineage. Ajmac, like Aj and Ix, is a good day for the "planting" in the foundation shrine of a new but as yet unborn child of the patrilineage. 8 and 9 Ajmac (like 8 and 9 Aj) are for washing the clothes of the saints by members of the confraternities.

In divination for an illness, Ajmac indicates that the person has sinned against a member of his own patrilineage and that he or she must ask pardon before his or her spouse and parents. The lower the number, the more recent or minor the sin, while the higher the number, the older or more serious the offense. If the question concerns whether a particular woman will marry the client, Ajmac is a positive answer: she will join in the patrilineage (*pa ri alaxic*).

Ajmac is also a good journey and money day; the higher the number, the better the financial outcome.

A child born on Ajmac will be lucky in business but irresponsible as a spouse or parent. Nevertheless, his or her adultery or other sins committed against the family will be forgiven, unlike the sins committed by people born on other days, so that his or her family will prosper.

No'j.—The mnemonics for No'j are *utzilaj no'j xuchomaj, itsel no'j xuchomaj* ("he was thinking good thoughts, he was thinking bad thoughts"), and *no'jinic chomanic* ("to think, meditate, argue, resolve, conclude, or worry"). No'j, one of the four Mam, has a good head and many thoughts, both good and evil.

In a No'j year, one expects members of the civil government to propose a new building or taxing plan, which could be either an excellent or a stupid idea. On each occurrence of No'j during a No'j year, the priest-shaman may think of novel solutions to long-standing family, canton, or town problems. Although there are no obligatory visits to community or family shrines on No'j, one could visit the community shrines on any low-numbered No'j in order to give thanks for a solution to a problem or else for a new blanket design.

In divination the day No'j, in combination with other day names, means both *chomanic* ("to think" in the sense of a calculative, argumentative, troubled train of thought) and *no'jinic* ("to think" in the sense of creative or meditative thought). For example, in a divination about illness, Can and No'j would indicate that one should think about which *ajnawal mesa* caused this illness. Aj and No'j or Ajmac and No'j would direct thought to family members, while C'at and No'j would direct thought to one's debts to another person or to the Mundo.

A child born on No'j will be a creative and innovative thinker and consequently an excellent daykeeper. Such a child, because of his or her problem-solving ability, could also become a civil or religious leader. No'j is a masculine day, and the child born on this day, regardless of actual sex, will have a masculine character.

Tijax.—The mnemonics for Tijax are *xak'abal chi'aj* ("telling lies, slandering"–literally, "trampling lips"), *k'abanic* ("to conceal" from one's family), and *ch'oj* ("fighting").

1 and 8 Tijax are two of the twenty-one permission days for the novice daykeeper. At this time, the student is reminded of the slanderous "trampling lips" *(xak'abal chi'aj)* of his or her friends,

who might call him or her a fool or a witch for undergoing the training. They will do this either because they are jealous that the Mundo has not chosen them, or else because the Protestant missionaries or the Catholic priest have filled them with lies about "pagans" each Sunday morning. On 1, 6, 8, and 9 Tijax, daykeepers visiting the community shrines may ask that religious slanderers fight *(ch'oj)* among themselves rather than with them. On the same visit, they also ask that there be no jealousy or concealment *(k'abanic)* over financial or sexual matters among members of their own patrilineage.

In divination, Tijax indicates that a missionary is trying to engage one in a religious dispute *(ch'oj)*, or else that one's spouse is angry and jealous about attentions paid to another man or woman. The higher the number, the more serious the dispute, ending (at 13) with the jailing of one or both parties and a public scandal. In divining for a marriage, journey, or business, Tijax would indicate that a fight would result. In an illness divination, Tijax would indicate slander, whether by an enemy or by the patient himself, as the cause.

A child born on Tijax will go through life as a victim and promoter of political, sexual, and religious lies, slanders, and fights. Such a person will not be trained as a daykeeper, for he or she will be so weakened as a result of disputes that he or she will be unable to act as the representative of a sick person before the Mundo.

Cawuk.—The mnemonics for Cawuk are *remelic tiquilic* ("to hold water, to plant or set out" in the sense of putting stew in a bowl on the table or leaving offerings from newly harvested crops in the church for Santiago and San Antonio Pologuá), and *mulom kuchum* ("gather together gossip, trouble, or harrassment").

On 1 and 8 Cawuk, permission days for the novice daykeeper, the teacher reminds the student that the rituals have already begun and that the offerings have now been placed on the table of the Mundo *(remelic tiquilic)* in his or her name. On 1, 6, 8, and 9 Cawuk, daykeepers visit the shrines in order to place offerings on the table of the Mundo, as well as to ask that any troubles *(mulom kuchum)* placed there by their enemies be returned to those same enemies.

In divination for an illness, Cawuk would indicate that someone set a table *(remelic tiquilic)* of offerings before the Mundo and the ancestors, asking them to send the illness to the client. The higher the number, the longer ago and the more serious the result of this request. However, in divining for the outcome of a business deal, "the table is set" (*remelic tiquilic*) indicates that the Mundo and the ancestors approve and that the proposed business deal is a good one.

A child born on Cawuk will have a troubled and harassed (*mulom kuchum*) life full of punishment from the ancestors. Such a person would not have the strength necessary to help others and thus would not be trained as a diviner.

Junajpu.—The mnemonics for Junajpu are *quik'ij ri Nantat* ("ancestors' day"), *chiquiwäch ri Nantat* ("before the ancestors"), and *quetaman ri Nantat* ("the ancestors already know").

1 and 8 Junajpu are permission days for a novice daykeeper. On 1, 6, 8, and 9 Junajpu, individual daykeepers make offerings at the communal shrines before the ancestors (*chiquiwäch ri Nantat*). On 11 Junajpu, the town priest-shaman from Los Cipréses visits Socop, the sacred western mountain of the ancestors. Here he asks the ancestors for blessings (rather than the illnesses they can also send) for all living Momostecans.

Junajpu days, like Aj days, are selected for house-building rituals; the priest-shaman specifically asks if the ancestors know (*quetaman ri Nantat*) and if they are in agreement concerning the new house. Junajpu days are also selected for the prayers and offerings that enable the spirit (*nawal*) of a dead person to enter the cold, dark room of the Mundo and thus join the other spirits. The younger and less powerful the person, the lower the number chosen. For example, the spirit of a baby enters the room on 1 Junajpu, a young married woman or man enter respectively on 5 and 6 Junajpu, while an old woman enters on 8 Junajpu and an old man on 9 Junajpu. A woman who has served as a midwife and/or daykeeper enters on 9 Junajpu, while a male priest-shaman enters from 9 to 12 Junajpu, depending on how high up in the priestly hierarchy he went. A person who has been town priest-shaman or second city manager (see chapter 2) enters on 12 Junajpu, and the powerful and capricious *ajnawal mesa* enters on 13 Junajpu.

In divination, Junajpu indicates the dead. If the question concerns the cause of illness, the number of Junajpu indicates the age and status (at death) of the dead person who sent the illness. If the question concerns whether or not the client will recover, and if the Junajpu number that would be selected for the entry ceremony of this client's spirit appears, it means that the client will not recover, for his or her spirit is already with the dead. In a marriage divination, Junajpu indicates that the client's own sister or another female relative will be lost to his patrilineage, going to join her husband's patrilineage. If a priest-shaman dies on 9, 10, or 11 Junajpu, it indicates that he or she was destined to die: the ancestors wished his or her presence among them. But if the death occurs on 13 Junajpu, this was an evil priest-shaman who took money from his clients and kept it rather than using it for the necessary offerings on their behalf.

A child born on Junajpu will have a close, perhaps unhealthy relationship with the dead. He or she may even become an *ajnawal mesa*, acting as a medium for the voices of the dead.

Imöx.—The mnemonics for Imöx are *camöxiric* ("one becomes possessed or crazy"), *nimalaj c'ulel* ("a big enemy"), and *cumatz rib chiquiwäch Mam* ("humble oneself before the Mam").

On 1, 6, and 8 Imöx, a daykeeper visits the appropriate public shrines, where he or she humbles him or herself *(cumatz rib)* before the Mam (Quej, E, No'j, Ik') so as not to be dominated by their power, which makes one crazy *(camöxiric)*. On high-numbered Imöx days, powerful calendar diviners go to mountaintop shrines to present themselves before the Mam, asking them to dominate persons who have used witchcraft against others. This domination comes in the form of an illness with a mental as well as a physical component. The diviner who calls directly on the power of the Mam in order to harm others in this way is the big enemy *(nimalaj c'ulel)* who brings divine punishment upon his or her enemies. This is considered a very dangerous practice, because the Mam, after hearing the case, could decide to dominate the person who asked rather than the intended victim. The nine or thirteen consecutive days of the two main witchcraft rituals always include an Imöx day for notifying the Mam of the intended victim.

In divination for an illness, Imöx indicates that an enemy *(c'ulel)* has asked for the illness; the lower the number, the less serious the illness. As an early result in a marriage divination, Imöx means that the desired woman would cause the client to become crazy *(camöxiric)*; through her unfaithfulness or other malicious actions, she would dominate the man. In divining for a journey or a business deal, Imöx indicates so many problems and so much complexity that one would become crazy.

A child born on Imöx will be dominated by the power of the Mam. As a result, he or she will be weak, inefficient, undirected, even insane. Although such a person cannot be effectively trained as a daykeeper, he or she will be quite interested in witchcraft and may patronize the traveling merchants who sell printed prayers to San Simón and other evil saints, published in Mexico, Honduras, and in Mazatenango, Guatemala. People who rely solely on printed materials in attempting such dangerous acts are said to drive themselves mad.

Ik'.—The mnemonics for Ik' are *eyawarinak* ("one became annoyed"), *contra c'ulel* ("an enemy is against one"), *lawalo* ("strong, wild, violent"), and *ch'u'j* ("frenzy, fury, madness"). Ik', one of the four Mam, is very *bravo (lawalo)*, bringing either violent rainstorms or else windstorms without rain.

Ik' is such a dangerous Mam that the usual ceremonies for the current Mam are performed only on 1, 6, and 8 Ik' during an Ik' year. On these days, priest-shamans ask that they, their families, and clients not be crushed by the violence of Ik'. They specifically ask that lightning, earthquake, flood, or landslide not destroy their homes, themselves, or their domestic animals. They also ask that the strong negative human emotions of hatred, anger, rage *(eyawarinak)*, and frenzy *(ch'u'j)* not fall upon themselves, their family, or their clients. A powerful and evil daykeeper or *ajnawal mesa* uses a high-numbered Ik' to induce these negative, destructive rages, in nature as well as in humans. On such days, people may be dominated to some degree by violent passions, no matter how hard they try not to be.

In divination for an illness, Ik' indicates that the client has an enemy against him *(contra c'ulel)* who induced a rage *(eyawarinak)* or frenzy *(ch'u'j)* within him. The result was illness. The lower the number, the more recent the rage and the less serious the resulting illness. In a marriage divination, Ik' is a negative answer, indicating that the woman named is an enemy *(c'ulel)*, since she is too passionate and emotional *(lawalo)* and will bring frenzy *(ch'u'j)* and destruction to the home and family. Ik' is such a bad day for a journey or business deal that most Momostecan merchants will avoid transactions altogether on high-numbered Ik' days.

A child born on Ik' will be a *bravo*, strong, wild, even violent person who could be trained as an *ajnawal mesa*. Although such

people are greatly feared and even hated, Ik' men often assume
high military or civil office because of their personal power.

Implications for Mayan Epigraphy

This presentation of the mnemonics, rituals, divinatory meanings, and character of each of the twenty day names, as taught and
practiced in Momostenango, should have made it apparent that
although some days have strong tendencies one way or another,
there are no absolutely "good" or "bad" days. Even though Ik', for
example, has a generally negative flavor, 1, 6, and 8 Ik' are used for
the positive purpose of guarding against disasters. Secondly, the
mnemonics for each day, which often embody sonic resemblances
to the day name, must not, as Thompson suggested, be ignored as
"fortuitous" or "spurious accretions,"[5] for they are central to the
oral system of calendar instruction and the practice of calendrical
interpretation. The mnemonics typically connect the days with
rituals by way of sound play or paronomasia rather than connecting
days with static symbols by way of etymology. For example, Batz' is
interpreted by way of *botz'oj* ("winding," referring to a wand with
flowers wound on it), which connects it with marriage proposals. It
should not be glossed as "howler monkey," as Thompson would
desire. In other words, the "theory" of day meanings is based on
living "practice," rather than on what Thompson would see as the
decayed or misused fragments of a once-perfect symbol system.

The mnemonics, like the twenty day names, are Quiché rather
than narrowly Momostecan; I have found people in Chichicastenango, Santa Catarina Ixtahuacán, and Chinique to be familiar with
these and other mnemonics. Paul Townsend has found similar
mnemonics among the Ixil in Cotzal.[6] It should also be noted that
the interpretation of the day names through paronomasia occurs in
the *Chilam Balam of Chumayel*, a Lowland Maya book of the
seventeenth century.[7]

Further, the mnemonics, rituals, and divinatory meanings of
these days, combined with the knowledge of their modifications by
the preceding number, resolve many apparent differences reported
in the literature as to the values of the days in different Quiché
towns. Perhaps the two best examples of such days are Ik' and

Ak'abal. Sapper characterized Ik' as a bad day in Quezaltenango and Momostenango—one on which an enemy would send an illness, [8] while Schultze Jena characterized it as a sacred day, a good day for performing rituals for the household idols in Chichicastenango.[9] This apparent disagreement is rather easily resolved by Bunzel's consultant's discussion of the ritual and divinatory meanings of the day Ik' in Chichicastenango:

> This is a bad day, a dangerous day. This is the day that is sacred to the idols. I, for example, have idols in my house. When this day comes I honor them by performing a rite in my house. This is done in the evening, with a little incense, *aguardiente*, roses, and pine needles and two candles of five pesos each which will burn all night. If divinations come out in īq' it is a sign of sin before idols. Divination in īq' and aq'bal signify slanders, perhaps on the part of an enemy, before idols. Painful swellings, and cancer are attributed to this day. (Bunzel 1952:280–81)

This more thorough discussion is in harmony both with Schultze Jena's information that Ik' is a sacred day for performing rituals for the house idols and with Sapper's information that the enemy can send an illness on this day. I found a similar interpretation of Ik' in Chinique (a community near Chichicastenango), where Ik' is a good day to feed liquor to stone idols (in the home and at shrines) in order to receive favors from them. But at the same time, it is a day when these idols may send destruction.

In the case of Ak'abal, Schultze Jena separated out what he felt were unresolvable differences in the meanings of this day between Chichicastenango, where it is a day of witchcraft, and Momostenango, where it is a good day to complete a marriage ceremony. In Momostenango, *ak'abil* ("at dawn"), which indicates the time for a marriage proposal, might be said to be a central mnemonic. That this is the case is clearly shown by Rodríguez's minimal presentation of the meaning of the day in Momostenango as a good one to ask for a woman,[10] and Saler's assertion that in El Palmar (a community founded by Momostecans), "any ak'abal, no matter what day number is combined with it, is 'a good day for looking for a girl.' "[11]

As I have already discussed at some length, Momostecans also associate Ak'abal, by way of the mnemonic *c'abal* ("opening") with the ill feelings that may enter lineage shrines on ritual days. The most common form of Quiché witchcraft is through the expression of dissatisfaction before an open lineage or other shrine. I myself have been the victim of it in Momostenango. I have also been present in Chinique when a daykeeper complained about a neighbor to the Mundo; he expected that his complaint would result in an illness for this man. In both cases, the daykeepers themselves knew that they were practicing witchcraft, although they felt it to be justifiable self-defense. This practice of complaining to the Mundo and ancestors about injustices in order to get revenge is called *chak'abaj* ("You blame!"), which is a mnemonic for this day in both Momostenango and Chichicastenango. Bunzel's description of Ak'abal would indicate that this mnemonic is the central one in Chichicastenango:

> Aq'bal (*oscuridad*, darkness, night). Symbolic of the evil in the hearts of men. "Aq'bal is a bad day, the day of slanderers. 8 Aq'bal is a day to ask protection against slanderers, if one wishes no evil. But the 'strong' day, 12 or 13 Aq'bal are days for working evil against others; for asking justice before the Lords of Justice that enemies may be punished for their slanders and calumnies. If divinations come out in Aq'bal it is bad; it means that some enemy is working sorcery against one. Then one must defend one's self with strong ceremonies." (Bunzel 1952:281)

It appears that this community no longer uses a particular day on the Quiché calendar for marriage ceremonies. Instead, the calendar diviners look for a Monday or Thursday on the Gregorian calendar.[12] This may explain why Maxeños apparently use only the mnemonic *chak'abaj* ("You blame!"), while Momostecans also think of *c'abal*, referring to the opening of the lineage shrines to ask permission to marry a woman and *ak'abil* ("at dawn"), the time of the proposal itself. The difference between the two communities springs not from confusion in a symbol system, but from a difference in the practices on which theories of day meanings are based.

Social actions, primarily consisting of ritual practices that underlie and limit the mnemonics selected for particular days, take precedence over paronomasia in the cases of five of the twenty days: Ajmac, Tijax, Cawuk, Junajpu, and Ik' all lack the feature of paronomasia in their mnemonics. The interpretation of the other fifteen day names, however, unites practice and paronomasia. Whatever changes may have come about in the ritual practices associated with the days since Precolumbian times, it is probable, from a linguistic point of view, that the phonetic constraints on paronomasia have remained the same. For this reason, any evidence concerning the rules governing sound plays in Mayan languages is of considerable importance to the decipherment of Mayan hieroglyphic writing, in which a given word might be spelled not with a glyph of its own but in rebus fashion, using glyphs of other words with similar sounds. Thompson claimed that in such rebus writing, a glottalized consonant would never be replaced by a plain one, and vice versa, a rule that is confirmed (with one complication) by Quiché day mnemonics: Ak'abal = *ak'abil, c'abal, chak'abaj;* C'at = *c'atic, c'at, c'asaj;* Can = *caban;* Came = *camej, camical;* Quej = *quejaj;* K'anil = *cak'anaric, ixk'anil;* Toj = *tojonic;* Tz'i' = *tz'ilonic, tz'iyalaj, catz'iyaric;* and Batz' = *cabätz'inic, cabotz'ic, botz'oj, tz'onoj.* The complication is that one of the mnemonics for Tz'iquin is *siqu'italic,* but here it might be argued that the *qu (c)* in the mnemonic has picked up its glottalization through metathesis— that is, through transposition from *tz'* in the day name—rather than through a complete contradiction of the rule that glottalized consonants are not acceptable plays on plain ones. Another of Thompson's rules is that *c* (or *qu)* and *k* are not interchangeable; the Quiché evidence is once again largely confirmatory (see the above examples), except where Ak'abal = *c'abal.* Thompson also forbids shifts in vowels;[13] here again, the Quiché evidence is largely in agreement, as may be seen in the examples already given and in Ix = *jix,* except that *all* of the mnemonics for Batz' (see above) involve a vowel shift, though the shift in Batz' = *cabätz'inic* is a small one.

In summary, Thompson's rule concerning glottalization remains unshaken, but the cases of Ak'abal = *c'abal* and the Batz' mnemonics suggest that his rules concerning *c/ k* and vowel shifts should not be thought of as absolute, as he seemed to insist, but as strong tendencies. The Quiché data raise one new possibility Thompson does not discuss, that of metathesis, exemplified not only by the transposition of glottalization in Tz'iquin = *siqu'italic* but by the reversal of vowel and consonant in Aj = *ja*.

While the sounds of the Quiché mnemonics for the day names may give clues to the rules for reading passages in ancient Mayan texts that happen to be written out phonetically rather than logographically,[14] these mnemonics should also serve to remind epigraphers that the ancient method of giving a full reading to a hieroglyphic text may have involved much more than serially assigning a particular phoneme, syllable, morpheme, or word to each glyph. The ancient reader, on coming to the logographic glyph for a day name or some other word heavily loaded with meaning, may not have been content with simply pronouncing that word (and then going on to the next glyph), but may have opened up its wider implications through the recital of just such interpretive words and phrases as are used by the Quiché diviner today.[15]

6.

The Blood Speaks

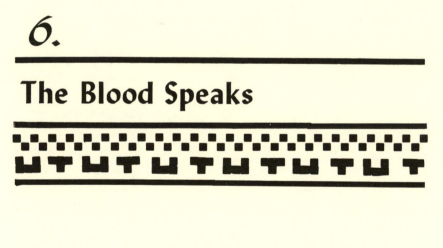

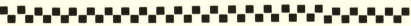

In a wide area of Mesoamerica, stretching from Sonora and Michoacán down through Oaxaca and Chiapas to the Guatemalan highlands and Belize, the blood is considered to be an animate substance, capable, in some individuals, of sending signals or "speaking." The reception of its messages takes two forms, internal and external. In the case of the internal reading, found throughout the Guatemalan highlands, the shaman has a sensation within his or her body, variously described in the literature as a tingling, jumping, twitching, or twinging in the blood or muscles. This sensation conveys information about the past or the prospects of patients or divinatory clients. In the case of the external reading, found in the remaining areas, the shaman receives information directly from the patient's blood by means of "pulsing," touching the patient's body at various pulse points. In both cases, the blood may be said to "speak," but otherwise these two phenomena would appear to be radical transformations of one another, with a mutually exclusive geographical distribution. For the Mam community of Todos Santos, which is in the Guatemalan highlands but very near the border of Chiapas, Oakes described what appears to be an intermediate case. A shaman put his left hand on the calf of his right leg, just below the knee, while asking himself who witched the patient;[1] in other words, he might be said to have pulsed himself rather than pulsing the patient. In the case of the internally sensed "tingling" or "jumping" of the blood, the shaman does not touch his or her own body.

Although it has never been described systematically, the internal speaking of the blood has received frequent mention in the ethnographic literature on highland Guatemala. An Ixil told Lincoln that although he had not as yet received the complete call to become a calendar expert, he had a certain feeling or signal in his upper and lower arms that told him when someone was coming, was crying, or was in jail.[2] Saler reported, for the Quiché-speaking community of El Palmar, "twinging 'of blood' in the legs of specially gifted persons, [with] the pulsations being interpreted according to some scheme for yielding binary answers—'yes' or 'no'—to any question."[3] Falla mentioned that an innate quality among native shamans in the Quiché municipality of San Antonio Ilotenango was a very fine sensitivity to their own blood signals and body.[4] In Chichicastenango, Bunzel found that during divination, the day-keeper would ask a series of questions of the patient or client until he is suddenly "answered by a twitching sensation in the forearms, which is said to be located in the veins, and to be the voice of the blood." This ability to divine with the blood was said to be a direct gift from the ancestors.[5] In this same community, Tax noted the existence of persons who experienced "muscle-jerking,"[6] and Rodas, Rodas, and Hawkins mentioned that when a diviner is praying, "if his left arm pit twitches, that is a bad sign while if his right arm pit twitches that is good."[7] Schultze Jena also reported this left/right, evil/good opposition.[8] Cosminsky noted that the midwives of the Quiché-speaking town of Santa Lucía Utatlán experience "twitches or tremblings" in their left hand if the birth will be delayed, and in their right hand if it will be quick.[9]

This same left/right, evil/good scheme was noted by Hinshaw in the Cakchiquel-speaking community of Panajachel, where "a twitching left arm, leg, or eye is a sign of impending misfortune; on the right side it is good luck." His survey concerning this specific proposition indicated a very high level of agreement among the other Cakchiquel and Tzutuhil municipalities ringing Lake Atitlán, as well as in ten out of twelve other western Guatemalan municipalities.[10]

Among the Chortí, the diviner chews tobacco and rubs the saliva on his right leg, questioning the spirit shaman in his calf. If the spirit answers yes, he receives a twitch in the calf; otherwise the answer is no.[11] At Colotenango, a Mam-speaking village where most of the shamans are women, the practioner sits with her legs extended in front of her and feels a "force" (*tipumal*) ascending her legs, telling her the cause of the illness and the possibility of its cure. For example, if the force moves up the inside of the legs, the patient will live, while if it is on the outside, the patient will die.[12] In another Mam community, Santiago Chimaltenango, Wagley described the shamans as "giving prognostications from the movements of the nerves in their feet"; if the diviner has "a male nagual his foot moves to the right," while if "he has a female nagual it moves to the left."[13] La Farge mentioned that in the Kanhobal-speaking community of Santa Eulalia, the soothsayers receive messages in their hands and legs.[14]

The external speaking of the blood, in which the practitioner receives messages through the body of the patient or client rather than directly through his own, would appear to have an obvious parallel with "taking the pulse," as practiced by physicians in our own culture. But Mesoamerican pulsing is never a simple matter of measurement of the heart rate. Isabel Kelly, for example, reported that in the Veracruz community of Santiago Tuxtla, "the curer touches our pulses and declares that they are very 'high' (not in the sense of pulse rate but of position above the wrist)."[15] Ralph L. Beals states that "in all [western] Mixe towns there are curers who first diagnose by feeling the wrists, elbows, and forehead. They at once know the cause of illness."[16] Mak found that among the Mixtec, the "pulse beat reveals such things as which spirits are responsible for the illness, what is the patient's nagual, what animal should be roasted and applied."[17] Pulsing has also been reported among the Zapotec in Mitla. There, "the standardized diagnosis for any ailment, *ver la sangre*, to see the blood, or *pulsar*, to take the pulse, is used."[18]

The most detailed data on pulsing in Mesoamerica come from Chiapas. In the Tzotzil commumity of Zinacantán, Evon Z. Vogt reported that the shaman feels the pulse of a patient at the wrist and inside the elbow, on both sides, and that "the blood 'talks' and provides messages which the shaman can understand and interpret."[19] In this community, according to Fabrega and Silver, "the blood not only tells the *h'ilol* 'shaman' the sources of illness, but also how many candles are wanted, what mountains and shrines must be visited, and so on."[20]

June Nash has called pulsing in the Tzeltal community of Tzoontahal "a form of 'sociopsy' comparable to biopsy in modern medicine"; pulsing rests "on the notion that the witch leaves his signature in the blood and the curer 'hears' it." In this community, the most common pulse points used are in the wrist, the inner elbow, forepart of the ankle, inner knee joint, and the temples. The theory of pulsing is that since "the blood passes from the heart and 'talks' at the joints, revealing the conditions and needs of the heart," the curer only need "listen to what the blood wants" in order to determine whether the illness is "good," the result of upset social relations, or "evil," the result of witchcraft. Nash further noted that "pulsing is not simply a monologue by the patient but rather a dialogue in which the curer's pulse from his thumb pressed on the patient's speaks to the patient and causes him to reveal his fears."[21]

The dialogical nature of pulsing is even clearer in the Tzeltal community of Oxchuc, where, if an abnormally slow pulse is found (a sign of witchcraft), the shaman questions the patient and his relatives—his spouse, parents, and children—naming the persons with whom he may have had a quarrel. While he does this, he waits for the blood to "talk," for the pulse to leap when he names the person responsible.[22] Likewise, in the Tzeltal community of Pinola, the curer first listens to the pulse in several different parts of the body—wrists, elbows, nape of neck, instep of foot, ankles, and forehead—and then proceeds to question the patient: "Have you offended somebody? Have you quarreled?" However, as it was explained to Hermitte, the curer does not actually need to elicit the information: he already knows the answer, since the pulse answers yes or no when he mentions the possible disease that is afflicting the patient and its cause.[23]

In the Tzeltal community of Tenejapa, Metzger and Williams have described pulsing as "the primary distinguishing characteristic of curers." The skill, which is a "gift of God," enables the curer to learn the etiology of the illness, what medicines to use, and the locations in which specific prayers must be said. The curer can also point out the person, usually a parent or ancestor, whose sexual misbehavior, either fornication or adultery, has resulted in the illness. All of this is possible because "the blood of the patient knows well what [are the] sins of the parents," and it "tells" the curer. However, a curer who makes obvious attempts to elicit from the patient or his family the information that pulsing alone should reveal is not highly respected;[24] in other words, the dialogical dimension of pulsing is minimized in this community and the individual shamanic gift is maximized.

For both the Tzeltal and Tzotzil, the blood is the location of the person's spirit. Villa Rojas found that the Tzeltal "curer talks with the spirit of the patient by taking the pulse."[25] Hermitte reported that "one curer said that sucking at the temples, the crown of the head, the nape of the neck, the elbows, the wrists and the feet of the patient was useful when curing *espanto* in order to 'awaken the spirit of the blood.' "[26] Holland found that "the pulse is the tangible, material expression of the human spirit" and that "the contemporary Tzotzil maintain the ancient Mesoamerican belief that the blood is the substance of the person."[27]

While "listening" to what the blood "says" is procedurally different in Chiapas and Guatemala, with the shaman attending to the blood of the patient in the one case and to his or her own blood in the other, messages in which binary oppositions indicate good or evil are frequently reported as the result in both areas. Because of these dualistic oppositions and because the messages focus on the individual, it would seem easy to assign the speaking of the blood to its proper place in Victor Turner's binary scheme for the classification of methods for exploring nonpresent time. He restricts the term "divination" to one of these methods, while assigning the term "revelation" to the other. Divination, in his sense, is analytical and dualistic, a taxonomic system that "seeks to uncover the private malignity that is infecting the public body." Revelation, on the other hand, is holistic and nondualistic, using connected sets of "authoritative images and root metaphors" to assert "the fundamental health of society grasped integrally."[28] In these terms, the speaking of the blood, as so far discussed, would seem to be a species of divination, using a dualistic scheme to investigate private malignity and lacking the grander symbolic claims of revelation. But recent research among the Kekchí in Belize considerably complicates this picture and leaves open the possibility that more detailed investigations might change it elsewhere.

The data for the Kekchí come from San Pedro Columbia where the speaking blood, which in this case is registered through pulsing, is directly connected to the four-directional "authoritative symbol" or "root metaphor" of Mesoamerican religion and world view. In fieldwork conducted among the shamans in San Pedro, James Boster found that the main pulse points, located at the wrists and ankles, are called the "four sides of one's being" (caxcutil acue), analogous to the four sides or corners of the milpa, home, and world. In Turner's terms, the act of pulsing in San Pedro is holistic, directly linking the patient to a connected set of images that integrate the social and natural worlds. Yet these same practitioners interpret what the blood says at the pulse points in terms of sets of oppositions: fast/slow, irregular/even, normal/ill, and good/evil.[29] In this Kekchí case, it would seem that the speaking of the blood involves a combination of Turner's divination and revelation, carrying out the analytical unmasking of the patient's private malignity (which is infecting not only himself but his family and even the society) within the larger metaphorical context of the world directional system. In the process, the patient is cured by the fundamental power and health of society, nature, and the cosmos. My own data from Momostenango clearly support a similar interpretation and show in detail both the divinatory and revelatory nature (in

Turner's senses) of the speaking of the blood, this time in a community where the speaking takes place in the blood of the diviner.

Lightning in the Blood

In Momostenango, the "speaking of the blood" (*cacha' uquiqu'el*) is caused by the rapid movement of "lightning" (*coyopa*) within the blood and muscles of diviners. The phonetic form of the latter term, meaning both "sheet lightning" in the atmosphere and "blood lightning" in the body of the diviner, varies slightly according to dialect area. Momostenango, with its use of *coyopa*, is in the central highland area. In San Cristóbal Totonicapán (southwestern highlands), the term I heard is *caypa*, while in Chinique (northeastern), it is *cayipa*. Tax reported the term as *kuixpa* for Chichicastenango (eastern). [30]

Momostecans whose blood speaks experience the movements of *coyopa* many times every day, whether or not they happen to be considering a question about past or future events at the time. For example, a person going about household tasks might receive a signal that a visitor is about to arrive, or a person about to set out for the town center might receive a warning that there is danger on the road. As was seen in chapter 3, a priest-shaman praying at a shrine might get an indication from the blood as to whether or not his apprentice is doing well. The occasion when movements of the blood are most expected is that of divination, though even then it is not known at what particular moments such movements might occur (see chapter 7 for examples). That some movements will occur during the counting of the 260-day cycle is certain enough that a calendar diviner can undertake the exploration of a client's question even when the *baraj* (containing the divinatory paraphernalia) has been left at home, or when the question has been asked in the public street and there is no place to go in order to use the *baraj*. In such a case, the diviner will simply count the days on the fingers (starting with the day to which the question pertains), stopping to give an interpretation whenever the blood speaks, until all twenty day names have occurred twice (see chapter 7 for examples of how the interpretation of days and of blood movements may be combined). Such a procedure is much less thorough than a full-scale divination and would not be used for such weighty questions as those concerning a serious illness or the asking of a bride, but it is thought adequate to such tasks as dream interpretation or advice concerning routine journeys.

Coyopa is received by a child born on Ak'abal, Can, Came, Quej, K'anil, E, Aj, Ix, Tz'iquin, or No'j (see chapter 3); such a child is a potential candidate for training as a daykeeper. After a series of dreams and/or illnesses, sometimes during childhood but more often in adulthood, he or she will become a novice and learn to interpret the movements of the lightning. Interpretation is taught indirectly through myth-telling, prayer-making, and dream analysis, but above all through direct discussion of the movements actually experienced by the novice and the teacher while they are together.

During the preinitation training period, the novice is carefully taught that the lightning within the body is similar to the sheet lightning over the sacred lakes of the four directions. When sheet lightning is seen at night from the direction of these lakes—Lemoa in the east, Pasocop in the west, Najachel (Atitlán) in the south, and Pachi'ul in the north—the priest-shamans know whether or not there will be rain. If the lightning is from the east or north, the rain will stop, while if it is from the west or south, the rain will come. However, since rain is desirable only at certain times and not at others, this association is not reduced to a simple positive/negative opposition. Rather, the point is that, just as external sheet lightning in any one cardinal direction gives information as to both good and bad weather, so internal human lightning in one of the body's own cardinal directions gives human information, whether good or bad. Whenever diviners visit these lakes, which is quite an undertaking since all except Pasocop are very distant from Momostenango, they gather a small container of water that they carry back to their own land and deposit in the spring or seep near their low "at the water" (*uja'l*) shrines. This water both purifies the spring and adds information from the cardinal directions, which are called upon in divinations and prayers on behalf of clients with illnesses.

Concerning the meanings of the lightning movements within the body, the novice is taught, at the most general level, that a blood movement on the front of the body indicates a present or future state, event, or action, while a movement on the back of the body indicates a past state, event, or action. Another general rule is that a movement on the left side of the body, whether the person is male or female, concerns the actions or thoughts of a woman, while a movement on the right side concerns a man. At the same time, these two rules align the diviner within the four-directional universe. When a daykeeper prays, he or she may begin by facing east (*chirelebal k'ij*, "at the rising sun"), the present or future. In this position, the back is toward the west (*chukajibal k'ij*, "at the sunset"), the past; the right, or male, side is aligned with south (*cajxucut kaj*, "four corners of sky"), and the left, or female, side is aligned with north (*cajxucut ulew*, "four corners of earth"). In other words, in orienting him or herself, the daykeeper becomes an epitome, or microcosm.

The symbolic alignment of body, gender, time, and direction is repeated on a larger scale when the priest-shaman of the town visits the sacred mountains of the four directions (see chapter 4). His visit to the eastern mountain is made on 11 Quej, a day associated with the ability to divine the future (see chapter 5). He visits the western mountain on 11 Junajpu, a day associated with the ancestors; Junajpu days are used for the ceremony for the entry of the *nawal* ("spirit") of a dead person into the cold, dark room within the earth. With 11 Aj comes the visit to the southern mountain; Aj is a special day for ceremonies performed by the priest-shaman for his patrilineage and it thus befits the southern mountain's corresponding with the right (male) side of the diviner's body. Finally, on 11 Came, comes the visit to the northern mountain; Came, a "feminine" day, one especially good for asking for a woman in marriage, is thereby associated with the left (north) side of the body. The same sequence of days (but with different numbers) is followed for a novice's permissions for the "mixing" (divining), which are done on 1 and 8 Quej, Junajpu, Aj, and Came. In effect, these permissions serve to introduce the individual to the macrocosm, while the teaching of the front-back, right-left scheme for reading lightning movements introduces the macrocosmic scheme into the very body of that individual. Figure 26 summarizes the macrocosmic–microscomic scheme.

Lest all of this seem highly abstract, it should be remembered that the temporal associations of the front of the body with the present and future (where a person is going), and the back of the body with the past (where a person came from), have an obvious experiential basis. To this basic scheme is added biological time, which flows from ancestors to descendants who, in turn, correspond

Descendants
Divination
Quej/diviners
Mundo Quilaja
present, future/birth
front of body

left side		EAST		right side
female				male
Mundo Pipil	NORTH		SOUTH	Mundo Tamanco
Came/marriage				Aj/patrilineage
Marriage Ceremony		WEST		Lineage Ceremony

back of body
past/death
Mundo Socop
Junajpu/the dead
Death Ceremony
Ancestors

26. The diviner's orientation.

to the spatial categories east and west and to the rising, or "birth," of the sun and the setting, or "death," of the sun each day. Further, the 260-day divinatory calendar is arranged so that Quej, the day on which the novice's first permission is asked before the Mundo, is followed thirteen days later by the same-numbered Junajpu, the day on which the *nawal* of a dead person is sent off by a priest-shaman to the Mundo.

The association of the front and back of the body with birth and death would seem to point toward a final reduction to a good/evil dualism, but the goodness or badness of a blood movement depends upon the nature of the question asked. For example, if the question is, "Why is this person ill?" and the shaman's lightning moves on his lower back, it means that a deceased member of the patient's patrilineage has caused this illness. On the other hand, if the priest-shaman is teaching something to his novice and the lightning moves in this very same place, it means that the dead relatives of the novice are in support of the apprenticeship.

The back of the body relates to both the good and evil done by the ancestors when they were living, and to the good and evil they daily send to the living from their home in the dark room of the Mundo. Consequently, if the question in a divination is, "Why is this person ill?" and the diviner receives a movement in the left buttock, the interpretation is that a female ancestor, so many generations ago that her name is unknown to the client, was involved in a serious dispute—over water rights, for example—for which she herself did not pay by becoming ill. Therefore, the client's illness is a result of the unresolved residue of evil remaining on earth. Another and potentially equally valid interpretation is that the client has not remembered the dead. Specifically, he or she has not regularly visited the graves of his or her dead relatives with offerings of candlelight, refreshing drinks of spring water, the pleasing odor and nourishment of flowers, and the bark of the copal tree, all of which the dead need in order to survive in the afterlife. On the other hand, if the question concerns what an animal symbol such as a dolphin represents in a novice's dream and the daykeeper receives a movement in the left buttock, it is clear that this symbol represents one of the novice's female ancestors, who is pleased that the novice is undergoing training, since the novice will soon be calling on her for help in divining and will also be making offerings to her.

In the case of the lateral set of terms, right-left, there are other Guatemalan ethnographic sources indicating a good/evil analytical opposition (I use here a slash for analytical oppositions and a hyphen for dialectical pairs), but the male-female pair under discussion here presents a different picture. It is true that a blood movement on the right side of the body might be said to represent a man's actions, but it also represents maleness in general, no matter who manifests it. Women born on the two extremely masculine days of the 260-day calendar, No'j and Quej (see chapter 5), might be signalled as men on the right side of the diviner's body. Likewise, men born on the two extremely feminine days, Came and Ak'abal, might be signalled as women on the left side of the body. These four days are powerful for ritual, and they are all possible birthdays for future daykeepers of either sex (see chapter 5); they cannot be arranged in a binary positive/negative set. Further, since the left side of a diviner's body is the location for a blood movement concerning either a woman or else an Ak'abal or Came man, and since the right side concerns either a man or else a No'j or Quej woman, what is operating here is not a simple binary opposition, but rather a dialectical complementarity in which the terms male-female and right-left encompass one another rather than opposing one another (male/female, right/left).

The facts from Momostenango are clear enough on this point, but my field notes from Chinique and San Cristóbal Totonicapán, as well as the published literature from Chichicastenango,[31] suggest that a simple binary opposition, with the right side of the body good and the left evil, might exist in these other towns. This scheme seems to be a transfer from the area of animal omens onto the human body. In these communities, as well as in Momostenango, the animals of the Mundo (i.e., wild animals) may suddenly cross the road in front of one; a movement toward the left is an evil omen, whereas a movement toward the right is good.

Even at Momostenango, there is a clear good/bad opposition in the proximal/distal directionality of blood movements on the fingers, but it lies at a lower, noncosmological level in the body system. A movement outward from the hand to the tip of the little finger means that a young child—male if on the right hand, female if on the left—will die, while a movement from the tip of this finger inward to the palm means this child will get well. Here, the age of the person concerned is governed by the hierarchy of the fingers.

The thumb or "big finger" (*nima cak'äb*) represents a great-grand-mother on the left and a great-grandfather on the right hand.[32] The index finger, called "first child" (*nabe alc'ualaxel*), represents a grandmother or grandfather, depending on the side. The middle finger or "second child" (*ucab alc'ualaxel*), represents a person from fifteen to thirty years old. The ring finger, or "third child" (*urox alc'ualaxel*), represents a child from five to fifteen years old. Finally, the little finger, called both "fourth child" (*ukaj alc'ualaxel*) and "lastborn child" (*ch'ip cak'äb*), represents a child up to five years old. These designations, from great-grandfather on down, are interpreted quite broadly, so that if a person asks a diviner about a third party who is unrelated to himself or the diviner but who is either the age of a grandparent (forty to sixty) or an unusually important person, then a blood movement to the tip of the index finger indicates that person's death.

Since the system of meanings for the fingers is identical for the toes, a diviner can be more certain of a prognostication by asking the blood if the person indicated will really die. If it is true, then the lightning should move within the next few seconds in the corresponding toe. This doubling of locales for an answer is a general pattern in the system. For example, both a movement up the side of the calf and one up the front of the thigh mean that someone is coming; however, some diviners find that one of the two areas is more consistent for them. While all the diviners I have talked with report that they experience the lightning in their fingers much more frequently than in their toes, the man who trained me has found that he usually receives the message that someone is coming to see him on his calf, while a diviner I came to know after my initiation receives this same message in his thigh. Both of them, however, report that they can ask again and receive confirmation in the other area. The palms of the hands and the bottoms of the feet are another pair, indicating getting something in hand or under foot (such as a business deal), or else being grabbed or trampled by an enemy. To trample (*tac'alenic*) or to grab (*majanic*) are two ways of saying that a powerful diviner is doing witchcraft to the person, "trampling" him into the grave or "grabbing," "pulling" him into the earth.

Death may be predicted by a movement under the eye or mouth, indicating the chief emotional responses at wakes: respec-tively, crying and drunkenness. If the person will merely see someone else's funeral party, the movement will be above the eye or mouth. The degree of social distance from any situation is also registered—in the arms, calves, and thighs of the diviner—by the location of the movement on the inside (within the family) or the outside (distant from, or outside the family) of the limb in question.

Like the proximal/distal dimension in the fingers, the opposition flesh/bone expresses the analytical oppositions good/evil, life/death. A movement near a bone, especially near the elbow or knee, may indicate the sudden death of the person being divined for, discussed, or even just passing by in the street. In these same contexts, a movement in a fleshy part, particularly in the thigh, indicates a good outcome of life situations. For example, if the question concerns whether or not to make a particular business trip and the lightning moves in the center of the diviner's left or right thigh, the answer is affirmative. But if the lightning moves across the shin bone, the answer is negative because there is a trap in the road. If the diviner is asking whether or not his client will recover from an illness and the lightning moves from the top of the thigh down to the knee and then around behind the knee, the answer is that the person's spirit will soon enter with the dead. Here, although the movement began inside the edge of a fleshy and therefore "good" place, it then moved toward and over a bony or "bad" place, finally ending up on the back, which is the west or ancestor side of the body. When this movement is very rapid, the person will die within a day or two; if it is slow, the person will die in two weeks to a month.

Among all these examples of lightning movements, only two pairs of terms can be resolved into a positive/negative opposition: flesh/bone and (on the fingers) proximal/distal. The other paired terms in the system of movements are in a dialectical relationship, not resolvable to a positive/negative opposition: front-back, left-right, over-under, inside-outside, and rapid-slow. Here, either term can be positive or negative, depending on the context. The front-back and left-right pairs map the entire body and enclose all the other pairs (including the positive/negative oppositions) within a larger system that is ultimately cosmological in its reference.

That the system of body divination is ultimately dialectical rather than analytical is confirmed by the meanings of the movements on or close to the front or back center line of the body, a line passing from the crown of the head down to the genitals. Analytical oppositions raise the possibility of middle, mediating, ambiguous terms. Dialectical pairs necessitate no such middle term because they already contain elements of each other. Rather than being the scene of meditation, the middle is the scene of unresolvable conflict, or a meeting of irreducible differences. In the body system, a movement in the center of the forehead indicates conflicting thoughts; the center of the throat or chest indicates a verbal quarrel; and the genitals indicate sexual intercourse. The polite name for the genitals of either sex is *awas* ("taboo, untouchable"), which is also the term for the hearth of a shrine, itself the place of meeting for the microcosm of the diviner's body and the macrocosm of the Mundo.

It can now be seen that the speaking of the blood, at least as it is interpreted in Momostenango (and among the Kekchí), does not fit into one or the other half of Turner's dichotomy between divination and revelation. In his terms, it might be said that the speaking of the blood carries out the analytical unmasking of the patient's private illness, which would seem to be a divinatory process, in the context of the "authoritative images or root metaphors" of the world directional system. Thus the speaking of the blood raises the proceedings to a revelatory level.[33] This is accomplished through the microcosm of the diviner's body, which in effect places the client's case before the world's mountains and lakes through the medium of sheet lightning. The "language" of the blood is indeed built of paired terms, which would seem to make it divinatory, but most of these pairs are not reducible to positive/negative binary oppositions of the kind Turner must have had in mind. Rather, the pairs enjoy a dialectical relationship, perhaps most clearly exemplified by the representation of Quej and No'j women on the right (and otherwise male) side of the body, and of Ak'abal and Came men on the left (and otherwise female) side of the body.

The speaking of the blood lends its combined divinatory and revelatory character to the larger ritual of which it is a part when its own messages are combined with those of the Day Lords in sortilege (chapter 7). If anything, the interpretation of the days shifts the final balance in sortilege even further away from Turner's basic notion of divination, since the language of the days (chapter

5), unlike that of the blood, does not involve paired terms in the first place.

The Red Dwarf

As befits a root metaphor, lightning occupies a central role not only in the language of the blood and in cosmology but also in Quiché conceptions of their own history and ethnic identity as well. I shall explore this question by examining various narratives and then the Conquest dance-drama.

In the Momostecan origin story of the various calendric rituals and the blood lightning, called "Old Words" (Ojer Tzij; see appendix A), the gamekeeper and guardian of the Mundo is the main character. Here he is variously called "shepherd or gamekeeper" (*ajyuk'*), Mam C'oxol, Tzimit, and Tzitzimit. In the first episode, he is in his Mam (Year-bearer) role as the spirit of Quilaja, the sacred mountain of the east. He meets a group of Momostecan political leaders at the foot of Quilaja and tells them that they are losing some of their leaders to the jaguar (*balam*) and mountain lion (*coj*) because they are without proper laws or religious customs. He then literally whips into them the knowledge of the proper customs for the town shrine (*awas rech tinimit*). As the story unfolds, three of the four Mam (the year-bearing days Quej, E, and Ik') and one of the two secretaries of the Mundo (the day Tz'iquin) speak to each other while the political leaders listen in, learning some of the intricacies of the solar calendar.

In the second episode, women and children suddenly began disappearing, and a group of men go out looking for them. Like the group in the previous episode, they meet the gamekeeper who tells them it is their fault that the women are being eaten by the jaguar and the mountain lion, for they do not have the patrilineage shrine (*awas rech alaxic*). Once again, the little guardian of the Mundo whips this knowledge into them. Shortly thereafter, merchants are being eaten by the jaguar and mountain lion, and still more customs are established by the dwarf shepherd.

In the last episode of the story, the C'oxol is clearly portrayed as teaching individual Momostecans their customs and awakening their blood. Here he explicitly becomes a red dwarf—called the C'oxol, Tzimit, or Tzitzimit—and he uses his stone axe—which, part of the time, the narrator identifies with the bag that holds divining equipment—to strike the lightning into their blood. This dwarf, who is called both "White C'oxol" (Sakic'oxol) and "Red C'oxol" (Quiakac'oxol), is identified as the manifestation of the spirit of the mountain or volcano by the Quiché, Cakchiquel, Mam, and Tzutujil of Guatemala.[34] In the excellent eighteenth-century ethnographic survey undertaken by Cortés y Larraz in nearly every community in Guatemala, the Sakic'oxol is universally described as a gamekeeper.[35] He appears in the *Annals of the Cakchiquels*, a native document written in the Cakchiquel language beginning in 1573, where he is called Zaquic'oxol and is portrayed as a small boy who is the guardian of the road on the slope of a volcano. When the two magicians, Qoxahil and Qobakil, come upon him and threaten to kill him, he says, "Do not kill me. I live here, I am the spirit of the volcano." Then he begs for clothing and is given "the wig, a breast-plate the color of blood, sandals the color of blood."[36] Zaquic'oxol also appears in the *Popol Vuh*, written in Quiché between 1554 and 1558. Here, during the final creation of the world, he becomes the guardian of wild animals by hiding in a tree. He thus escapes the fate of the biting animals—the jaguar, mountain lion, rattler, and yellowmouth (fer-de-lance)—who were turned to stone when the sun, moon, and stars appeared and dried up the earth.[37]

The C'oxol is very much alive today in stories Quiché calendar diviners tell about their own or others' encounters with him. This little dwarf can be met in Los Riscos in Momostenango, on Patojil near Chinique, or on Canchavox near San Cristóbal Totonicapán. One diviner I know possesses the stone shoe of the original C'oxol or Tzimit; he found it in the mountains near Chinique and keeps it with his divining seeds and crystals. He explained that at the time the earth became hard, the Tzitzimit was hiding in a tree and dropped his shoe. Like the animals, it turned to stone. Momostecan diviners visit Minas, a foothill of the Cuchumatanes, where they find small stone concretions that are the animals who were turned to stone by the sun during the creation of the world. These concretions are placed in the family shrine called the *mebil*, which consists of a small box containing various ancient items (see chapter 3).

Diviners from many municipalities near Santa Cruz del Quiché make pilgrimages, on 8 Ix and 8 Ik', to a cave under the sacred city of Utatlán where they hope to encounter the Sakic'oxol or Tzitzimit. This cave is reached by first buring copal and asking permission to enter, which is done at the entrance of the long man-made tunnel leading to the cave. Next, the diviner goes inside until he reaches the fork in the tunnel; again he burns copal and asks permission to enter. Now he takes the narrow left path and goes down, down, down to the corral, where there are all kinds of miniature animals—goats, deer, mountain lion—and tries his luck at pulling one of them out of the group. If he is lucky, the keeper, the little Tzitzimit or C'oxol, all dressed in silver, allows him to do this and even gives him money. If taken home and placed in a small box, such a gift will multiply until he is forced to buy bigger and bigger boxes. If he is not lucky, he meets not the C'oxol but an open mouth more than four yards wide and will fall into it and be swallowed by the Mundo. This recalls the mountain lions and jaguars that ate the ignorant Momostecans until the Tzitzimit whipped religious knowledge into them.

Sol Tax has also recorded visionary experiences in the tunnel under the ruins of Utatlán. A man from Santa Cruz del Quiché had told one of Tax's consultants from Chichicastenango that for many nights Tecum, Quiché, C'oxol and other "princes" of the old days appeared to him in dreams and told him to go alone at night to the ruins and enter the tunnel. He finally entered with an *ocote* torch and went farther and farther inside. At the very end of the tunnel, he saw the characters of his dreams, all decked out as royalty, and talked with them.[38]

The Tzitzimit or C'oxol is portrayed annually, in more than fifty different municipalities in central and western Guatemala, in the popular dance-drama known as *The Dance of the Conquest*. The dance-drama was written by Spanish missionaries (with the aid of native consultants) during the first half-century after the conquest of Guatemala. Although the text was undoubtedly intended to aid in the conversion of the indigenous people, the drama as a whole is interpreted today in a way that is strongly biased against the conquerors and their conversion techniques. The three main characters, in Momostecan opinion, are Rey Quiché (Quicab), Tecum Umam (or Tecúm Umán), and Rey Ajitz, the red dwarf Tzitzimit who carries a stone hatchet. Rey Quiché is portrayed as terrified by the Spanish forces; he gladly receives baptism and thereby survives the conquest. The brave Tecum Umam marches into battle against the Spanish; he refuses baptism and dies. The C'oxol or Tzitzimit correctly divines the defeat; he also refuses baptism, but instead of taking arms, he runs off to the woods to live after being knocked around by the Spanish soldiers. According to Momostecan accounts, the C'oxol gave birth to Tecum's child, which is represented in the drama by a small doll. The moral of the drama seems clear. The political leader accepted baptism, the military leader accepted death, and the customs survived the conquest by going into the woods, where the lightning-striking hatchet of the Tzitzimit continues to awaken the blood of novice diviners and where the child of Tecum still lives.

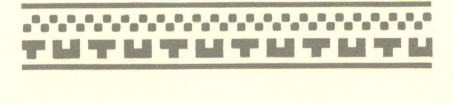

7.

Understanding

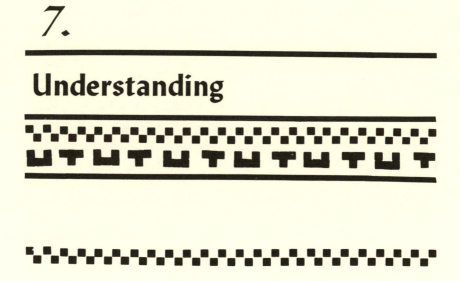

In Momostenango, sortilege, or divination by lots, is an event called *ch'obonic* (literally, "to understand"). Understanding is achieved by a combination of several actions: the mixing, grabbing, and arranging of piles of *tz'ite* seeds; the counting and interpreting of the 260-day divinatory calendar; and the jumping and speaking of the diviner's blood. The diviner, who is chosen by the client, is often a relative but need not be. Both clients and diviners come from all the traditional occupational groups (see chapter 2). Certain diviners have many more clients than others, depending on both their achieved and ascribed status in the community. For example, the priest-shaman who was the head of the Auxiliary Organization, the "watcher of our town" *(ilol katinimit)* during my fieldwork, had so many clients that it was impossible to visit him in his home in the town center for longer than one hour before someone would arrive with a question. He was popular as a diviner partly because he was at that time in the second year of his four-year tenure as the chief civil officer of the Auxiliary Organization and partly because of his intensely shamanic personality, which manifested itself in constant movements of his blood.

Sortilege takes place in Momostenango at all times of the day and night, whenever a client comes to the diviner with a question and the diviner decides to try to answer it. These questions may concern virtually any topic: illness, accident, land disputes, house-building, inheritance, lost property, business transactions, travel, marriage, adultery, quarrels, birth, death, dreams, or omens. Sortilege is usually done in the diviner's home on a table-top, but the formal multiperson divinations for finding the priest-shaman of the town take place inside a municipal building around a large circular table. Theoretically, a sortilege may be done on any day, but high-numbered days are usually avoided because their intensity might distort the result. Further, a diviner will not divine on a day in which he or she has had sexual intercourse, since to do so would cause the divining paraphernalia to be jealous of the spouse of the diviner and thus not cooperate in providing an answer to the client's question. Consequently, when a client asks a diviner, "Do me the favor of doing a question for me," the diviner may either say, "With much pleasure, what is your name and what is your question?" or else he or she may say, "Please come tomorrow or the next day with your question." Since clients will understand that the particular day they have chosen to approach the diviner may be the problem, they know not to be offended by a rejection; they simply come the next day.

The formal divination event itself begins after the client has stated his or her question, for example, *La c'o rajaw wa' c'äx?* ("Does this pain [illness] have an owner?"), or *La qu'el pa sak wa' viaje?* ("Will this journey come out [in the light] well?"), or *La qu'el pa sak wa' c'ulanem?* ("Will this marriage come out well?"). At this point, the diviner will set out a small, low, rectangular table and spread a clean cloth on it. Then he or she will take out the bag with the divining paraphernalia *(baraj)* and place it in the center of the table. Now the client will place his or her payment (usually equivalent to ten or twenty-five cents) on the table, which will remain there during the entire divination process. The diviner will sit down at the table on a low stool, with both feet planted firmly on the earth (novices are specifically trained not to cross their legs or place one foot on top of the other) and "open" his or her body to the cosmos. The client sits directly across from the diviner, on a stool or on the ground. In the case of a divination for a marriage, the client may be accompanied by his father; in other cases, the client's spouse may be present.

To begin the divination act itself, some diviners make the sign of the cross over the divining bag and then repeat the Paternoster and the Salve María in Spanish. Diviners who use these Christian prayers say that "it is like asking permission before God." Other diviners omit Christian prayers altogether and, after touching the divining bag in the four directions, say:

En el nombre del Padre Tecum Umam y Rey Quiché Mundo, C'oxol Mundo, Tzitzimit Mundo, principa mundo quinwaj jun mayij jun tok'ob—Alcalte Quej, Alcalte E, Alcalte No'j, Alcalte Ik', Secretario C'at, Secretario Tz'iquin—quinwaj ri tok'ob.

In the name of the Father Tecum Umam and King Quiché Mountain [spirit], C'oxol Mountain [spirit], Tzitzimit Mountain [spirit], the first mountain [spirits] I ask for one blessing, one favor—Alcalde Quej, Alcalde E, Alcalde No'j, Alcalde Ik', Secretary C'at, Secretary Tz'iquin—I want the favor.

Here, the three main characters of the Conquest Drama—Tecum Umam, Rey Quiché, and the C'oxol or Tzitzimit—and the four Mam of the solar calendar are all asked permission to go ahead with the divination, rather than God, Christ, the Holy Ghost, and the Virgin Mary.

After either (but not both) of these framing prayers, the diviner will pick up the divining bag in his or her hands and begin a long prayer addressed to the actual task of divination. This prayer opens by asking pardon before both God and the Earth— *Sachaj la numac Tiox, sachaj la numac Mundo* ("Pardon my sin God, pardon my sin Earth"). Then the diviner announces that he or she is taking hold of the divining bag and borrowing the breath of the particular day on which the divination is taking place:

Quinkajaxtaj ri uxlab la ri k'ij la wa' cämic. Pa wa' jun santo y laj k'ij día lunes, Jun Came quinchapo wa' k'ani piley saki piley, k'ani chok' saki chok'.

I am now borrowing the breath of this day, today. On this holy and great day Monday, 1 Came, I am taking hold of these yellow beans white beans, yellow crystals white crystals.[1]

At this point, the notion of "borrowing" can be elaborated to include not only borrowing the power of the particular day on which the divination is being done, but specifically borrowing the *coyopa* ("lightning") from the lakes of the four directions:

Quinkajaxtaj ri k'ani coyopa saki coyopa, ri casilobic chuwi' ri nima cho ri ch'uti cho, chirelebal k'ij, chukaji-bal k'ij, cajxucut kaj, cajxucut ulew.

I am now borrowing the yellow sheet-lightning white sheet-lightning, the movement over the large lake little lake, at the rising of the sun (east), at the setting of the sun (west), the four corners of sky (south), the four corners of earth (north).

At this point, sensing that the "blood" and the days are ready to respond, the diviner, after saying *cuyaxtaj ri jun sak k'alaj* ("one is now giving the clear light"), then proceeds to frame the divination question in a formal way. For example, the first formal question in the case of illness would be, *La c'o rajaw, uwinakil wa' c'äx* ("Does this illness have a master, an owner")? Here the term *uwinakil* ("person") is always used to refer to the client, whether the diviner is related to the person or has never met the person before. This is the first formal question in all divinations concerning illness, and the answer determines the subsequent curing techniques used by the client, his or her family, and/or the diviner. Another example of a formal divining question is, *La qu'el pa sak wa' quiviaje wa' quivisita pa ri Chichicastenango* ("Will their journey, their visit to Chichicastenango turn out well [in white]")? This type of question is frequently asked for Momostecan merchants, who employ diviners to help them decide whether or not, and precisely when, to set out on a particular long-distance business trip. A third very common divination question is asked for a prospective groom and his father before they go to the trouble and expense to hire a "road guide" *(c'amal be)*, or marriage spokesman: *La qu'el pa sak, wa' María, Trix, Julia, Pal, María, wa' wukub utzil wukub chomal c'aslemal ri caraj wa' Anselm, Andrés* ("Will this come out in the clear, these [name of the girl, her father, her mother, her paternal grandfather, and her paternal grandmother], these seven goodnesses seven fatnesses that these [name of the boy and his father] want")? In other words, will the marriage ceremony and the life that this boy and his father want strike the girl and her family well?

The girl's parental and grandparental relatives are mentioned in the prayer, whether dead or alive, because their willingness is extremely important; it is their patrilineage that permanently loses her if the marriage is successful. On the other hand, if the marriage is unsuccessful, then it is to their home, land, and shrines to which she will be drawn in times of trouble, especially if her relatives did not completely release her to her husband's patrilineage. When a woman marries, she is removed from the home, land, and shrines where she was "sown" and "planted" before her birth in the ritual called *awex ticon*. The removal is called *kopinic cotz'ij* ("to cut the flower"), and it involves a symbolic cutting of two geraniums, one representing the boy and the other the girl. The flowers are then tied together firmly in a cloth and taken to the boy's home with the newly married couple.

The "seven goodnesses" (*wukub utzil*) and "seven fatnesses" (*wukub chomal*) mentioned in the divination question echo the formal oratory delivered during the marriage ceremony not only in Momostenango but in many other Quiché towns as well. In Chichicastenango, for example, Bunzel recorded the phrase, "seven favors, seven blessings" in the marriage ceremony, which she said meant, "May you have six daughters, six sons."[2] In El Palmar, Saler recorded "seven excellences, seven fatnesses," but he could find no one who was certain of the meaning of the phrase.[3] Schultze Jena recorded "six favors six benefits," probably for Chichicastenango, but it might also have been for Momostenango.[4] Some Momostecan diviners say that *wukub utzil chomal* refers to the daughters and sons the young couple will bear, but one diviner I talked with had a different explanation. The *wukub utzil* ("seven goodnesses") according to him, are the seven sacraments of the Roman Catholic Church, while the *wukub chomal* ("seven fatnesses") are the seven fat cows that predicted seven plentiful years in a prophet's dream (Joseph) in the Old Testament.

After formally framing the divination question, the diviner then says something like, *Quinkajaxtaj ri uxlab la, ri tew, ri cakik', ri sutz', ri mayul chirelebal k'ij, chukajibal k'ij, cajxucut kaj, cajxucut ulew* ("I am now borrowing the breath, the cold, the wind, the cloud, the mist at the rising sun [east], at the setting sun [west], four corners of sky [south], four corners of earth [north]"). Here, one may list as many different terms as one wishes, in both Quiché and Spanish, for the chilly, moist air in which ancestral and divine knowledge, gathered from the four directions, travels. Some diviners elaborate the listing of the four sacred lakes and mountains in the same directional order: Lemoa (east), Pasocop (west), Najachel (south), Pachi'ul (north); Quilaja (east), Socop (west), Tamancu (south), Pipil (north). This leads to a general mention of mountains and volcanoes: *ri nima juyub ch'uti juyub, ri nima xcanul ch'uti xcanul* ("large mountain little mountain, large volcano little volcano"). At this point in the prayer, some diviners repeat these latter phrases, using the same Quiché syntax but substituting Spanish synonyms for the Quiché nouns *juyub* and *xcanul—ri nima monte ch'uti monte, ri nima volcán ch'uti volcán*. They may then go on to name each mountain and volcano in Guatemala to which they may have made a pilgrimage. Among the most commonly mentioned are Santa María, Cerro Quemado, Belejeb Silla, Santiago Atitlán, and Minas. After mountains, in whatever degree of elaboration, come the valleys: *ri nima tak'aj ch'uti tak'aj, nima liana ch'uti liana* ("the large flat little flat, large plain little plain").

Next, the diviner calls upon the three main community shrines: *Nima Sabal Ch'uti Sabal, K'ani Pila Saki Pila, K'ani Mar Saki Mar, ri cho ri plo* ("Large Declaration Place Little Declaration Place, Yellow Spring White Spring, Yellow Sea White Sea, the lake the ocean"). Unlike Nima Sabal and Ch'uti Sabal, Paja' is never referred to by name; rather, it is called upon as representing all springs, lakes, and oceans. Lakes and springs are highly curative, whereas the ocean is polluted, since everything from the earth is eventually washed down into it. Paja' is near a spring of pure water, but the small river that runs past it carries away the illnesses mentioned in the prayers at the shrine and takes them down to the ocean. The prayer is closed by stating, *Quinkajaxtaj ri k'ani coyopa saki coyopa, ri casilobic chuwi' ri nima cho ri ch'uti cho* ("I am now borrowing the yellow sheet lightning white sheet lightning, the movement over the large lake little lake").

Having summoned the cosmos and borrowed its breath and lightning, the diviner begins to untie the divining bag and empty the mixture of *tz'ite* seeds and *chok'* ("crystals") onto the table. He mixes the seeds and crystals, usually with the right hand and in a counterclockwise direction, while softly repeating phrases from the opening prayer. It is at this time that gifted diviners often have the experience described as "his blood speaks" (*cacha' uqui-qu'el*). The message, which the diviner immediately speaks aloud but in a low voice, is extremely brief, most often consisting of the simplest type of Quiché sentence (a verb followed by a subject), for example: *Cape rixok* ("The woman is coming"). A blood message at this juncture rarely concerns the specific question at hand, but rather something extraneous to the question. If this message were received while divining for an illness or a marriage, it might mean that the client is about to receive a high military or political office. It would probably not indicate that the illness was caused by a woman or that the prospective wife was on her way to marry the client. This piece of extraneous information may or may not be discussed and interpreted at this point, depending on the client. If the client is interested in the message, he or she may volunteer a possible interpretation, and the diviner may then receive a confirmatory movement.

The movement that causes the diviner to say *cape rixok* ("the woman is coming") is either up the side of the left calf or up the front of the left thigh. If the client says, "Perhaps my sister will visit today from San Cristóbal" and the diviner's blood moves a second time, this time in the other of the two locales, then the diviner will say, "Yes, your sister is coming today." If there is no confirmation the matter will simply be dropped.

Next, the diviner will spread out his seeds and crystals and begin to pick out ten of the crystals. Some diviners in Momostenango have only these ten crystals in their bag, while others have additional, smaller crystals that remain mixed with the seeds. The largest of the ten crystals is called *ilol* ("seer") in Quiché or *alcalde* ("mayor") in Spanish (pronounced *alcalte* by Quiché speakers). The diviner addresses it: *Sa'j la alcalte justicio* ("Come here mayor justice"), and then he places it in the center of the table. On each side, touching the mayor are then placed the two crystals that serve as his aldermen, called *rach'il* ("helper") in Quiché or *regidor* ("alderman") in Spanish. Next to the right-hand helper comes the *ajtz'ib* or *secretario* ("secretary"), and next to the left-hand helper the *c'olol pwak* or *tesorero* ("treasurer"). Among these five most important crystals there is usually at least one that contains a small yellow fleck or star. The diviner holds this crystal up to the light and carefully examines it for any movement before beginning an important question—for example, one concerning a grave illness or a recent death. The next five crystals are the "messengers" or "policemen" *(tako'n* or *ajch'amiy)* for the other five, and they are carefully lined up with the others, to the left and right of them, touching one another.

The ranking of these ten crystals duplicates the authority structure of the Auxiliary Organization of the municipality (see chapter 2). In addition, the five leading crystals are intimately connected to the solar calendar. The center crystal, besides being the mayor, represents the two most powerful Year-bearers (Mam), Quej and Ik' (see chapter 4). The two aldermen are the two less dangerous and less powerful Mam, E and No'j, while the treasurer and the secretary are Tz'iquin and C'at. The ten crystals, when lined up for divination, serve as the authorities before whom the individual calendar days are summoned to speak; they also draw the lightning from the four directions. As one diviner explained it, "These little crystals have contact with the lightning, they pull the electricity just like a radio."

While the ten crystals are being lined up, approximately along the center line of the table between the diviner and the client, the diviner will address them:

> *Sa'j la alcalte justicio. Sa'j la nabe regidor ucab regidor.*
> *Sa'j la ajtz'ib c'olol pwak. Cämic k'ij, cämic hora, caya*
> *alak jun sak k'alaj; y xukijelo ri casilabaxic k'ani coyopa*
> *saki coyopa, k'ani relampago saki relampago, cuya ri sak*
> *cuya ri k'alaj.*

> Come here, mayor justice. Come here, first alderman, second alderman. Come here, secretary, treasurer. Today this day, today this hour, you are giving a clear light; and also that the yellow sheet lightning white sheet lightning be moved, the yellow lightning white lightning, give the light the clarity.

Then the diviner will begin mixing the remaining crystals and seeds rapidly, saying, *Xukijelo, ri comon Nantat, queletzijonok jun rato chi rech wa' chanim chi rech wa' jun pregunta, chi rech wa' jun sak k'alaj* ("Also, dead Ancestors, let them come out to converse a moment for this instant, for this one question, for this one clear light"). Thus the ancestors, particularly those who were priest-shamans, are the last of the beings summoned by the diviner, and, at the same time, they are the most intimate, separated only by death from the diviner and his client.

Now the diviner will stop and blow into his right or left hand and grab as many seeds and crystals as possible. This act must be done "without calculation," as my instructor put it. Next, the diviner will place the handful aside and push the remainder toward the right side of the table, then spread out the handful and begin separating the seeds and crystals into groups of four without picking them up. These groups are lined up from left to right across the table, in front of the diviner and separated from the client by the row of ten crystals previously set out (see fig. 27). It will take several rows of groups of seeds to count out an entire handful. The

27. Sortilege under way before burning offerings on the mountain of Tojil, one of the principal shrines of the ancient Quiché kingdom. The man at left, a lineage priest-shaman, has posed his question. The diviner has set out rows of seeds and crystals and is ready to begin counting.

number of piles in each row varies from five to eight; some diviners line the groups up so that each successive row has the same number of groups as was chosen for the first row, but others do not. The final row (the one closest to the diviner) is, of course, a matter of chance: it may be as long as the others, or have only one group, or anything in between. Within the final group, there may be one, two, or four seeds and/or crystals, but not three. If there are three items left over after the last full group of four, then two of the three are arranged as a second-to-last group, with one left over for the last place.

This first arrangement of the seeds is crucial to the divination, since it is considered a test of both the diviner and the client. If the result is one seed, that means that the divination may not come out clearly, through some fault of the diviner or client. The diviner may be in arrears in his calendrical shrine visits, or it may be that the client does not trust the diviner. If, however, the number is even, and especially if it is four, then the result will probably be quite reliable, although it ultimately depends on the outcome of the three further arrangements. If the first arrangement comes out even, and two or even all three of the remaining arrangements come out even as well, then the result of the divination as a whole is quite certain. If two of the remaining arrangements come out odd, the result is half certain, and if three, it is uncertain. If the first arrangement comes out odd, there will remain some uncertainty even if the other three results are even; an all-odd series would be considered the fault of the diviner or client, and the divination would proceed no further.

When all the seeds of the first arrangement have been set out, the diviner addresses the first group of seeds by the name of the day on which he is divining, for example, *Sa'j la Ajaw Jun Quej, cabixtaj la* ("Come here Lord 1 Quej, you are being spoken to"). If Quej were the current Year-bearer, the diviner might say, *Sa'j la Alcalte Quej, cabixtaj la* ("Come here Mayor Quej, you are being spoken to"). In the case of an illness, the day the client first became ill is "borrowed" and addressed, replacing the day of the divination itself. After the first day has been addressed and summoned, the diviner will repeat or allude to the question being asked. In a marriage divination, one might say, *Jun Quej, cabixtaj la rech wa' wukub utzil, wukub uch'omal* ("1 Quej, you are being spoken to about the seven goodnesses, seven fatnesses"). Then begins the counting of the days according to the groups of seeds and crystals, starting with the day first addressed. Some diviners "read" the seeds as a book is read in modern Western tradition, starting with the top left group and then counting each row from left to right; others reverse direction with each row, reading back and forth after the fashion of ancient Greek boustrophedon writing.

The counting may or may not be interrupted by the speaking of the blood. The moment it speaks, the diviner stops counting, noting the day name and stating the message. For example, if the blood moves in the right hand on the day 5 Batz', the diviner will say in a low voice: *Uchapom rachi, cacha'* ("Already he has it grasped, it says"). Now there is a moment's pause. If the message does not come again in the same locale or in the paired place—in this example, under the right foot—then the diviner may ask 5 Batz', *La kastzij ri cabij la* ("Is it certain that it is you who speaks")? If the blood speaks again, the message is confirmed. What it is that is "grasped" depends on the client's question and the point in the day count at which the blood indicates this grasping. Let us suppose that the question concerns whether or not the client should hire a marriage spokesman to do the "asking" *(tz'onoj)* for a woman. In this case, the diviner, after receiving the confirming blood movement, will announce in a normal voice, *Tz'onoj, cacha'* ("The asking, it says"), since it was the day Batz', which has as one of its mnemonics *tz'onoj* ("asking") that spoke through the blood. The diviner will remark to his client that it seems he already has the woman in his hand.

Now the counting of the piles of seeds will resume. Let us say that in this case, it comes to 4 Ak'abal on the last group (fig. 28). This indicates that the marriage would seem to be certain, since one of the mnemonics for Ak'abal is *ak'abil* ("at dawn"), which would be the time of day to begin the "asking." The diviner will count through these seventeen groups again, this time arriving at 8 Junajpu on the last group. He may then say, *Quetaman ri Nantat* ("The ancestors already know"), which would indicate that the ancestors are in accord with the marriage.

At this point, the diviner will remove two seeds and place them next to the ten large crystals as a mnemonic for 4 Ak'abal and 8 Junajpu, the two results of this first arrangement. Then he will gather together all the remaining seeds and the smaller crystals, mixing them while praying in a low voice that the lightning and the

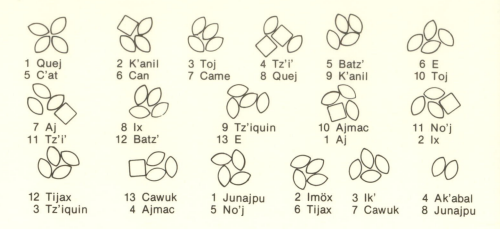

1 Quej 5 C'at	2 K'anil 6 Can	3 Toj 7 Came	4 Tz'i' 8 Quej	5 Batz' 9 K'anil	6 E 10 Toj
7 Aj 11 Tz'i'	8 Ix 12 Batz'	9 Tz'iquin 13 E	10 Ajmac 1 Aj	11 No'j 2 Ix	

12 Tijax 3 Tz'iquin	13 Cawuk 4 Ajmac	1 Junajpu 5 No'j	2 Imöx 6 Tijax	3 Ik' 7 Cawuk	4 Ak'abal 8 Junajpu

28. Model divination, first arrangement.

days may speak again. The diviner may also ask not to be deceived by them: *Mäc'ajisaj! Mäbän la ri mentira* ("Do not deceive! Do not tell a lie")! Once again, he will blow into his right hand and quickly grab as many seeds and crystals as possible, setting them apart and arranging them in groups of four. If there were nine more seeds and crystals than in the previous handful, the result would be as in figure 29. Here the final result, one seed, indicates less certainty than does the first arrangement.

The diviner addresses the first pile of seeds: *Sa'j la Ajaw Jun Quej. La caya'ic* ("Come here Lord 1 Quej. Will it be given")? In other words, will the woman be given to the client in marriage? Now begins the count. The diviner may well pause on arriving at 5 Batz', since this day answered before. But if the blood does not immediately speak again, the count will continue until some other day answers or until the last pile is reached, which is 7 Came. Here the diviner will speak the mnemonic for Came that is appropriate in this context: *C'ulanem cacha'* ("Marriage it says"), and then quickly will count through again. This time, 12 Batz' may answer, *Botz'oj cacha'* ("Winding it says"), indicating the flower wands (*botz'oj*) given to the woman's family by the man's family during the "asking." Since there were twenty groups of seeds this time, the count will end up with the day name Came again, this time 1

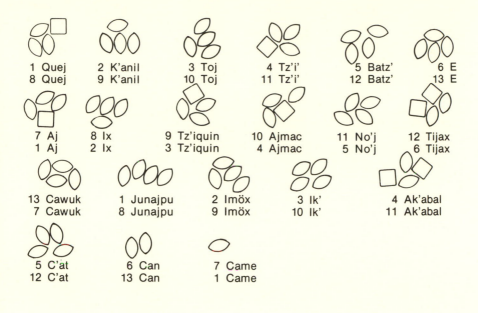

29. Second arrangement.

Came, which in this context means the same thing as 7 Came: *c'ulanem* ("marriage"). The diviner will now place a second seed in the row of crystals to remind him of this result.

The gathering and mixing of the seeds and crystals for a third arrangement is again accompanied by prayer. This might include the following phrases: *Caya' la ri sak k'alaj. Mäbän la ri mentira! La qu'el pa sak wa' María* ("You are giving the clear light. Let there not be a lie! Will this come out well [in white] with this Mary")? If the third handful of seeds was larger than the second by seven seeds, it would give the result shown in figure 30. Now the diviner will again greet 1 Quej and ask the question, *Sa'j la Ajaw Jun Quej. La qu'el pa sak wa' María* ("Come here Lord 1 Quej. Will this come out well with this Mary")? Then begins the count. But this time, when the diviner arrives at 4 Ak'abal, the blood moves across his or her throat. This movement suddenly darkens what until now had been an extremely positive result, for it indicates, as one diviner would put it, that "someone is cutting off one's head without motive." Since the blood moved on the day 4 Ak'abal, it indicates

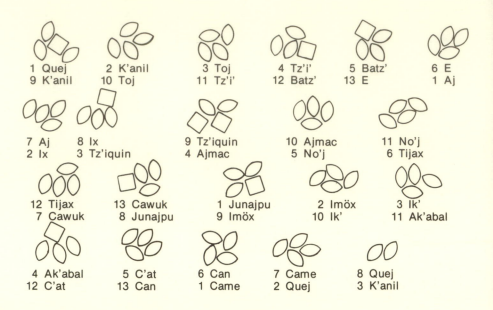

1 Quej   2 K'anil   3 Toj   4 Tz'i'   5 Batz'   6 E
9 K'anil   10 Toj   11 Tz'i' 12 Batz'   13 E   1 Aj

7 Aj   8 Ix   9 Tz'iquin   10 Ajmac   11 No'j
2 Ix   3 Tz'iquin   4 Ajmac   5 No'j   6 Tijax

12 Tijax   13 Cawuk   1 Junajpu   2 Imöx   3 Ik'
7 Cawuk   8 Junajpu   9 Imöx   10 Ik'   11 Ak'abal

4 Ak'abal   5 C'at   6 Can   7 Came   8 Quej
12 C'at   13 Can   1 Came   2 Quej   3 K'anil

30. Third arrangement.

the "asking" as the possible scene where the client or his marriage spokesman will be verbally attacked. The diviner will probably not alarm his client by saying something here, but instead will continue the count, arriving at 8 Quej, which indicates a priest-shaman. Perhaps the woman's marriage spokesman or her lineage priest-shaman will make this attack, but the diviner may still remain quiet and simply begin the second count.

On the second count of the present arrangement, the diviner might pause to address the day that begins it: *Sa'j la Ajaw 9 K'anil. La qu'el pa sak wa' tz'onoj* ("Come here, Lord 9 K'anil. Will the asking turn out well")? Then, counting through, the diviner will pause on the day 11 Ak'abal, and if the blood moves again, either across the throat or else in the center of his chest (the latter indicating a quarrel), he will say, *K'abaj* ("You blame")! This broadly indicates a lie, a trick, or slander. The count will then quickly resume and arrive at 3 K'anil. This day could mean *cak'anaric* ("to harvest"—in other words, the girl is ready to be harvested) or else it could mean *tzukunel* ("feeder"), which is another name for a priest-shaman. Both of these readings would indicate that the woman's lineage priest-shaman rather than her marriage spokesman may be the source of the "blame" indicated by the blood movement on 4 Ak'abal. Now the diviner will ask the client and his father whether the priest-shaman of the girl's family ever quarreled with anyone in their own family. The father says, "Yes, but it was a land dispute that took place . . ." Here the diviner interrupts him, saying, *ojer tiempo* ("long ago"), since his blood moved in his right buttock, indicating that this quarrel between males took place two or more generations ago (see chapter 6). The father says, "Yes, the quarrel was between my great-grandfather, who was the canton priest-shaman at the time, and the girl's great-grandfather, who was the priest-shaman of her patrilineage." The latter man was illegally removing water and wood from another man's land for the use of his lineage. The client's great-grandfather was called in to settle the dispute but instead became involved in the quarrel. The result was that his wife died because of all the anger.

The diviner, without commenting, will set aside two seeds as a reminder of the results of this arrangement and begin mixing and praying over the seeds and crystals, asking not to be deceived by the days. Then the diviner grabs a handful and makes the fourth arrangement (figure 31). This time, the result is the same as for the first arrangement (4 Ak'abal), but now the last group has a full complement of four seeds, which indicates a more certain answer. Once again, 8 Junajpu indicates that *Quetaman ri Nantat* ("The ancestors already know") about the marriage proposal (4 Ak'abal). But now the combination of the diviner's blood movements and the client's revelation of a quarrel between the two families points to an additional interpretation. The number of this Junajpu is 8, which specifically indicates a dead person of high enough status to have been a priest-shaman. This would be the girl's great-grandfather, who may well cause trouble.

Except for the matter of the priest-shaman who was the girl's great-grandfather, the results of the first four arrangements, all starting from 1 Quej, have been quite favorable to the marriage. Now the diviner, having isolated a problem, will look for the solution, questioning days chosen from among the previous results. In this case, the obvious days are 8 Quej, which indicates a priest-shaman, and 8 Junajpu, which indicates a dead person who could

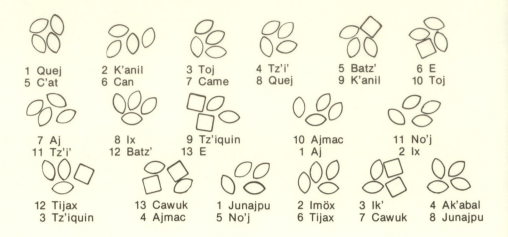

well have been a priest-shaman. The diviner will ask for the name of the girl's great-grandfather and include it in the prayers to these two days, asking whether this ancestor might accept an offering and allow this woman to marry the client. The diviner may address both these days at once (but start his count from only one of them) or else ask them in separate arrangements. If the answer is favorable, then the next question will concern the day (or days) and places at which these offerings would be accepted. The diviner is most likely to propose, if possible, days and places that are already on his own schedule of obligatory rituals, beginning on the nearest one-day and covering a total of at least four consecutive ritual days. Since the present divination was performed on 1 Quej, the earliest day for beginning to set things right with the girl's great-grandfather would be 1 Junajpu and the place would be Paja' (see chapter 3), to be followed by offerings on 8 Quej at Ch'uti Sabal, on 1 Aj back at Paja', and on 8 Junajpu at Ch'uti Sabal again (fig. 32). Following procedures like those used in questioning 1 Quej, the diviner will ask 1 Junajpu, the beginning date, whether such a schedule of offerings would be accepted.

Once an acceptable schedule has been found for the offerings, the diviner will then question 4 Ak'abal, 1 and 7 Came, and 3 K'anil (the remaining results from the initial four arrangements) to find out which of these four days would favor the asking itself. In these

32. Several hearths at Ch'uti Sabal, the mother and father shrine for all the lineage foundation shrines of the municipality. Strewn about are the leaf wrappers of copal incense packets; sprouting from among the potsherds at left is a *tz'ite* tree.

follow-up questions, a diviner is likely to make only one or two arrangements for each day questioned rather than four, especially if the results seem clear.

With all the questions answered, the diviner will gather all the seeds and crystals (including the large ones) together and pray over them: *Maltiöx che ri Tiox Mundo* ("Thanks be to God Earth") for answering the questions. Then he will grab a handful, kiss it, and put all of the seeds and crystals back into the bag, twisting the string around the opening and tying it.

At this point, if the divination called for offerings on particular days of the 260-day calendar in order to correct any problems discovered during the divination (this is a frequent outcome), the diviner will collect money for the offerings (approximately forty cents per day) and for his prayermaking services (twenty to forty cents per day). The diviner will also instruct the client, who is now his or her "burden" *(ëkomal)*, not to make love or quarrel on the offering days. Now the client will say, *Cuje' ba na* ("We have to go now"), and the diviner will answer, *Jat ba', chabana cwenta* ("Well go then, be careful").

This detailed narration of a model divination seems the only fitting summary for the various processes that are brought together in red seed sortilege. Together, they constitute a larger process of "understanding" *(ch'obonic)*, which comes through the interweaving, in sortilege, of the counting of the calendar, the speaking of the blood, the facts of the case, and the rapport of diviner and client. It is precisely this full, polysystemic combination that has either been unrecognized or else considered evidence of error or fraud by previous Guatemalan ethnographers. Both Wagley and La Farge reported instances in which Mam diviners misinterpreted what they took to be the fixed meanings of particular day names, Wagley wondering aloud about possible "fakery," La Farge pointing to "mistakes,"[5] and neither of them exploring the possibility that the outcome of a divination might rest on more than a monosystemic process of day-counting. In the Quiché community of El Palmar, Saler wondered whether a diviner might be influenced, in the case of a marriage, by knowing in advance that the bride's father was in opposition, but he felt that to ask a diviner about this might be taken as an accusation of trickery.[6] We can now see that such a question would not have been taken amiss. Information as to a bride's father's opinion would be fully relevant to the diviner's discussion with the client, something to be brought out in *sak k'alaj* ("white clarity") rather than hidden behind a "tricky" counting of the days. The participants are not expected to act as if they knew nothing, totally surrendering themselves to a mechanical procedure. Divination is *applied* epistemology: it does not operate independently of the particular question before the diviner and the client.

8.

Astronomy and Meteorology

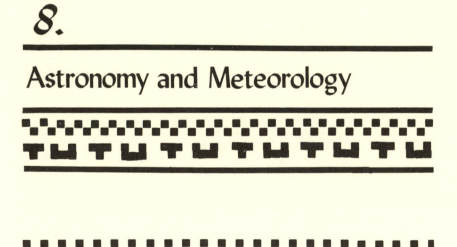

The Mayan universe consists of a many-tiered upper world, a middle world, and a many-tiered underworld. The sun, moon, stars, planets, and (since the Spanish invasion) Christian deities and saints reside in the upper worlds. Humankind, *winak* or *winic* in Mayan languages, reside in the middle world. The underworld, *xibalba* ("place of fear"), is an evil location that is entered by human beings at death, through a cave or the standing waters of a lake or ocean. The Sun is the ruler of the cosmos for the majority of contemporary, as well as ancient, Mayan peoples, and his two annual passages across the zenith are used to fix dates for sowing and harvesting.[1] Today, as in the past, the eastern and western directions are established through the observation of the intersection of the daily path of the sun with the horizon, and time is marked by the sun's progress along the horizon. Further, since the movement of the sun defines both space and time in all Mayan languages, the spatial categories east and west are not distinguished from the temporal categories sunrise and sunset.

The Directions

Classic Mayan directional symbolism has been described as referring to the daily path of the sun across the sky and through the underworld (east, zenith, west, nadir) rather than to the cardinal directions (north, south, east, west). At the heart of this proposal are the twin-pyramid groups of Tikal, depicting the Maya cosmos. Each of these clusters consists of eastern and western pyramids, a stela enclosure to the north, and a nine-doored structure to the south. The group represents a horizontal cosmogram of the daily path of the sun, in which it rises at the eastern pyramid, passes the zenith at the royal portrait stela in the northern enclosure, sets at the western pyramid, and passes the nadir at the nine-doored southern building.[2]

The directional glyphs in Classic inscriptions and Postclassic codices have been deciphered and read phonetically in Yucatec Maya as *lak' k'in, chik' k'in, yax,* and *mal,* which translate as "east, west, zenith, and nadir." Further evidence for this reading has been given by the recently discovered wall paintings in a tomb at Río Azul, in which each of the four walls has a directional glyph. Directly above each of them is a glyph that has been called by

33. Glyph blocks on east wall of Tomb 12, Río Azul.

34. Glyph blocks on west wall of Tomb 12, Río Azul.

epigraphers the "ben-ich superfix," or T168, and another glyph indicating day, night, moon, or Venus. The hieroglyph indicating day, or sun (*kin*), is infixed in the ben-ich superfix above the directional glyph on the eastern wall (see the four-petaled flower affix on the upper left side of the top glyph in fig. 33), while the hieroglyph indicating night, or darkness (*akbal*), is infixed in the ben-ich superfix on the western wall (see the upper left affix on the top glyph in fig. 34).[3]

On the remaining walls, the hieroglyph indicating the moon is infixed in the ben-ich superfix above the directional glyph at the north (see the affix on the upper left side of the top glyph in fig. 35), while the hieroglyph indicating Venus is infixed in the ben-ich superfix above the directional glyph at the south (see the affix on the upper left side of the top glyph in fig. 36). These two hieroglyphs could represent the moon and Venus in opposition, above and below the horizon, during the night when the occupant of the tomb, Ruler 6 Sky, was buried. The fact that the tomb contains an inscription giving the date of burial as 8 Ben 16 Kayab on the Calendar Round (see chapter 4), combined with the style of the painting, suggest three possible historical dates for this event. On only one of these, March 6, 502 A.D. (by the 584,283 correlation constant), was the moon less than 5° from true zenith and Venus within 4° of true nadir. During this particular night, Venus and the moon were never visible simultaneously. Moreover, at no time was the moon in the northern part of the sky, and Venus could not have been in the south. Thus, the directional glyphs associated with the moon and Venus cannot be read as referring simply to north and south, but must involve zenith and nadir. These same Classic Maya directional glyphs can also be read in Chol as *hok' k'in* ("east/sunrise"), *k'ah k'in* ("west/sunset"), *xin chan* ("zenith/north"), and *mal puy* ("nadir/south").[4]

Evidence of a zenithal, rather than northern, interpretation can also be found in other Classic Mayan inscriptions on the northern panels in the eastern and western doors of Temple 11 at Copán, Honduras. In this unusual temple, consisting of two exceptionally wide, noncorbeled vaults running east-west and north-south, crossing in the center, the glyphic inscription divides into two discourse sequences that begin at the north door, in the front of the building. While the subject matter of the inscription in the north-south corridor concerns the accession of the ruler and the dedication of a reviewing stand, in the east-west corridor the north panel on the east door contains the phrase *xay tu pa chan* ("crossroads of the sky"), referring to the dedication of the cross-corridors of Temple 11 itself. In this same east-west corridor, the north panel of the west door indicates a location called *ch'ul chan* ("holy heaven").

35. Glyph blocks on north wall of Tomb 12, Río Azul.

36. Glyph blocks on south wall of Tomb 12, Río Azul.

Both of these texts, each located on northern panels, clearly refer to the zenith as the direction of the events in question, rather than to north.[5]

The compilers of Spanish Colonial dictionaries translated the Yucatec directional terms *xaman* and *nohol* as equivalent to the European cardinal points "north" and "south," and some epigraphers and archaeologists continue to describe Mayan directions in terms of our Western compass-point tradition, despite the evidence from Río Azul and Copán. Meanwhile, linguists and ethnographers have been finding that none of the contemporary Mayan directions are precisely equivalent to our Western notion of horizontally fixed cardinal points.[6] Thus, for example, in Kekchí, a Quichean language, the terms for the directions come from intransitive verbs indicating motion. East is *relebaal sak'e* ("sun's coming out place") and west is *roquebaal sak'e* ("sun's entering place"), while south is *relebaal ik'* ("wind's coming out place"), and north is *roquebaal ik'* ("wind's entering place").[7] In Tzeltal, the important directions of orientation are east, or the "coming out of the sun," and west, or "the sleeping place of the sun." North and south are topographically referred to, respectively, as "highland" and "lowland," or "above" and "below," and north can also be called *kini ha'al*, which designates a violent wind, specifically a rain-bearing wind.[8] In recent interviews with Cakchiquel speakers, I learned that east and west indicate the daily rising and setting motion of the sun, while north is *cak ik'* ("violent wind"), and south is *xoco-mil* ("left-handed"), which is the name for the treacherous south wind that comes up suddenly each summer afternoon across Lake Atitlán, threatening boats.

The pattern is similar in the lowland Mayan languages. Today in Chol, the terms for east are *pasel k'in* or *ba mi lok'el k'in* ("sun's coming-out place" or "place where the sun is taken out") and the terms for west are *majlib k'in* or *ba mi yoche majle k'in* ("sun's going-in place" or "where the sun enters"). North is *chak ik'lel* ("red wind"), referring to strong winds that bring bad weather, and south is *nool*, cognate with Yucatec *nohol*. In Mopán east is *hok'eeb k'in* ("the sun comes out"), west is *okeeb k'in* ("the sun enters"), and when one insists on eliciting terms for our concepts of the cardinal directions north and south, consultants will provide the Spanish terms *norte* and *sur*. In contemporary Yucatec, *lak'in* ("next sun") is the place where the sun rises in the east, and *chik'in* ("eaten sun") is the place where it sets in the west. Both are considered to be located along a line between two corners of a flat, four-cornered earth. The entire northern side of the world is referred to as *xaman*, while the southern side is *nohol*; also, north is on the right-hand side of the sun god, while south is on his left-hand side. In colonial times, these two terms were also used to designate winds, with the north wind being *xaman ik'* and the south wind being *nohol ik'*.[9]

In Tzotzil, a Mayan language spoken in highland Chiapas, the eastern and western directions do not refer to fixed cardinal points, but rather to the daily motion of the sun; thus, east is *lok'eb k'ak'al* ("emerging sun") and west is *maleb k'ak'al* ("disappearing sun"). North and south are both *xokon vinahel* ("side of the sky"), which are differentiated according to whether they are on the right or left hand of the sun. North can also be referred to as *xokon vinahel ta batzi k'ob* ("edge of heaven on the right hand") and south as *xokon vinahel ta tz'et k'ob* ("edge of heaven on the left hand"). In Mam, a highland Mayan language spoken in Guatemala, all of the directional terms are derived from intransitive verbs of motion, with east as *okni* ("move toward the east"), and west as *elni* ("move toward the west"). The term for north is *jawni* ("to go up") and south is *kubni* ("to go down"); both together may be referred to as *iky'ni* ("along"). Since *jaa'wal*, from the intransitive verb *jaaw* ("go up"), refers to the termination point of the sun's ascent, it might best be translated as "sun's meridian" rather than "north."[10]

Among speakers of Quiché, several sets of terms have been reported as translations for Spanish *norte* and *sur*; depending on the specific sociolinguistic context, they can be paired with other terms designating east and west. For example, when a speaker of the Achí dialect of Quiché in Cubulco is asked to name the directions—north, south, east, west—he or she calls north *ajsic* ("above" the town center), and south *iquem* ("below" the town center); however, if this same speaker is referring to a distant place, then north is *wiqabim* ("on the right") and south is *moxim* ("on the left"). East is *pa quel ka kajaw* ("where our father [the sun] comes from") and west is *pa ca caj wi ka kajaw* ("where our father descends"). Similarly, an Achí speaker from Rabinal lists north as *wiquik'ab* ("right side") and south as *moxk'ab* ("left side"), while the directional terms for east and west are *chukajibal sak* ("where the sun rises") and *chirelebal sak* ("where the sun sets"). When a speaker of Quiché proper is asked to name the directions, he or she may reply that east is *relëbal k'ij* ("sun's rising place") and west is *ukajibal k'ij* ("sun's falling place"), while north is *uwiqui ak'äb relëbal k'ij* ("right hand of the rising sun") and south is *umöx ak'äb relëbal k'ij* ("left hand of the rising sun"). In formal discourse, however, while the east-west terms remain the same, the other pair varies: for example, *xcut ri caj, xcut ri juyub* ("corner of sky, corner of earth") or *caj xucut caj, caj xucut ulew* ("four corners of sky, four corners of earth"). Quiché speakers think of these words as referring to the north and south, respectively, but at the same time they fit the above-below or zenith-nadir pattern found in other Mayan languages and suggest, as well, that both the sky and the earth have four sides. Another set of contemporary Quiché terms, *unic'ajal caj, unic'ajal ulew* ("middle of sky, middle of earth"), occurs together with the usual terms for east and west in the *Título C'oyoi*, an important sixteenth-century document. Thus the pairing of terms indicating a vertical axis with others indicating an east-west horizontal axis has considerable historical depth in Quiché.[11]

Mayan speakers today, whether highland or lowland, describe the sun as a human or godlike figure with a brilliant round face, who rises each day on the eastern horizon and faces his universe with north on his right hand and south on his left hand.[12] After he reaches his meridian, at noon, he pauses briefly, then continues across the sky, entering the earth in the west, reaching a point opposite his meridian at midnight, and remaining in the underworld until he begins his eastern rise once again. The terms for east and west in all Mayan languages indicate a line, or vector, along which the sun rises and sets, depending on the season of the year. The other two directional terms are missing altogether in the dictionaries for about half the Mayan languages; when they do appear, they variously indicate the right and left hand of the sun god, the direction of prevailing or rain-bringing winds, highland and lowland, above and below, and/or zenith and nadir. Thus, Mayan directions are *not* discrete cardinal or intercardinal compass points frozen in space, but rather are sides, lines, vectors, or trajectories that are inseparable from the passage of time.

Astronomy

There are more than three thousand stars and planets an observer can pick out with the naked eye at any one moment on a clear night. It might be expected that at least the planets and the Milky Way, as well as all of the first- and second-magnitude stars visible in the latitudes of the Mayan world, would be of considerable interest to Mayan peoples. Unfortunately the ancient Mayans left us no star or constellation catalogues, no treatises on astronomical theories or methods, and no measuring instruments. We also lack records of the astronomical observations that lie behind the tables and almanacs in the Dresden, Paris, and Madrid codices. It is left to us to decipher what problems ancient Maya astronomers addressed and what methods they employed to arrive at the textual solutions that survive.

In order to reach some understanding of Precolumbian Mayan astronomical concepts and practices, one needs to study inscribed stone monuments and architectural alignments; incised bones, shells, and pots; painted ceramics and murals; and the four extant hieroglyphic codices, together with Colonial manuscripts written by Mayans in the roman alphabet. One should also study Colonial dictionaries, Spanish chronicles, and the current astronomical and cosmological ideas and practices found in both the religious ceremonies and the oral and written literature of the living Maya of today.

In Momostenango, all of the celestial bodies—including the sun, moon, planets, comets, meteors, stars, asterisms, constellations, and the Milky Way—constitute a single category, labeled *ch'umilal caj* ("starry sky"). The diurnal, monthly, and seasonal paths and positions of these celestial bodies along the horizon and across the night sky are observed and discussed by Momostecan naked-eye astronomers, who are initiated daykeepers. The daily path of the sun, known as *ube sak, ube k'ij* ("road of light, road of day"), is described in Quiché as *oxib utzuk', oxib uxucut chupam sakil* ("three sides, three corners in the light"). It is visualized as a triangle, whose angles are the three transition points in diurnal time. This solar triangle stretches from the sun's rising position to its noon position, and on to its setting position. By analogy, heavenly bodies that rise, cross the night sky, and set in opposition to the sun, in reasonable proximity to its path, are said to form *oxib utzuk', oxib uxucut chupam k'ekum* ("three sides, three corners in the dark").

Stars are used to tell the time of night, and they also herald the time of year for both ritual and agricultural purposes. Both the winter and summer solstice sunrise and sunset positions are called *xolkat be* ("change of path"). This term, unlike our own Latin-derived term, solstice ("sun stand"), stresses the back-and-forth movement of the sun. The most important change of road is the winter solstice, *rakan k'ij* ("sun's reach"), which annually marks the end of the high-altitude corn harvest, in December. At the latitude of Momostenango (15° 04' 38″ north of the equator), the zenith passages of the sun occur on May 1 or 2, during the sun's north-ward movement, and on August 11 or 12, during its southward return. The sunrise and sunset positions on both zenith passages are referred to as *jalbal* ("place of change"), indicating the location of a change in the nature of the sun's path, rather than a change of paths.

The planets, as a group, are known as *cak ch'umil* ("red stars"). When Venus (or any other planet that takes the role of eve-ning star) appears in the western sky after sunset, it is called *rask'äb* ("of the night"). Venus in its morning-star aspect is called Junajpu, a day name that is also the personal name of a mythic hero in the *Popol Vuh*. When Venus or any other planet appears as a bright star in the east before dawn, it is referred to as *ëko k'ij* ("sun carrier"), and its path is known as *ubeal ëko k'ij* ("sun carrier's road"). Comets are referred to as *uje ch'umil* ("tail of the star") and are considered omens of pestilence. In Colonial Yucatec Maya, comets were called *ikomne* ("windy tail") or *kaktamay ek* ("fire ill-omened star").

In Quiché, a shooting star, falling star, or meteor is referred to as *ch'abi k'ak'* ("flaming arrow"). Here *ch'abi* refers to the tip, or point, of an arrow, dart, dagger, or spear, while *k'ak'* means "fire." A Colonial Quiché term for meteor was *ch'olanic ch'umil* ("star that makes war"). Among the contemporary Tzotzil, falling stars are called *ch'ob* ("torch"); in Yucatec they are called *halal ek'* ("arrow star"); and the Lacandon describe them as "arrowheads."[13] Ob-sidian points and blades found by Momostecans in their cornfields today are considered to be the remains of falling stars. These ob-jects are gathered and placed, together with other sacred objects, in the family *mebil*, the traditional household shrine (see pp. 81–82).

Some highland and lowland Mayan peoples describe meteors or comets as the cigar butts of the gods, and it may well be that the cigars smoked by the hero twins of the *Popol Vuh* are to be understood as meteors. Throughout the Mayan area, meteors are thought to be evil omens forecasting sickness, war, and death. It is also widely believed that obsidian points can be found at the precise location where a meteorite lands. The cognitive links among obsidian, war, death, and sickness are due to the past use of instruments of warfare and human sacrifice that had obsidian points or cutting edges, together with the past and present use of obsidian blades in bleeding procedures and in surgery.[14]

Individual stars identified in Momostenango include Regulus, or *jun ch'umil* ("one star"), and Spica, or *pix* ("spark"), both of which lie along the ecliptic. Certain Quiché asterisms are rather similar to Western ones; for example, *xic* ("hawk") is recognizable as Aquila, the Eagle. Others are not at all the same. Two or more stars or asterisms may share a single name, while single stars or asterisms may have more than one name. For example, Acrux (in the Southern Cross) and Polaris (in the Little Dipper) together are called *xucut ch'umil* ("corner stars"). There are two asterisms known as *ripibal elak'omab* ("thieves' cross"); one of them is in the Southern Cross and the other is the seven-star grouping within Sagittarius consisting of Sigma, Phi, Delta, Gamma, Lambda, Epsilon, and Eta. Similarly, both the Pleiades and Hyades are called *mötz* ("handful"), and both the Big Dipper and Little Dipper are called *pac'ab* ("spoons"). The Milky Way, on the other hand, has two separate designations, depending on which end is being indicated. The undivided segment is *saki be* ("white road"), while the part with the dark cleft, or rift, is *xibalba be* ("underworld road"). The bright stars Castor and Pollux, in Gemini, have two designations: *quib chuplinic* ("two shiny ones") and *quib pix* ("two sparks").

Within the constellation of Orion, known as *je chi k'ak'* ("dispersed fire"), there are two asterisms with a one-star overlap: Orion's belt, or *je oxib chi k'ak' ajaw* ("tail of the three fire lords"), and Alnitak, Saiph, and Rigel, called *oxib nima ch'umil* ("three big stars"), of which the brightest, Rigel, is called *nima k'ak'* ("big fire"). This asterism is also referred to as *oxib xc'ub* ("three hearth stones"). The Great Nebula, M42, located within the triangle marked out by these three stars, is described as smoke from a celestial cooking fire. Although this vast cloud of glowing gases is visible to the naked eye, the Orion Nebula was not mentioned in ancient or medieval records, and its European discovery did not come until 1610. The description of certain key stars as "fiery" is also found today among Yucatec Mayans. In the town of Yalcobá, near the archaeological ruin of Cobá, Orion's Belt and the Hyades each have *u k'áak'* ("their fire") in the form of the bright stars Rigel and Aldebaran. [15]

Stellar movements, especially the ones Western astronomy calls achronic and cosmic, are used by Momostecans to mark the progress of the solar year. An achronic star rise takes place on the eastern horizon at the moment of sunset on the western horizon, while a cosmic star set takes place on the western horizon at the moment of sunrise on the eastern horizon. During the dry half of the year, between harvest and planting (November through April), stellar risings and settings are observed and used in timing ritual events. Each of six such events, spaced from twenty to thirty days apart, singles out a particular star or constellation as *retal ak'äb* ("the sign of night"). Thus, in mid-November, the Pleiades rise near the sunrise position during evening twilight, cross their meridian at midnight, and go down near the sunset position in the dawn twilight. Other key stellar rise and set events occur in mid-December, with Orion; in mid-January, with Gemini; in the third week of February, with Regulus; in mid-March, with the Big Dipper; and around April 1, with Acrux.

The moon also has achronic and cosmic risings and settings. At the beginning of the month, the moon is momentarily visible as a slim crescent, low on the western horizon at sunset, called *ch'utin ic'* ("little moon") or *alaj ic'* ("baby moon"). According to knowledgeable Momostecans, the moon is reborn each month at what we call its solar conjunction, or the astronomical new moon, *mixalaxic ic'* ("the moon has been born"); however, since the new moon is visible only during solar eclipses, they reckon the age of a given moon from the first appearance of the slim crescent moon in the west, which follows conjunction by a day or two. That this practice may be more generally Mayan, and quite old, is demonstrated by a dictionary source from Yucatán that assigns the number thirteen to the full moon, indicating that moon ages were counted from the first visibility of the waxing moon. [16] When full moons are reckoned from conjunction, they come when the moon is fourteen to sixteen days old. But the age of a particular moon and the problem of reckoning time by a unit equal to a complete lunar cycle are treated by Quichés as two different matters. Because of the difficulty of sighting the newly waxing moon, midwives and farmers today find it best to reckon months from full moon to full moon.

As the month progresses, the waxing crescent moon rises in the western sky, slightly north of the setting sun, and is observed edging its way slowly eastward until it has reached what Western astronomers refer to as the first quarter, so named because the moon at this time is on the meridian one-quarter of a full circle (90°) from the sun. Momostecans, however, refer to this phase as *nic'aj ic'* ("half moon"), which emphasizes the degree of the moon's illumination rather than its position in relation to the sun. The moon reaches its meridian, or *pa nic'aj* ("in the center"), at sunset, then sets at about midnight. For the next week, as it approaches the full phase, it rises and sets later and later. During this time of the waxing gibbous moon, or what Quichés call *chak'ajic* ("maturing," or "ripening"), it is in the eastern sky at sunset and sets after midnight. Throughout this waxing period it is addressed in prayers as *kanan* ("our mother").

Two weeks after the new moon, the full moon, or *setel ic'*, literally "rounded moon," is seen in the east, near the sunrise point. For Momostecan observers, the true full moon is the first one that is seen rising shortly after the sun sets in the west. It travels across the entire night sky and sets in the west near sunrise. The night of the full moon, or *jun ak'äb ube* ("one night its road"), is particularly dramatic. Both moonrise and moonset are clearly visible, and the moon's path, like that of the sun, makes a complete triangle, or *oxib uxucut* ("three corners"). This night of the moon's achronic rise and cosmic set, in opposition to the sun, is the only time that Momostecans find the moon's movements to resemble those of the sun. The spectacular oppositional journey of the full moon, known as *oxib utzuc' oxib uxucut chupam k'ekum* ("three sides three corners in the dark"), consists of moonrise in the east, *relebal ic'* ("moon's rising place"); midnight at the meridian, *pa nic'aj ic'* ("at the middle of the moon"); and moonset in the west, *ukajibal ic'* ("moon's falling place"). On this one night, the moon takes on a male aspect and is considered the nocturnal equivalent of the sun, with its full bright disk and complete transit of the sky. It may even be referred to, figuratively, as "the sun." This helps to explain the seeming anomaly in the *Popol Vuh*, where Xbalanque (one of the hero twins) is said to rise as the moon, although he is male. He may have corresponded only to the full moon, while Blood Woman (his mother) may have been the waxing moon and the elderly Xmucane (his grandmother) was perhaps the waning moon.

Women and children are admonished not to look directly at the moon during an eclipse, but rather at its reflection in water. If a pregnant woman should bathe in the middle of a river or a lake under a full moon that is undergoing an eclipse, which is to say *uyabil ic'* ("moon's sickness") or *ucamic ic'* ("moon's death"), she will bear a stillborn child or else a deformed one—mute, lame, or albino. Babies conceived on the night of a full moon, especially during a partial eclipse, or *k'ekum ic'* ("darkened moon"), will become either twins or transsexuals. These ambiguous babies are said to change back and forth, rapidly at first (every three or four days), from male to female, and female to male. Later they change their behavior and gender identification more slowly, eventually alternating between female and male behavior, dress, and identification every three or four years.

Mayan people fear the sudden darkening of celestial bodies and believe that both solar and lunar eclipses signal famine and other sicknesses. Despite their fears, both Quichés and Lacandones watch the reflection of eclipse events in containers of water set outside in the yard. Zinacantecos set out pails of water during lunar eclipses, but the stated purpose is not to view the moon, but rather to enable her to wash her face. In some communities the proper behavior during an eclipse is to make a great outcry, shouting and banging on tables, beating on drums and pots and pans, ringing the church bells, shooting off firecrackers or guns, and lighting great bonfires. Failure to do so during an eclipse of the moon in May of 1918 was considered the cause of a measles epidemic in the Mam-speaking community of Santiago Chimaltenango.[17]

During the waning of the moon after the full phase, it is considered by Momostecans to be an old woman, and is addressed in prayers as *katit* ("our grandmother"). Until the beginning of the last quarter, marked by the *nic'aj ic'* ("half moon"), it is described as *rij ic'* ("curved surface," or "back of the moon"). On this date, the moon rises quite late in the evening, until the old woman enters her final waning phase, called *catzujubic*, "drying up." At the beginning of the last-quarter phase, the moon rises at midnight and is at the meridian at sunrise. After that, the ever-shrinking crescent moon rises later and later and is farther and farther east when the sun rises, until, near the end of its waning phase, the sun begins to catch up with it. The cycle ends with the moon rising at dawn, lagging farther and farther in the east, until it is *mukulic* ("buried") at *camibal ic'* ("moon's death place").

Butchering, harvesting, woodcutting, and sexual intercourse are all avoided during the earlier part of the moon's two-week waxing period, since at this time animals, crops, trees, and people are all considered immature and tender. The annual planting of dried maize kernels and black beans is the one activity that is considered appropriate for any part of the waxing lunar period. If the field to be planted is new, the men go out and fell the trees, burn off the undergrowth, and turn the soil in February, when the Pleiades, or *mötz* ("fistful"), reach the meridian shortly after sunset. In the case of an established field, the men simply turn the soil and chop up and turn under the previous year's cornstalks. The precise date of sowing corn kernels and beans, together with the length of the vegetative period in a given year, are determined by a combination of the altitude of the fields, soil fertility, hawk migration, astronomy, and calendrics.

Agronomy, Meteorology, and Hawk Migration

Although many scholars have reported that there is a connection of some sort between Mayan astronomy and agronomy, there has been a notable lack of agreement concerning the precise nature of the correlation. While the appearances, disappearances, and paths of the sun, moon, and stars have been described as useful in timing agricultural activities, the relationship between these key events and hawk migrations has never been considered.

Each year the change of season from cold and dry to warm and wet, in March or early April, and back again, in October or early November, is heralded by the migratory flight of huge flocks of hawks. In the *Popol Vuh*, there is mention of a flock of migrating birds, *tz'iquin molay* ("birds joined together," or "throng birds"). These "throngs" may well have been flocks of Swainson's hawks (*Buteo swainsoni*), given that they are so numerous as to present an obstacle to the hero twins, Hunahpu and Xbalanque, and given that the twins encounter them at harvest time. Further, a dictionary source gives *mo* as a term for a "large black hawk." There is a black hawk (*Buteogallus anthracinus*), whose entire plumage is slate black, but it is extremely shy and does not join together in huge flocks; some individuals migrate from South and Central America as far north as Tucson, Arizona, but most never migrate. Swainson's hawks have a dark, or melanistic, phase, when they are sooty brown all over, including the wings as seen from below. It seems likely that the *Popol Vuh* passage refers to flocks of these hawks in their dark phase, during the autumn migration.[18]

Ornithologists have often commented on the biannual migratory flights of Swainson's hawks over Central America, calling the sight one of the more remarkable in the bird world. After breeding in North American basins and plains, stretching from California and Texas to Alaska, nearly the entire population funnels through Central America each autumn. In just a few days, massive flocks of more than two thousand individuals each make their 13,000–16,000 kilometer flight from North America to the pampas of Argentina.[19]

These huge flocks of Swainson's hawks, known as "boils" or "kettles," sometimes include a few broad-winged hawks (*Buteo platypterus*). Since their migration corridors, or "flyways," follow leading lines such as mountain ridges, river valleys, and coastlines, these diurnal migrants apparently utilize a combination of topographic, ecological, and meteorological landmarks to determine their flight pattern. Where mountains are parallel to their flight direction, as are various ridges in Guatemala, they can soar with relatively little effort for long distances, supported from below by upwardly deflected winds. Since these winds can attain speeds of more than 25 miles per hour, their deflection yields a vertical component of over 1,600 feet per minute. During their fall migration, when convection in the air over land occurs in the form of isolated bubbles of rising air known as "thermals," or chains of bubbles known as "thermal streets," the rate of air ascent may be as much as 20 feet per second, providing an excellent means for migrating hawks to gain altitude by ascending on one thermal and then gliding to the next.[20]

Updrafts are also created by sea breezes along coastlines and by light winds over water during the change of season from cold to warm. Since water warms more slowly than land, and since cold water cools the air over it while warm land warms the air over it, on bright sunny days the surface temperature of air over land rises above that of air over water. In this situation, pressure over the land decreases, causing the air to flow toward the land, creating a small cold front, before which air can rise at the rate of several hundred feet per minute. Hawks observed soaring in a narrow line along the shores in the Great Lakes area of North America are apparently using these updrafts. A similar meteorological situation may explain the movements of Swainson's hawks in Guatemala on March 23, 1966, when more than four thousand of them were observed passing along the shore of Lake Atitlán.[21]

Hawks are often seen flying before thunderstorms and squall lines located in front of advancing cold fronts and associated low-pressure areas. The most spectacular hawk flights occur in close conjunction with particularly intense low-pressure areas, or storms, during both the spring and the autumn. On April 7, 1976, the hawks flew over Momostenango just hours before the season's opening thunderstorm. The next day our teacher told us, "Yesterday hawks passed by in masses, by the hundred, by the thousand. Our seeds were planted. When they pass by again, in October, they drop the thieves' cross, the bent one, into the sea. The water shuts off, we bend the cornstalks. Each year when they arrive they lift the thieves' cross up out of the sea and the water comes. I saw them yesterday by the thousands, now today it's raining." Although we couldn't immediately understand the meaning of what he said, I had it on tape, so that I could listen to it again, after I myself had learned enough natural history to understand it. Once I was aware of the correctness of the linkage of migratory hawk flights with seasonal change, I began to wonder how hawk migratory patterns, together with broad climatological patterns and local meteorological phenomena, might correlate with the movements of constellations, the calendar, and agricultural practice.

During their annual northern migration, in March or April, Swainson's hawks are referred to by contemporary Quichés as *torol k'älaj* ("openers of the rainy season"), since they "lift" the Southern Cross out of the sea and above the horizon, bringing rain. The Southern Cross is first observed briefly, on the southeast horizon, at about 11:00 P.M., in February. In March, it can be seen lying along the horizon, by nine o'clock in the evening. It is not until after the Swainson's hawks have passed overhead and "lifted it out of the sea" that the Southern Cross can be seen from a hilltop shrine just outside the town center, rising in the southeast, close to the time of sunset. The Southern Cross is known as the "thieves' cross" because during the period of its longest visibility (from about 8:00 P.M. until 3:00 A.M., in early April), migrating Swainson's hawks are carnivorous and actively prey on birds, reptiles, and small mammals.

Swainson's hawks radically change their dietary habits during their southern migration, in October or November, becoming almost entirely insectivores. At this time, they are called *torol sak'ij* ("openers of the dry season"), and they are said to drop the thieves' cross into the sea and stop the rain. However, this dry-season thieves' cross is not the same constellation as the wet-season thieves' cross. The "bent cross" that our teacher mentioned is not the wet-season Southern Cross, but rather a seven-star asterism in Sagittarius that centers on Delta. He explained that the star cross in Sagittarius, unlike the Southern Cross, has been bent just as he bends his corn plants each fall, before harvest. The same two thieves' crosses were reported for the Quiché of Quezaltenango: the Southern Cross and another cross, "not straight but rather inclined to its left," which was identified, with the help of star charts, as the group of seven stars consisting of Sigma, Phi, Delta, Gamma, Lambda, Epsilon, and Eta in Sagittarius.[22]

In addition to the Sagittarius thieves' cross, Swainson's hawk is associated with the "hawk," or *xic*, constellation. From a natural-history perspective, the Quiché name of this constellation makes more sense than its Latin name, Aquila, or "Eagle," since the dihedral, or V-shaped, pattern of the wings matches the way Swainson's hawks hold their wings during flight. A V-shaped outline is used by observers to distinguish Swainson's hawks from related species, including eagles, that extend their wings almost straight out during flight.[23]

Each year, from mid-October until early November, when Swainson's hawks are migrating southward, the hawk constellation can be seen at the zenith soon after sunset, flying high, just as hawks do. At this same time, the bent cross in Sagittarius lies to the southwest, below the hawk, at about 50° above the horizon. Sagittarius sets at about 10:00 P.M., and Aquila sets at midnight. By late October or early November, when Swainson's hawks mi-

grate through Guatemala, the hawk constellation sets around nine
o'clock in the evening. Or, as my teacher described it, "the hawk
drops the cross down into the sea." During this same period, the
full moon's arrival at the zenith at midnight coincides with the time
of the sun's nadir. By December, the hawk constellation sets at
sunset and is invisible until early February, when it undergoes
heliacal dawn rise, and the full moon once again reaches the zenith
at midnight, coinciding with the second solar nadir.

Good agricultural lands in Momostenango range from 1,500 to
2,500 meters above sea level. At the higher altitudes, the planting
of clusters of mountain maize mixed with black beans begins in
March, even though the dry season stretches from November
through April. The early planting is possible at these altitudes because of the combination of low temperatures, mist, and fog, which
retard the evaporation of moisture from the soil, compensating for
the lack of rain. In December, 260 days after sowing, the maize is
harvested. At lower and dryer elevations, found in the cantons of
Canquixajá and Xequemeyá (see map, p. 19), the planting of valley
maize and black beans begins on the full moon nearest the first
solar zenith passage, or on May 1 or 2. The Chortí Maya, who live
at the same altitude as the Momostecan farmers of Canquixajá and
Xequemeyá, also use the first zenith passage to time their corn
planting.[24]

On the day of its zenith passage, the sun moves into conjunction with the Pleiades, heralding the first of the three- or four-day
heavy rains that open the rainy season. During this time, the twin
bright stars, Castor and Pollux in Gemini, travel near the zenith
and mark the most extreme horizon positions the sun will reach at
the summer solstice, the time of the heaviest summer rains. Valley
planting is also heralded by the reappearance of the rift in the
Milky Way. These celestial occurrences coincide with the annual
fiesta of the Holy Cross, May 2 and 3, which is widely celebrated
in the western highlands of Guatemala with masses for rain, together with music and dancing for the fertility and growth of the
crops. The harvesting of valley maize begins shortly after the second zenith passage, which occurs on August 11 or 12.

Mountain maize, like humans, is sown or conceived on a particular day name and number, but the long stretch of time between
then and harvest, or birth, is noted by moons rather than by days.
Reckoning moons is easy for farmers, who finish sowing in March

each year, before the first full moon. A midwife carefully notes the phase of the moon on which her client failed to menstruate, or see her "sign of the moon," but then counts by full moons and re-adjusts, at the end, for the phase first noted. After sowing, maize plants or babies vegetate or gestate for nine months and (ideally) come to fruition on the same day number and name of the 260-day calendar as they were sown.

The nine-month growing period of mountain maize, like the human gestation period, may help account for the 260-day length of the sacred almanac (see p. 93). On the other hand, given the nature of seed selection, the observation of hawk migration, and the speeding of the ripening of the maize by the doubling over of the stalks, the 260-day calendar may have had a determining role in the development of agricultural practice. Then again, since the date for seeding or reseeding a cornfield and for doubling over the cornstalks is timed (in part) by the migration of huge kettles of Swainson's hawks, and since the southward migration can fall at any point between October and early November, the 260-day ideal corn almanac can be overridden and the crop can be allowed a slightly shorter or longer cycle. Since hawks move according to local meteorological phenomena, including winds and low-pressure areas, they provide a potential mechanism for correcting the agri-cultural calendar according to the actual weather conditions in a given year.

Astronomical Commensuration

Classic Mayan astronomy, cosmology, and calendrics have en-gaged many scholars during the past hundred years, and there ex-ists an enormous published literature on the topic. Ethnographic studies of ongoing Mayan astronomical, cosmological, and calen-drical concepts and practices, however, have concerned but a handful of scholars, who have produced only a small literature during the past forty years. The question of commensuration of astronomical cycles in Precolumbian written Mayan calendars con-tinues to engage scholars, but the investigation of extant indige-nous methods of commensuration has largely been ignored. My own field research in Momostenango has revealed a cycle of rituals that provides a means for coordinating lunar observations with the 260-day and 365-day calendars.

The patrilineage leaders, or mother-fathers, of Momostenango follow a schedule of visits to the high shrine of Nima Sabal according to the following sequence of days: 9 Quej + 13 days = 9 Junajpu + 13 days = 9 Aj + 13 = 9 Came + 13 = 9 Cawuk + 13 = 9 E + 13 = 9 Can + 3 = 12 K'anil = 82 days. This total is equivalent to three lunar sidereal months (3 x 27.32167 days = 81.96501 days). The visits are made in order to bring an abundant harvest and keep the lineage healthy. Shortly after sunset on the first day of the series, the mother-father opens a particular altar that pertains to his own patrilineage. Nima Sabal belongs to a category of shrines called *tanabal* ("elevated" or "stepped place"), which offer an extensive view of the horizon. Mother-fathers remain there for some time, burning incense, praying to their dead predecessors by name, and observing the night sky. In their prayers, they mention the specific phase of the moon and its position in the night sky relative to certain bright stars, planets, asterisms, and constellations. They are interested in the seasonal variation in the moon's path through the stars and across the cleft, or dark rift, in the Milky Way.

Several patrilineage leaders are known for their ability to predict rain by noting the precise position and phase of the moon on all seven days of this series. The great majority, however, only observe the night sky seriously on the opening day, 9 Quej, then again on the second day, or 9 E, and finally on 12 K'anil, the closing day, which falls 82 days after the opening.

This 82-day ritual period is referred to as *chac'alic* ("staked," or "stabilized"). The point of astronomical interest is that wherever the moon (if visible) might have been located among the stars on a given 9 Quej, it will be in nearly the same position 82 days later, on 12 K'anil. However, since a sidereal month (27 days, 7 hours, 43 minutes, 11.5 seconds) is shorter than a synodic month (29 days, 12 hours, 44 minutes, 2.8 seconds), the moon will not be in the same phase when it returns to the same position in the night sky.

The mother-fathers of cantons and wards have the responsibility of greeting the Mam ("Year-bearer") on each occurrence of the day name, at one of four hilltop shrines, located a short distance from the town center. In a Quej year, for example, a group of these mother-fathers, led by the head mother-father of Xeque-meyá, will visit the hilltop shrine on Paturas once each twenty days, on days named Quej. In an E year, this same group will be led, on each day named E, to the shrine at Chuwi Akan, by the head mother-father of Los Cipréses. Their dawn and dusk visits involve not only ritual activities such as praying, burning copal incense, and setting off fireworks, but also the observation of the sun's position along the horizon. This is an important task, since the careful observation of sunrise and sunset positions at twenty-day intervals helps these naked-eye astronomers properly to anticipate the zenith passages of the sun.

Above these leaders, at a still higher rank, are two *chuchka-jawib rech tinimit* ("mother-fathers of the town") who, after they are selected by the canton and ward leaders, serve for life (see p. 35). Once a year, a group of these ward, canton, and town leaders makes a pilgrimage, in order to welcome in the new Year-bearer at a shrine located on a distant mountaintop. In addition to this visit to the key mountain of the year, the town mother-fathers also visit four mountaintop shrines, on a cycle of days that coordinates the four 65-day periods of the 260-day almanac with four overlapping 82-day periods (see table 5). This cycle of visits provides them with an opportunity for observation and gives them a conceptual scheme for coordinating lunar time reckoning with the 260-day cycle and the 365-day solar year in a more orderly fashion than would be possible through synodic lunar reckoning alone. Noting the motion of the moon against the backdrop of the stars at 82-day intervals offers the possibility of conceptually linking the course of the daytime sun with that of the nighttime stars. This, in turn, opens the cognitive pathway leading from observations of achronic and cosmic risings and settings of the stars to the mapping of a sidereal solar path.

Commensuration of astronomical observations with calendrical cycles is accomplished in Momostenango through the use of days with the same four names—Quej, E, No'j, and Ik'—to mark the beginnings of the 65-day quarters of the 260-day cycle, the 82-day lunar sidereal period, and the 365-day solar cycle, or vague year. But unlike the case of solar Year-bearers, which occur in such sequences as 9 Quej, 10 E, 11 No'j, 12 Ik', the prefixed number of the four days that mark the beginnings of 65-day and 82-day cycles remains constant: 9 Quej, 9 E, 9 No'j, 9 Ik'. These four days divide

Table 5. The 65-day cycle, with overlapping 82-day cycles

Quej	*9	3	10	4	*11	5	12	6	13	7	1	8	2
K'anil	10	4	11	5	*12	6	13	7	1	8	2	9	3
Toj	11	5	12	6	*13	7	1	8	2	9	3	10	4
Tz'i'	12	6	13	7	1	8	2	9	3	10	4	11	5
Batz'	13	7	1	8	2	9	3	10	4	11	5	12	6
E	1	8	2	+9	3	10	4	+11	5	12	6	13	7
Aj	2	9	3	10	4	11	5	+12	6	13	7	1	8
Ix	3	10	4	11	5	12	6	+13	7	1	8	2	9
Tz'iquin	4	11	5	12	6	13	7	1	8	2	9	3	10
Ajmac	5	12	6	13	7	1	8	2	9	3	10	4	11
No'j	6	13	7	1	8	2	#9	3	10	4	#11	5	12
Tijax	7	1	8	2	9	3	10	4	11	5	#12	6	13
Cawuk	8	2	9	3	10	4	11	5	12	6	#13	7	1
Junajpu	9	3	10	4	11	5	12	6	13	7	1	8	2
Imöx	10	4	11	5	12	6	13	7	1	8	2	9	3
Ik'	11	5	12	6	13	7	1	8	2	!9	3	10	4
Ak'abal	12	6	13	7	1	8	2	9	3	10	4	11	5
C'at	13	7	1	8	2	9	3	10	4	11	5	12	6
Can	1	8	2	9	3	10	4	11	5	12	6	13	7
Came	2	9	3	10	4	11	5	12	6	13	7	1	8

Key to the overlapping cycles
* =   Opening (9 Quej) and closing (11 Quej, 12 K'anil, 13 Toj) of Paturas and Quilaja shrines (A and A' in fig. 37)
\+ =   Opening (9 E) and closing (11 E, 12 Aj, 13 Ix) of Chuwi Akan and Tamancu shrines (B and B' in fig. 37)
\# =   Opening (9 No'j) and closing (11 No'j, 12 Tijax, 13 Cawuk) of Nima Sabal and Socop shrines (C and C' in fig. 37)
! =   Opening (9 Ik') Cakbach'uy and Pipil; closing (11 Ik', 12 Ak'abal, 13 C'at) would occur during the following 260-day cycle (D and D' in fig. 37)

the 260-day cycle into segments that follow one another without gaps or overlaps. On these days, the town mother-fathers visit Nima Sabal, then walk to another hill closer to the town center, and continue to one of the mountaintop shrines that lie some distance from town.

The 82-day periods, unlike the 65-day periods, overlap with one another (see fig. 37). Thus, after opening the shrines on Paturas and Quilaja (designated A) on 9 Quej, the mother-fathers return there 80 days later, in order to begin a three-day closing ritual spanning 11 Quej, 12 K'anil, and 13 Toj (A'). Since the total distance from 9 Quej to 12 K'anil is 82 days, or 3 sidereal lunar months, the opening and closing rituals permit sidereal reckoning of the moon. But the next sidereal period overlaps with the first, so that on 9 E, 15 days before the closing rituals begun on 11 Quej, they open the second set of shrines, at Chuwi Akan and on the mountain of Tamancu, both of which are located in the south (see map on p. 19 and B in fig. 37). This 82-day period is then completed with the closing of these shrines, on 11 E, 12 Aj, and 13 Ix (see table 5 and B′ in fig. 37). A third such period, begun 15 days before, on 9 No'j, in the west at Nima Sabal and Socop (see C in fig. 37), is completed on 11 No'j, 12 Tijax, and 13 Cawuk (see C′ in fig. 37). The fourth period, in the north at Cakbach'uy

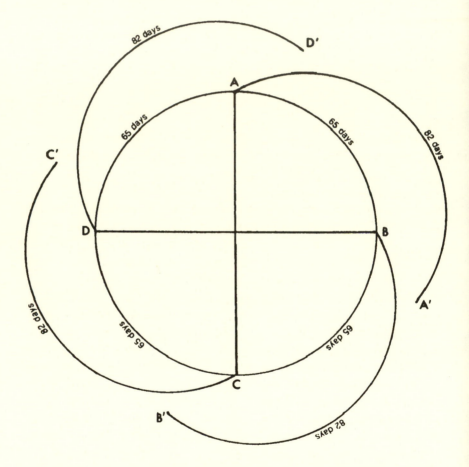

37. Quartering of the 260-day almanac with overlapping sidereal lunar reckoning. On this drawing A = 9 Quej, A′ = 12 K'anil, B = 9 E, B′ = 12 Aj, C = 9 No'j, C′ = 12 Tijax, D = 9 Ik', D′ = 12 Ak'abal.

and Pipil (see D in fig. 37), having started 15 days before, on 9 Ik', is completed on 11 Ik', 12 Ak'abal, and 13 C'at (see D' in fig. 37).

Simultaneously with the sidereal rhythm, these same visits contain a synodic rhythm. For any two successive mountaintop shrines, such as A and B, the phase of the moon observed at the opening of A will repeat itself 147 days later, at the closing of B (located at B' in fig. 37), and yet again when shrine B is opened, 178 days after it was closed, a total of 325 days after the opening of shrine A. Here it should be noted that the same sum is reached by adding the two canonical lunar intervals used in the Dresden eclipse table, which are 148 and 177. In Momostenango, the event on the 147th day falls half a day short of 5 synodic moons, the one on the 178th day falls less than a day beyond 6 synodic moons, and the event on the 325th day falls just a little less than 4 hours beyond 11 synodic moons. Summarizing the arithmetic, we find that $147 = 65 + 82$ and $325 = 147 + 178 = 4 \times 65 + 65$. To state the pattern in another way, repetitions in phases of the moon move forward by one shrine each time around the full circle of shrines. Over a period of years, the precise locations of the moon within its sidereal and synodic cycles during the shrine visits will shift, but the locations during any given visit remain good predictors of what will happen over the space of a year or more. It remains for future fieldwork to investigate whether these shifts might be read as auguries of changing fortunes in human affairs.

The overlapping pattern of synodic and sidereal lunar reckoning discussed above is commensurable with the 260-day cycle. Further, the selection of four days from this 260-day cycle that can also serve as Year-bearers brings this combined synodic and sidereal lunar scheme into partial alignment with the solar calendar. Thus, in any given circuit of the four shrines, three and sometimes four of the days on which openings are performed, or closings are started, will fall on days bearing the name of the current Year-bearer, a day which is itself marked by ceremonies throughout a given year. In 4 out of 52 years, spaced 13 years apart, the opening of a shrine will correspond to the first day of that year, or *nabe mam* ("first grandfather"). In another 4 years, the beginning of the closing ceremony will correspond to the first day.

There is also evidence for the combination of synodic and sidereal lunar reckoning in Precolumbian times. The period assigned by the Dresden Codex to the visibility of Venus as the morning star, 236 days, has been rounded off so as to equal the duration of eight synodic moons. The actual visibility of Venus as morning star averages 263 days, or 27 days longer than 8 synodic moons. Since 27 is the nearest whole-day approximation of a sidereal moon, there could have been a rule of thumb for following the progress of the morning-star Venus that went something like this: starting when it first appears, count 8 moons (of the synodic kind) and then expect Venus to disappear when the 9th moon has made one complete circuit of the zodiac. Evidence for an intricate network of multiples of synodic and triple-sidereal lunar cycles has been recently found at Palenque, El Perú, and in the almanac on pages 23–24 of the Paris Codex. These cycles may indicate a knowledge of celestial coordinate astronomy, one in which bodies are tracked with respect to one another, rather than with respect to the horizon. The zodiacal character and the approximate positions of the 13 constellations in the Paris almanac have recently been determined.[25]

The discovery, in a contemporary highland Mayan community, of the notation of achronic and cosmic risings and settings of individual stars and asterisms, combined with the use of 82-day periods anchored to the 260-day and 365-day cycles, provides indirect evidence that Classic Mayan society may have developed a common frame of reference for understanding the movements of the sun, moon, and stars. Although there is as yet no evidence of past or present use of angular calculations as such, it seems likely that ancient Mayan peoples combined horizon astronomy with coordinate astronomy.

The multimetrical temporal rituals described here involve dialectical thought patterns that go beyond the simple dialectics of polarization (thesis, antithesis, synthesis), as historically exemplified in Hegelian and Marxist thought, to include the dialectics of overlapping or mutual involvement. It appears that Mayan peoples used differing systems of timekeeping in the separate provinces of their biological, astronomical, psychological, religious, and social realities, and that at some point in the past, these various systems underwent a process of totalization within the overlapping, intermeshing cycles of their calendars. Given the complexity of this cosmology, which is ritually reenacted, shared, and thus maintained today, the knowledge of contemporary Mayans ought not to be dismissed, as J. Eric S. Thompson once did, as nothing but the degenerate remains of Classic Maya glory. Rather, current cosmological theory and practice ought to be respected as a precious living resource, providing the conceptual tools for reconstructing the meaning of the material objects that happen to have survived from the Classic and Postclassic periods of Mayan history.

9.

Conclusions

My account of Mayan cosmology, calendrics, meteorology, and astronomy is based primarily on my own research among the Highland Maya in Guatemala during the mid-seventies and again in the late eighties. The book opens with my entrance into the particular Quiché context of communicative interaction known as *ch'obonic* ("to divine" or "to understand"), a context in which past, present, and future time are explored through a combination of the counting of the 260-day calendar and the speaking of the blood. A subjective account of such an experience would be solely in the language of the observer, keeping Mayan peoples at a considerable distance. This is precisely the stance involved in a natural science approach to a social science problem: what is claimed to be objectivity is in fact the subjectivity of the observer. Thus, the objectivity of the present account rests on a foundation of human intersubjectivity, a field of investigation that belongs solely to the social, or human, sciences, and whose primary medium is language. Further, the account rests not only on talk *about* Mayan calendars, astronomy, and divination, but also on the learning of calendrical, astronomical, and divinatory language itself. It is a study of the practical knowledge, or mastery, of diviners and skywatchers. As such, it is a contribution to what has come to be called "practice theory."[1]

Daykeepers cannot be sorted out according to an anthropological distinction between priest and shaman that separates ritual acts done for the public good from those done for private interests. It does not solve this problem to tighten up the definition of shaman by appealing to the classical Siberian example. Even the two Momostecan elders who perform priestly duties on behalf of the entire municipality are shamans; they have suffered an illness that leads to initiation as a diviner, and they possess both spirit wives and the divine gift of blood lightning. The terms "priest" and "shaman" might still be separated when it comes to particular roles on particular occasions, but when it comes to status, what is required is an interlaced concept of "priest-shaman" and "shaman-priest," depending on the proportion of public and private services rendered by a particular practitioner. A similar interlacing prevails elsewhere among the contemporary Highland Maya, both in Guatemala and Chiapas, but there are no other reports of a hierarchy like that of Momostenango, with three levels of priest-shamans above and a large group of shaman-priests below.

The Momostecan calendar embraces both the 260-day cycle and 365-day solar year, with the four Classic Mayan Year-bearers, or Mam, systematically connecting the two. The 260-day cycle is linked firmly to worldly, or earthly, affairs, mirroring no astronomical period, but rather the period of gestation or vegetation for humans and corn plants. Past ethnographic accounts of this cle contain various conflicting opinions as to what its first day is, but a comparison of the present results and those of previous studies indicates that there is no fixed first day. When a consultant is asked to describe the calendar, he or she simply begins with the current day or the current Year-bearer, thus following divinatory practice rather than an abstract theory as to what "the" first day is. When the ethnographer asks the unprecedented question, "What is the first day?" the consultant either denies that there is one or else develops a "theory" on the spot. This theory is always based on practice; he or she simply chooses an important ritual day, such as 8 Batz'. This is a perfect illustration of what Pierre Bourdieu calls "the dialectic between the schemes immanent in practice and the norms produced by reflection on practice."[2] In this example, theory is based on practice, rather than being prior to practice.

While scholars have sought to fix the meanings of the calendar day names to an etymologically constructed symbol system, Quiché calendrical practice reveals that the days are interpreted through a series of mnemonics that are frequently linked to the names by paronomasia, or sound play. These mnemonics refer not to an abstract symbol system, but to the ritual practices associated with the various days. Furthermore, variations among Quiché communities in the interpretation of specific days can be accounted for by differences in ritual practice. Thus, the "theory" of day meanings is based on schemes immanent in practice. When scholars dismiss these present-day schemes in favor of their own reconstructed symbol system, they commit what Bourdieu called "the fallacy of treating the objects created by science . . . as realities endowed with social efficacy."[3] There is little reason not to suppose that the ancient Mayan interpretations of the days operated much like those of the present-day Quiché, although there were undoubtedly considerable differences in the content of particular mnemonic phrases and in the rituals to which they alluded.

In addition to the counting and interpretation of the 260-day cycle, Momostecan divination employs another major technique:

the interpretation of jumping or twitching movements in the blood and muscles of the diviner, movements that reflect, on a microcosmic level, the flashing of sheet lightning over the lakes of the macrocosm. The divinatory interpretation of blood movements has been reported over a wide area of Mesoamerica. In Chiapas and other parts of Mexico, and in Belize, the diviner feels such movements in the body of the client, but in Guatemala they occur in the diviner's own body. My research demonstrates a clear and direct link between the speaking of the blood and the counting of the calendar within a single divinatory performance and also reveals that blood movements may occur anywhere on the entire body. The meanings of these movements are mapped according to a multidimensional scheme.

The systems of interpretation of the day names (among the Quiché in general) and for the blood movements (among Momostecans and perhaps more broadly) are dialectical rather than analytical in their logical patterns. Although some days are predominantly negative and others are predominantly positive, no one day name is totally negative or totally positive in its possibilities. In the blood system, the paired terms proximal/distal (with reference to the fingers) and flesh/bone are in analytical positive/negative opposition; however, the front-back, left-right, over-under, inside-outside, and rapid-slow pairs are in an interpenetrating, dialectical relationship. The center line of the body is not the place where ambiguity or mediation emerges, as it would be in an analytical scheme, but is rather the one vantage point from which differences appear to be in open conflict.

The interpretation of blood movements poses problems for the anthropological attempt to divide rituals for the exploration of nonpresent time into "divination," which is a dualistic, analytical system that uncovers private illness within the public body, and "revelation," which is a nondualistic, holistic system that emphasizes the health of society and nature at large.[4] From this point of view, the blood system would appear to be a species of divination, insofar as it proceeds according to binary opposition and is directed to the investigation of private illness. Yet at the very same time, it incorporates dialectical complementarities (a holistic dualism whose possibility has not been seriously considered before), together with metaphors that tie it to the world directional system and thus raise it to a cosmic level. The red dwarf C'oxol, who strikes blood lightning into the bodies of diviners with his stone axe, is not merely an occupational divinity venerated by diagnosticians of illness, but is also a symbol of continuing Quiché resistance to spiritual conquest.

Quiché resistance to the replacement of old customs with new ones is based, in part, on Quiché conceptions of time. As in other matters, thought proceeds dialectically rather than analytically, which means that no given time, whether past, present, or future, can ever be totally isolated from the segments of time that precede or follow it. This does not mean that innovations must be resisted, but that they should be added to older things rather than replacing them. My own teacher, in addition to employing traditional agricultural techniques and rituals in his milpa, unhesitatingly uses insecticides and commercial fertilizers. In the same spirit, during a 1976 discussion of Catholic Action converts, who advocated the replacement of the rituals of Mundo with their own, he summed up his own position by flatly stating, *"One cannot erase time."* The net result of this attitude is that the burdens of time do not so much change as accumulate. That is why the "traditionalists" of Momostenango could actively resist attacks on what they view as customs that are older than any in the Church and at the very same time show no interest in a nativistic purge of such Catholic customs as have long since become a peaceful part of community life.

Even such successive creations and cataclysmic destructions of the world as are described in the *Popol Vuh* involve no analytical compartmentalization of time; rather, each retains heritages from all previous ages. Deer and birds date from the first age, for example, and monkeys from the third; even gods overthrown in previous ages remain a part of later pantheons. Among the contemporary Quiché, the miniature stone animals and fruits collected for household shrines are regarded as relics of a previous age. On a smaller scale, this cumulative sense of time can be seen in the fact that a man who rises from the status of an ordinary daykeeper to that of a lineage, then a canton or ward, and finally a town priest-shaman does so not by passing from one job to another, but by piling one job on top of another.

Accumulation appears again in the list of predecessors that a lineage priest-shaman recites before his shrines, or the statement of one such priest-shaman, that "these shrines are like a book where everything—all births, marriages, deaths, successes, and failures—is written down." Theoretically, there is no limit to the potential length of such a book. This is an important point, because too much emphasis has been laid on the cyclical, or repeating, nature of the Mesoamerican concept of time, in order to contrast it with Western lineal, or historical, time. From the point of view of the 260-day cycle and the blood movements, time and events certainly repeat themselves, but when the day Junajpu or a movement on the back of the body points to the deed of an ancestor, as they have pointed many times before, the questions next asked will be directed toward discovering the uniqueness of that deed and the actual name of the ancestor.

The investigation of the events of another time, then, involves a dialectic between the cyclical and lineal aspects of time. The interaction of these same two forces in present time produces a strain along the localized boundaries where one named and measured segment of time must succeed or replace another. The strain is accommodated by treating that boundary as an imbrication, or overlap, rather than an instantaneous transition. The small-scale imbrication of two successive named days is illustrated by the problem of divining the meaning of a dream. Instead of attempting to determine whether the dream occurred before or after midnight, the diviner will question both of the days involved, since one of them "handed the dream over" to the other. In other words, night is a time when the influences of two "successive" Day Lords overlap. The series of permissions sought for the "mixing-pointing" of a novice daykeeper does not get underway all at once but has a partial beginning on 1 Quej and is not considered to be in full swing until twenty days later, on 8 Quej. Further, the end of this series is imbricated with the beginning of the series of permissions for the "work-service." The latter begins when the "mixing-pointing" has partially, but not fully, come to an end, just as the end of the "work-service" series will be imbricated, in turn, with the time that follows it. A similar process occurs at the boundary between two solar years; the new year is not considered to have finished arriving until its Mam has occurred twice (twenty days apart). That imbrication was a general Mayan pattern is shown by an example (on a still larger scale) from Prehispanic Yucatán, where the idol that ruled a katun (a twenty-year period) had to share its first ten years in the temple with its predecessor; further, it remained ten years after the end of its own reign, to keep company with its successor.[5]

The intervals and imbrications of the 260-day and 365-day calendars are formal and fixed, requiring no ongoing observations of natural phenomena. To track the progress of the seasons, Momostecans watch the comings and goings of stars and the migrations of hawks. During the dry half of the year, achronic and cosmic risings and settings are observed and used in timing agricultural events. The date for sowing corn kernels is determined by a convergence of favorable agronomical, meteorological, and calendrical conditions. Each year, the change of season, from dry to wet and back again, is heralded by the migratory flight of huge flocks of Swainson's hawks. Since the thermals they ride are created in the vicinity of thunderstorms, the observation of hawk migration accurately predicts changes in agricultural conditions. Swainson's hawks are also cognitively associated with two important Mayan asterisms: the thieves' cross in Sagittarius and the hawk, the latter corresponding to Aquila. Each year when Swainson's hawks migrate southward, in late October or early November, the hawk constellation can be seen at the zenith soon after sunset, with the bent cross in Sagittarius just below it, toward the southwest. Between the disappearance of the actual hawks and the cross, on the one hand, and that of the hawk constellation, on the other, there is a period of imbrication, in which the hawk lingers on as a sign of what has passed.

High-altitude planting of maize begins in Momostenango during March, and in December it is harvested. Mountain maize is sown, as humans are conceived, on a particular day name and number, and plants or babies vegetate or gestate for nine months, ideally culminating on the same day name and number of the 260-day calendar as they got their start. Thus, the growing period of mountain maize, like the human gestation period, may help account for the length of the 260-day calendar. However, given the nature of seed selection and the doubling over of maize stalks, the 260-day calendar may have had a determining role in the development of agricultural practices. On the other hand, since the date for seeding a cornfield and for doubling over the cornstalks is timed by the migration of Swainson's hawks, and since the southward migration can fall at any point either in October or November, the 260-day almanac can be overridden and the crop allowed time to mature properly. Since the hawks move according to local meteorological phenomena, they provide a mechanism for correcting the agricultural calendar according to the actual weather conditions in a particular year.

The selection of the same four days—Quej, E, No'j, and Ik'—to mark the beginnings of the 65-day quarters of the 260-day cycle, the 82-day lunar sidereal period, and the 365-day solar cycle serves to commensurate lunar observations with formal calendrical cycles. This is accomplished by allowing each of the successive 82-day periods to imbricate with the next one. The ward, canton, and town priest-shamans of Momostenango visit four mountaintop shrines on a cycle of days that takes all these intervals into account and that allows them to observe the night sky. Coincidentally with the sidereal rhythm, these visits contain a synodic rhythm, such that repetitions in the phases of the moon move forward by one shrine each time around the cycle of sidereal visits to the shrines. Precolumbian evidence for the mixing of synodic and sidereal lunar reckoning can be found in the Venus almanac of the Dresden Codex, in the Paris Codex, and in the inscriptions of Palenque and El Perú.

Noting the motion of the moon against the backdrop of the stars at 82-day intervals makes it possible to link the course of the daytime sun with that of the nighttime stars. This, in turn, opens the cognitive pathway leading from observations of achronic and cosmic risings and settings of the stars to the mapping of a sidereal solar path. The discovery, in a contemporary Mayan community, of the notation of such stellar movements, combined with the use of sidereal lunar intervals anchored to the 260-day and 365-day cycles, suggests that Classic Mayan society may also have combined horizon astronomy with coordinate astronomy.

Further evidence bearing on ancient Mayan astronomy is provided by Mayan directional systems, nearly all of which have both vertical and horizontal dimensions. In all Mayan languages, the terms for east and west indicate a line, or vector, along which the sun rises and sets, depending on the season of the year. The other two directional terms variously indicate the right and left hand of the sun god, the direction of prevailing or rain-bringing winds, highland and lowland, above and below, or zenith and nadir. Mayan directions are not discrete cardinal or intercardinal compass points frozen in space, but rather are horizontal and vertical lines, sides, vectors, or trajectories that are inseparable from the passage of time. They not only map out the flat world of horizon astronomy, but open the sky to coordinate astronomy as well.

The multimetrical temporal and astronomical observations and rituals described here involve thought patterns that go beyond the simple dialectics of polarization, exemplified by Hegelian and Marxist thought, to include the dialectics of overlapping or mutual involvement. It appears that Mayan peoples once had differing systems of timekeeping for separate areas of their biological, astronomical, religious, and social realities, and that these systems underwent a process of totalization within the overlapping, intermeshing cycles of their calendar.

Afterword

Even the most formal aspects of ritual life can carry the marks of unique historical events. Such is the case with the Quiché day named C'at. One of the mnemonics that serves to interpret it, *pa c'at, pa chim* ("in nets, in heaps"), incorporates the literal meaning of the day name, "net," which is symbolically conceptualized as a container for one's debts. The names for this day in other Mayan languages carry similar meanings, suggesting that we are dealing with an idea too ancient to permit a glimpse of its moment of origin.[1] But there is a second Quiché mnemonic for C'at, *c'atic* ("to burn"), and this may well have its origin in a traceable event. According to the colonial document known as *The Annals of the Cakchiquels*, it was on the day 4 C'at that the Quiché rulers named 3 Quej and 9 Tz'i' were burned at the stake by Alvarado, in 1524.[2]

It remains to be seen whether the 260-day calendar of our own times will go forward with any traces of the Guatemalan government's counterinsurgency campaign of the early 1980s, touted by the army as a "reconquest." One thing is certain though, and that is that numerous Mayan communities in the departments of Huehuetenango, El Quiché, Chimaltenango, and Alta Verapaz suffered direct military attacks on unarmed civilians, accompanied by the destruction of their homes and crops.[3]

Members of Catholic Action became key counterinsurgency targets, after revolutionaries gained their sympathy by singing the praises of liberation theology.[4] In the department of El Quiché during the early eighties, fourteen Catholic priests and hundreds of catechists were assassinated.[5] Throughout the highlands, the Guatemalan army linked the presence of large numbers of catechists to guerilla activity, and entire communities were classified and labeled on maps with red, pink, yellow, and green pins. Villages labeled "red" were considered to be in the hands of the guerrillas and thus open to direct attack, "pink" and "yellow" communities were closely watched and received random violence, and those labeled "green" were left alone, because they appeared to be free of subversion.[6]

Momostecan political leaders began hearing of army violence against catechists in 1979; their source was local members of Catholic Action, who had migrated into the Ixcán Grande area of Huehuetenango. They also received word from Momostecans living in the Ixil community of Chajul that the military considered catechists subversives. In the summer of 1979, during what was to be our last visit to Momostenango before the counterinsurgency campaign accelerated, we talked with a youth leader of the catechists, who declared that he no longer participated in Catholic Action. One of the older leaders of the movement had fallen ill, was scarcely able to move about, and had lost the ability to speak. Upon our return, in 1988, we learned that the youth leader had been initiated as a daykeeper and had received his divining bundle. As for the older man, during the early eighties he had given up consulting the local nurses and doctors in Quezaltenango and had turned to traditional Mayan healing. He was diagnosed as having a case of *cumatz*, or "snake" (see pp. 54–56). By the summer of 1988, he was completely recovered and had become the leading daykeeper, or mother-father, of his patrilineage.

In the context of Guatemalan state violence, it appears that the Momostecan shift in religious affiliation may have functioned in such a way that the absence of large numbers of active catechists protected the community from being labeled "communist" and thus a prime target for military repression. The Momostecan political perception that Catholic Action might attract military violence to the community was followed by a nativistic revitalization movement, committed to a return to the traditional religion and world view. In the face of potential annihilation, the indigenous leaders of Momostenango made an analytical decision to abandon their dialectical accommodation with the Catholic Action movement (see pp. 42–44). The long history of Momostecan political conservatism, combined with militarism (see pp. 20–22), encouraged members of the community to attack rather than embrace the guerrillas, with the result that the municipality was understood as nonsubversive by the counterinsurgency forces.

Even though Momostenango was never directly attacked by the army, sporadic guerrilla activities and the high level of counterinsurgency violence elsewhere curtailed the travels of local merchants and caused economic hardship. The response to the sharp drop in commerce was to intensify farming (especially corn production), wild food collection, and the production of traditional craft items such as clothing and pottery. These strategies lessened dependence on outside markets and products. Currently, many more Momostecan women are wearing the traditional, hand-woven *po't* ("huipil") and using locally produced pottery vessels for food preparation and water storage than they did during the prosperous seventies.[7]

Between 1978 and 1985, from 50,000 to 70,000 Guatemalans were killed, the great majority of whom were Mayans. Another 500,000 became internal refugees, 150,000 fled to Mexico, and more than 200,000 escaped to other countries.[8] This violent process of uprooting and dispersion, like the earlier Jewish and Armenian diasporas, may lead to a cultural and political regrouping into an ethnic nation that transcends the boundaries of established nation-states.[9] That this may be what is, in fact, currently taking place is indicated by several simultaneous social and cultural developments among Mayans living in Guatemala, Mexico, Belize, Canada, and the United States.

By the mid-eighties, the priest-shamans of Momostenango took the unprecedented step of publishing a mimeographed Mayan calendar, titled *Rajil b'al q'ij maya* ("Mayan day count"). Rigoberto Itzep Chanchavac was the official compiler of this impressively accurate document, which correlates the Gregorian calendar with the 260-day Mayan calendar. It came to be so much in demand that it was distributed widely in other communities. In 1989, I was shown an updated version, compiled in the Quiché community of San Andrés Xecul by Juan Chuch Paxtor, who titled it *Wuj ub'eal raqan q'ij-mayab'* ("The book of the road of the count of Mayan days").

In 1986, Guatemalan linguists who are native speakers of Mayan languages organized themselves nationally as the Academia de las Lenguas Mayas de Guatemala (ALMG) and voted in new alphabets for writing the twenty-six Mayan languages and hundreds of dialects spoken in Guatemala.[10] Despite the bitter opposition of Protestant missionaries, who wished to keep their own writing systems for the indigenous languages of Guatemala, President Vinicio Cerezo signed the new alphabets into law, on November 23, 1987. The activities of the members of this Mayan academy include advocating the use of the new alphabets for writing Mayan languages and pressing for bilingual education; at the same time, they encourage indigenous customs, such as the wearing of distinctive clothing and the use of the Mayan calendar. Soon after the academy's inception, two new all-Mayan research organizations were founded: the Centro de Documentación Maya and the Centro de Investigación Social Maya. In 1990, the latter organization published a Quiché appointment book called *Cholb'äl chak: Calendario maya* ("Instrument for ordering one's work: Mayan calendar"), accurately correlated with the Gregorian calendar.

While these events were taking place in Guatemala, the Kanhobal Mayan refugee community in Los Angeles founded a nonprofit, mutual-help group known as Integración de Indígenas Mayas or IXIM (a term for corn in all Mayan languages) and began publishing *El Vocero de IXIM*, a newsletter that features trilingual (Mayan/Spanish/English) versions of traditional stories and information about Mayan hieroglyphs and calendars. Meanwhile, in Belize, at the other end of this expanded Mayan world, Mopán and Kekchí Mayan women were embroidering the twenty day names into their handicrafts, using hieroglyphic script.

Catholic priests and nuns in Latin America have recently begun to change their long-standing position, supporting rather than attacking Mayan ethnic and religious revitalization. For example, the parish church in the Mopán community of San Antonio, Belize, actively supports the Toledo Crafts Association and the Toledo Maya Cultural Council. Both of these organizations are involved in economic ventures that could raise the standard of living for their community as well as promoting and preserving Mayan culture. Since the mid-eighties, the Toledo Maya Cultural Council has been petitioning the Belizean government and attending international conferences to request "freehold title" to five hundred thousand acres of land in the Toledo district for the establishment of a Mayan Homeland.[11] Mayan catechists in Belize have recently taken a serious interest in the prophetic visions of Guatemalan Kekchí catechists, concerning the proper care of sacred corn and the worship of the earth deity, Tzuultak'a ("Mountain-Valley").[12] Guatemalan catechists, despite the colonialist cultural indoctrination they received during their earlier religious training, have been transformed by their contacts with Mayans from diverse communities. A catechist who helped organize the Academia de las Lenguas Mayas states the matter this way: "I used to speak against the traditional religion. We can be the worst destroyers of our own culture. But now that I am more involved, I understand the barbarity I've committed and the need to support our traditions."[13] Several other university-educated catechists have recently begun to undergo formal training as daykeepers in the towns of Momostenango and San Andrés Xecul.

Guatemalan Mayans have recently formed a new organization, called Mayahuil ("New Dawn," in Mam), to protest governmental promotion of the quincentennial of Columbus's so-called "discovery" of America. In 1991, they joined with other indigenous groups from throughout the Americas in a campaign entitled "500 Years of Indigenous and Popular Resistance," devoted to creating a more truthful history of the Americas and to stopping environmental destruction.

New communal cultures of resistance to Western domination and control are clearly emerging today in the context of the Mayan diaspora. Mayan languages, traditional dress, the sacred earth, and the ancient 260-day calendar have emerged as key cultural values and core symbols in the construction of a transnational Pan-Mayan identity. What we can read in these symbols is that Mayan peoples are demanding their own conceptual world, their own ethnic identity, their own land, and, as always, their own time.

Appendix A

Old Words (Ojer Tzij)

Before this, there was a wooden plank like this [points to his spinning-wheel].[1] But now a drum is done in a pretty way; it is tied and is heard well in the street. But before, it was merely a board that was struck with a stick. Before, the *calpul* gave the order to the drummer or town crier *(ajk'ojom)* for the announcement. Today, in each hamlet, the town crier sounds the drum, giving the order for the assembly of the elders, but before it was in each *calpul*.

In the words of ancient time, the *calpul* gave the orders for the assembly of the lords. The town crier called out, "Come to the *calpul*, come to the assembly, come before the elders, we are looking for people. We have lost the mayor *(alcalte)*, we have lost the alderman *(regidor)*, we have lost the policemen *(alguaciles)*."

After the assembly, some people left; they went to look for these lost people. They went and went and went until suddenly they were in the midst of the mountain, and the night entered. It was dark, dark, dark when they realized it was night. They didn't have a match, they didn't have anything, nothing, since it's been very little time since matches came out. When they began, they were looking for an animal trail, a little path, when suddenly the night began, the darkness came. Then they began crying out: "*Alca—lte! Ajch'ami—y! Alcalte! Tata Jue—z*, where are you?" They were answered: the jaguar and the mountain lion began to shout, there in the mountain. "My God! What direction is that coming from?" one said, as they went along carrying their staffs, their walking sticks. Now, when the remains of animals, when the remains of beasts are left for a time in the mountains, other animals come and pluck them until the skeleton appears. So that when the animals arrived, they had eaten the [missing] people, all the flesh, all the body, until they were sheer skeletons.

After this [discovery], an announcement was made: "We have lost the *alcalte, regidor, ajch'amiy;* they went to the animals, they were lost in the dark. What meaning does this have?" They thought and thought. "What does this consist of? In what manner have we lost the *alcalte, regidor, ajch'amiy,* all of them?" Then they had an idea, a sense of what it was. They lifted it up, it is said, they lifted it up. The town crier announced that an animal had eaten them, that they were pure skeletons, the *alcalte, regidor, ajch'amiy, juez de obra.*

The first lords of the *calpul* are speaking among these same elders. "How did this happen? Well, let's see." They unfolded it: sure enough, when they went, they encountered the Mam. They went to the mountain, well they went to the sierra and at the foot of Quilaja, a boy of this size [gesturing, indicating a boy about three feet tall] appeared with his whip. He was a shepherd. He asked, "Where are you going? Where are you going to?" Various directors had come out, since there are many employed in each *calpul*. Each *calpul*, since before, it was [called] *calpul*. But now there are Santa Ana, Tunayac, Tierra Colorada, Cipréses, Xequemeyá, Canquixajá, Patulup, Pitzal, Tzanjón, Tierra Blanca, Xolajab, Pasajoc, Chicorral, San Vincente Buenabaj [all cantons]. Now the names have changed, but before, when the world began, it was *calpul*. So, the lords went. Good, they encountered a shepherd, the Mam. "Where are you going? Who are the servers *(ajpatanib)*? Who has the service *(patan)* here?"

The *alcalte* said, "I am the *alcalte* of the pueblo."

"Oh, how nice, how rare that you are the *alcalte!*" said the shepherd. "Why isn't there law, why isn't there an example?" Then he whipped the *alcalte* with his whip. He was carrying his whip, this *ajyuk'*, this shepherd. "How pretty that you are *alcalte! Aj! Baw! Baw! Baw!*" [whipping gesture]. How many lashes!

"No sir, no, no, no, no, don't strike me, since I don't know where they went, where they are to be seen, the *alcalte*, *regidor*, the *juez de obra* with his *ajch'amiy*."

"I'm telling you, rogue, you must comply, you must comply in setting up the burning place of the town *(porobal rech tinimit)*, the shrine of the town *(awas rech tinimit)*."

"Of course, why not?"

"Ah, crafty one. And you too! *Chiw! Chiw!* [as if whipping a second person with his empty bag of divining seeds]. And you too, rogue! *Fiw!*" [as if hitting a third person].

The hour had arrived for the planting of the town. Then the mountains, then Tamancu and Quilaja spoke. They spoke directly, personally! Tamancu said, "I am Tamancu, I am the *alcalte*."

"Ah, no!" said Quilaja. "I am the first *alcalte;* you are Tamancu, so you must wait."

"No, I am the first *alcalte;* I am 11 E, 13 E, 9 E."

"Now I say, I am Quilaja; I am the *alcalte* 9 Quej, 11 Quej, 13 Quej, 12 Quej, 7 Quej," as they [the numbers] skip around. "I am the first *alcalte* and Tamancu is second. But I'm lacking my secretary, lacking my *ajtz'ib*."

Then the secretary appeared and he spoke, "I am Pipil, I am

the secretary, but who will serve with you, Tamancu? You don't belong with me. You belong with your secretary, Carsa Joyan."

Then Tamancu said, "Ah, very well, now you don't belong with me."

"No, I don't belong in your time. No, Carsa Joyan belongs in your time," said Pipil.

"Good, and me?" said Quilaja.

"Well with me, with me you will pass."

Alcalte Socop spoke, "Are you my secretary?"

"Yes," said Pipil. "I have two years of service, but you have only one year of service. I serve one year with you, Socop, and then the next year with you, Quilaja. Now, Tamancu is with his secretary, Carsa Joyan, but a secretary does not serve for only one year. Oh, no, no, no, no; the secretary serves two years, two years of service for the secretary. First, one year with *alcalte* Tamancu, and then one year with *alcalte* Joyan."

Let's say *alcalte* Joyan is right now, only one year of service, but his secretary two years. He belongs with Tamancu, and he belongs with Joyan. Now this changes, it rests with Socop and his secretary Pipil. Then he comes out of his year, and it rests with Quilaja and his secretary Pipil. The four *alcaltes* change each year. Early in March, they'll not be employed. It'll touch on Socop and on Pipil, and, in 1978, Quilaja will be *alcalte*. In 1977, Socop takes his position. Now Socop is *alcalte* Ik', and his secretary is Tz'iquin, 11 Tz'iquin, right? It's what we were talking about.

Yes, 4 Tz'iquin, 11 Tz'iquin.

[At this point he arranges six of his divining seeds on the table and indicates the name of each *alcalte* or *secretario* and the mountain shrine where he is received at the beginning of his service (see figure 33).]

There it is, it's pretty, the four Mam with the two secretaries in between. First Quilaja [picking up the divining seed at lower right in figure 33], second Tamancu, third Joyan, fourth Socop. Good. Now, first secretary, second secretary.

"Good, now answer me. Who's going to be made priest-shaman of the town *(chuchkajaw rech tinimit)*? You [as if choosing someone], because you have the service *(patan)*," he said.

Because of this, I personally have my employment here in the center. I am the Síndico Segundo Municipal. I am the first of the pueblo [see chapter 2 for a discussion of civil government]. Because of this, I arrange for the customs. I am the one who has the right to make this, this movement. Into this a helper *(alguacil)* doesn't enter, another person doesn't enter. No, only the *alcalte* is the president of the pueblo, the Síndico Segundo is what I am. Because of this, I know each part, for this goes by a scale.

At first, there came out the custom of the pueblo. Then in each *calpul*, or as it is said now, in each canton, there in each *barrio* the women were dying. Well, when the women went out for water, when they went out with the children looking for firewood, when they went out, the jaguar and mountain lion killed them. The people weren't killing them—no, there came the jaguar and the mountain lion, and they carried the women away. Why? Why? Why? Why? Because the Mundo opened and they all went together. How many women! They were becoming skeletons, sheer skeletons. They were being finished off, the women and the children. Now there were no women, not even the bones were recovered. Only the bones of the children were found.

When the town crier came around looking for a message, there the husbands said, "So many women have been lost."

The men went out looking, and they came to the shepherd, who said, "What are you looking for?"

"Well, my woman was lost, my children at such-and-such an hour."

"Ah, indeed—your women passed away, for you are fools!"

"Ah, good sir."

"Why didn't you take care? The blame is yours! Your women are not to blame, for you lack the shrine, the patrilineage shrine *(awas rech alaxic)*. The patrilineage shrine, just like the town shrine, you fool! [whipping the man]. Good, this must be arranged. You will put the foundation of the animals *(warabalja rech wawaj)*—the 4 E, 5 Aj, 6 Ix—here," said the shepherd of the Mundo. "And here you must put the 7 Quej, 8 K'anil," he said. "And also the 7 Ix, 8 Tz'iquin, the treasure, here" [see chapter 3 for a discussion of all these shrines].

Good. Then he went away, and it remained so. The man had his cows and his horses, but then the wild animals came, they came to eat them. So again the shrine was raised up. This time the *awas rech quej* [horse]—9 E, 10 Aj, 11 Ix—was completed.

Later, when the merchants were going out on their trips—

suddenly the animals jumped out of the mountains at them. They came out and carried off the poor travelers.

When the criers came around, the families gave them the message—at such-and-such a place, such-and-such a place.

"Ah, now how are you fixed?"

The shrine was not yet complete, for today we have 6 E, 7 Aj, 8 Ix as well as 5 E, 6 Aj, 7 Ix. So they completed it, they finished it.

Then came the divining bundle *(baraj)*. Again, the shepherd was out walking, he was whistling, he was singing. What song was he singing, with his knapsack on his back?

Now the hour had arrived, when he was carrying his knapsack behind him. Suddenly the women went into the water. They went in all at once. When they where putting their jars into the water— suddenly they were thrown! *Pum!* All at once, they were thrown into the water hole! At the same time the men—well, their bellies swole up. Suddenly, when they were eating their tortillas, drinking their *atolito,* their stomachs inflated.

When, *ah, chu chu chu*—almost all the people were this way. Then it began. There, in the main road, the town priest-shaman passed the Tzimit. The Tzimit came out. The C'oxol, the C'oxol came out. Ah! He was like this [gesturing as if playing a *chirimía*]. Look, he was dancing, with his *chirimía* and his hatchet.

"What's happening to you people, what's happening? Well, you have passed me."

"Well, Oh God! My woman suddenly fell into the water hole. Oh, my God! My son, oh God, my daughter-in-law, are vomiting. They fell down and their stomachs just ripped, all the belly is torn." What happens is *ra—k!* It is torn, the stomach is ripped. It is inflated; then it rips.

"Ah, what am I going to say to you about this?" Well, the Tzitzimit, the real Tzitzimit came out—the C'oxol, and he was dancing with his hatchet.

"Now today is the last day, the last one."

"Ah, very well."

"Because you don't remember, you have the town priest-sha-man, patrilineage priest-shaman." Then he struck him, saying, "You don't remember, but if you'll receive me, I'm going to show you" [the narrator strikes himself all over with his empty divining bag]. *"Pun! Pun! Pun! Pun!"*

Then, because of this, it jumps, the lightning speaks, the signal, it jumps.

Because of this, we carry the divining bag—women, men, at fifteen, twelve, thirteen years, they already have their bag. It was left here for them by the Mundo.

The Mundo spoke, "I'll show you! But are you going to receive it?"

"Ah, forgive me, yes, I'm going to receive."

"Indeed, I'm going to show you. Now that I have given you the divining bag, you must answer the questions. You must mix. You have your sister, your neighbor, your *calpul* coming to ask a question. Here it will speak [strikes his knee] on the knee. There are those who are kneeling, who are attacking you in your road. Once and for all, may it stick with you."

He struck him with the same bag over and over in every place. Because of this, the blood speaks. Here behind the neck, here too—the Tzimit struck him. Here! And here! And here! And here! Look! And here too, *phew!* Here too, when it speaks here [throat], someone is cutting off one's head without motive. And here in the nape of the neck, there is envy. Someone is tossing bad things over one.

Yes, with this same bag [gesturing with his empty divining bag], the Tzimit opened it here, here, here, here around behind, including the seat [striking himself on the buttocks]. He gave him a blow here, so it would stick.

When we drink—when we will take our drink, we feel it here [below the lower lip]. When our neighbor dies and we will take our drink, we feel it here [same place].

"I'm going to show you," said the first Tzimit, this crafty one who left us the study. This is the teacher who—yes, indeed [blood movement] you are understanding, you are believing me. This is the matter of the Tzimit, the first one—yes, indeed [points to blood movement in center of his thigh].

Well, for this reason, the three testaments—the custom of the town, the custom of the shrine, and the custom of the divining bag were left—the three. But the teacher was only one. The shepherd is the one who left it. He was the one who showed the town priest-shaman the customs of the town, the lineage, and the divining seeds. The shepherd was the one to show it. He was the first one— the little bitty one, the Tzimit. He was the one who said, "I'm going to show you," and he grabbed his hatchet and began striking the town priest-shaman. "When there is evil, here, here, here, here," he said. "I'll show you well," he said, and struck him so that he would learn well.

The first Tzimit said, "Perhaps you didn't see it, but I'm coming to show you. Good! Good! Good! [striking] Everywhere." So it was left that when one begins to mix, mix, mix, then it is for this reason that one is being given signals—given signals. It speaks here, here, here, here—almost the whole body.

This is the story. "Are you going to receive or not?" [strikes himself three times on 'not']. Then they receive—men, women, even girls, even boys.

Mundo Joyan No'j (Mam)	3 ◯	◯ 4	Mundo Socop Ik' (Mam)
Mundo Joyan C'at (Sec.)	◯ 2	1 ◯	Mundo Pipil Tz'iquin (Sec.)
Mundo Tamancu E (Mam)	2 ◯	◯ 1	Mundo Quilaja Quej (Mam)

38. The Mountains of the Mam, or Year-bearers.

Appendix B

Prayers

The reader will notice immediately that Quiché prayers are constructed in groups of phrases that are parallel in their meaning and in their syntax. Edmonson insists on the couplet as the sole form of Quiché parallelism,[1] but the present texts contain clear exceptions including single phrases (without parallel), triplets, and (in the case of the list of numbers in the "Initiate's Prayer on Wajxakib Batz' "), parallel series of potentially indefinite length. I have chosen to treat each couplet, triplet, or longer parallelistic entity as a single line—beginning at the left hand margin with the continuation of long lines indented—rather than as a series of shorter lines because speakers of Quiché themselves tend to treat each such entity as a single utterance with scarcely any intonational marking of the divisions between the parallel parts and without the intervention of pauses.[2]

Divining Prayer

Sachaj la numac Tiox Mundo.
Pardon my sin God Earth.

Quinchapo k'ani baraj, saki baraj
I am taking hold of the yellow mixing, white mixing

k'ani piley, saki piley
yellow beans, white beans

k'ani chok', saki chok'
yellow crystals, white crystals

k'ani chachal, saki chachal
yellow necklace, white necklace

chiwäch la, Tiox Mundo.
before you, God Earth.

Quinkajaxtaj jun rato
I am now borrowing for a moment

ri uxlab la y xukije' wa' kajuyubal.[3]
your breath and also our body.

Quintaxtaj ri mayij, ri tok'ob
I am now asking for the blessing, the favor

chi rech jun sak k'alaj
for this one clear light

chi rech wa' nuchac, wa' nupatan
for this my work, my service

wa' nubaraj, wa' nupunto.
my mixing, my pointing.

Y xukijelo, k'ani sutz', saki sutz'
And also, yellow clouds, white clouds

ri mayul, ri tew, ri cakik'
mist, cold, wind

ri cabinic tzan juyub, tzan tak'aj.
walking over mountains, over plains.

Y xukijelo, ri nima loma, ch'uti loma
And also large hills, little hills

nima liana, ch'uti liana
large flats, little flats

nima xcanul, ch'uti xcanul
large volcanoes, little volcanoes

nima tak'aj, ch'uti tak'aj.
large plains, little plains.

Quelech'awok! Quetzijonic ri jun rato
Let them come out and speak! They are conversing a little while

chi rech wa' jun sak, chi rech wa' jun pregunta
for this one light, for this one question

chi tewal, chi cakik'al.
in chilliness, in windiness.

Quetzijonic pa wa' jun santo y laj k'ij
They are talking on this holy and great day

chi tewal, chi cakik'al
in chilliness, in windiness

quetzijonic jun rato
they are talking for a little while

chi rech wa' jun pregunta
for this one question

pa wa' Ajaw Wajxakib E.
on this Day Lord 8 E.

Quinchapo k'ani baraj, saki baraj
I am taking hold of the yellow mixing, white mixing

k'ani piley, saki piley.
yellow beans, white beans.

Y xukijelo, ri nan, ri tat[4]
And also, the mothers, the fathers

quech'awic, quetzijonic
they are talking, they are conversing

jun rato, jun momento
a little while, a moment

chi rech wa' jun pregunta.
for this one question.

Cakabano wa' chanim,
We are doing this at this very moment,

sachaj la numac.
pardon my sin.

Teacher's Prayer on Wukub Tz'i'

Sachaj la numac Tiox. Sachaj la numac Mundo.
Pardon my sin God. Pardon my sin Earth.

Wa' cämic quinjacho wa' quipatan,
This day I hand over their service,

chirij rakän uk'äb wa' (name), chirij rakän uk'äb wa' (name).
behind the legs the arms of this (name), behind the legs the arms of
      this (name).

Tunulic chac, tunulic patan[5]
The united work, united service

baraj punto
mixing pointing

k'ani piley, saki piley
yellow beans, white beans

k'ani chok', saki chok'
yellow crystals, white crystals

quinjach chirij cakän quik'äb, chuwe'k k'ij, chuwe'k hora.
I hand over behind their legs their arms, on tomorrow's day, tomor-
      row's hour.

Cämic, Wukub Tz'i'
Today, 7 Tz'i'

are c'u wa' upresenta, c'u wa' ri (name)
here is his present, here is (name)

cuc'am uchac, cuc'am upatan, cuc'am ubaraj, upiley
he is receiving his work, he is receiving his service, he is receiving
      his mixing, his beans

uk'ani chok', saki chok'.
his yellow crystals, white crystals.

Chuwe'k k'ij, chuwe'k hora cubano recibir.
On tomorrow's day, tomorrow's hour he receives.

Caya c'u rumemoria, caya c'u rusentido
Giving then his memory, giving then his sensing

catz'akatisaj rajilabal k'ij pa ri ujolom, catz'akatisaj rurazón.
completing his calendar in his head, completing his reason.

Cubano chuwi' casakiric, cak'an k'ij, canic'ajar k'ij
He is doing (his customs) after dawning, yellowing sun, becoming
     midday

pa ri wa' ujunabal, pa ri wakibal
at the one-place, at the six-place

pa ri wajxakibal, pa ri ubelejebal.
at the eight-place, at the nine-place.

Rech c'u ri baraj, rech ri punto quinjach
And his mixing, his own pointing I hand over

chirij rakän, chirij ruk'äb
behind his legs, behind his arms

chuwe'k k'ij, chuwe'k hora.
on tomorrow's day, tomorrow's hour.

Wa' baraj, wa' punto xpe chila' pa ri Xiquinabaj Mundo,
This mixing, this pointing came there from Stone Ear Mountain,

c'ambal rech, chokbal rech.
the receiving place, the crystal place.

Quinjach chirij rakän uk'äb
I hand over behind her legs her arms

wa' chac, wa' patan rech (name).
this work, this service of (name).

Are c'u wa' ri nupresenta
And here this is my present

quinjach c'ut wa' chac, wa' patan
I hand over then this work, this service

chirij rakän, chirij uk'äb
behind her legs, behind her arms

wa' chichu', wa' (name)
this woman, this (name)

cuc'amo wa' ruk'ij ralaxic[6]
she receives this his birthday

wuchac, wupatan
her work, her service

rech c'u k'ani baraj, saki baraj
her own yellow mixing, white mixing

k'ani punto, saki punto
yellow pointing, white pointing

k'ani piley, saki piley
yellow beans, white beans

tunulic chac, tunulic patan
united work, united service

quinjach chirij rakän, chirij uk'äb.
that I hand over behind her legs, behind her arms.

Chuwe'k k'ij, chuwe'k hora cabantaj recibir,
On tomorrow's day, tomorrow's hour it is being received,

catz'akatisaj pa ri ujolom.
completing it in her head.

Student's Prayer on Wukub Tz'i'

Quinc'amo wa' nuchac, nupatan.
I receive this my work, my service.

Caban la ri tok'ob, caya la pa ri nujolom
You sirs do the favor, you give it in my head

ri rajilabal ri k'ij.
the counting of the days.

Ri k'ani coyopa, saki coyopa casilabaxic,
That the yellow sheet-lightning, white sheet-lightning be moved,

quinta ri mayij, quinta ri tok'ob
I ask the blessing, I ask the favor

rech c'ut k'ani baraj, saki baraj
for her yellow mixing, white mixing

k'ani punto, saki punto
yellow pointing, white pointing

k'ani piley, saki piley.
yellow beans, white beans.

Quinc'amo wa' ruk'ij ralaxic.
I am receiving this her birthday.

Cajach chirij wakän, chirij nuk'äb
Handing it over behind my legs, behind my arms

rumal wa' chuch, wa' kajaw.
by this mother, this father.

Y xukije, wa' k'ani baraj, saki baraj
And also, this yellow mixing, white mixing

k'ani piley, saki piley
yellow beans, white beans

quinc'amo wa' k'ij ralaxic;
I am receiving this his birthday;

mä chi c'ut k'oxowinak jolom,
that there not appear headaches,

mä chi c'ut yi'tz'inak pomaj,
that there not appear twisted stomach,

mä chi c'ut chokej,
that there not appear cramps,

mä chi c'ut cumatz,
that there not appear snake,

mä chi k'oxowinak ware,
that there not be toothache,

juntiri quesachic.
that they all be forgotten.

Cakaj ne',[7] kanegocio
It is showing up, the beginning of our business

cakaj ne', kapwak
it is showing up, the beginning of our money

cak'aj k'ulew, cakaj kachoch
our land is showing up, our house is showing up

cakaj jun kacarro, cakaj jun ka avión;
our car is showing up, our airplane is showing up;

cayaba' la chi quech Mundo, chuwe'k cäbij.
you are causing the giving of all this to them Earth, tomorrow or
    the day after tomorrow.

Rumal ri', cakaj quetzukumijic chila' chiwäch la.
Because of that, it happens that they are giving food there before
    you.

Initiate's Prayer on Wajxakib Batz'

Sachaj la numac Tiox. Sachaj la numac Mundo.
Pardon my sin God. Pardon my sin Earth.

Quinya'o ri numulta, nupresenta
I am giving my fine, my present

chiwäch la Tiox, chiwäch la Mundo.
before you God, before you Earth.

Quinya'o wa' jun nuceracandela, nutac'alibal[8]
I am giving my wax candle, my stake

pa ri akän k'äb la Tiox
toward the legs arms of God

chirelebal k'ij, chukajibal k'ij
at the rising of the sun (east), at the setting of the sun (west)

cajxucut kaj, cajxucut ulew.
the four corners of sky (south), the four corners of earth (north).

Sa'j la rech c'ut nuchac, nupatan
Come here then my work, my service

nubaraj, nupunto.
my mixing, my pointing.

Chila' ch'upum wi ri k'ani piley, saki piley
There were cut there the yellow beans, white beans

k'ani chok', saki chok'
yellow crystals, white crystals

pa ri Santa Catarina y Tzan Poklaj[9]
at Santa Catarina and Tzan Poklaj

pa ri oriente, chirelebal k'ij.
at the east, at the rising of the sun.

Ch'upum tamom
The cutting the chopping

ri k'ani chachal, saki chachal
of the yellow necklace, white necklace

pa ri Xiquinabaj Mundo.
at Stone Ear Mountain.

Chiwäch la nujuyubal, nutak'ajal
Before you my mountain, my plain

ri nima xkanul, ch'uti xkanul
large volcano, little volcano

ri nima loma, ch'uti loma
large hill, little hill

ri nima liana, ch'uti liana
large flat, little flat

nima tak'aj, ch'uti tak'aj.
large plain, little plain.

Sa'j la Ch'uti Sabal, Nima Sabal
Come here Little Sabal, Large Sabal

K'ani Pila, Saki Pila
Yellow Spring, White Spring

ayin cho, ayin plo
all lakes, all oceans

y xukijelo, comon Nantat, comon chuchkajawib.
and also, all ancestors, all diviners.

Are c'u wa', chiquiwäch comon (name)
Here it is then, before all (name)

cäpe aläk chi rilic, chuta'ic
you who come here to see, to hear

wa' nucompesión, salvación
this my confession, my salvation

rech ri kavida, kac'aslemal
for our own life, our very own life

ruc' wajaw wixokil/wachajil
with my lord my wife/husband

ilol wech, tal wech[10]
my looking after, listening to [the needs]

pa ri ja, pa ri c'olibal.
in the house, in the place.

Xa junam quilic cäbän la cuc' ri cok'ic chi rech quiwa kuqui'a[11]
But equally you look after those who weep for their own food and
    drink

chi rech ri k'ani quetzal, saki quetzal
for their own yellow dollar, white dollar

k'ani plata, saki plata.
yellow silver, white silver.

Caya' la chakech ri jun kacinco, diez, quince, veinte, veinticinco,
    treinta, cuarenta, cincuenta, cien, doscientos, trescientos, cua-
    tro cientos, quinientos, mil, dos mil, cinco mil quetzales
You are giving us our five, ten, fifteen, twenty, twenty-five, thirty,
    forty, fifty, one hundred, two hundred, three hundred, four
    hundred, five hundred, thousand, two thousand, five thousand
    dollars

rech jun kachoch, rech jun kulew
for our house, for our land

rech jun kawaj, rech kanegocio, diligencia
for our animals, our business, diligence

y rech ri kestudio.
and for our study.

Mäpetic jalum, k'abam
Let there not come falsehoods, blame

chirij kakän kak'äb.
behind our legs our arms.

Uj c'o waral pa wa' tinimit Santiago Chuwa Tz'ak.
We are here in this town Santiago Momostenango.

Cujwacatic tzan juyub, tzan tak'aj.
We wander over mountains, over plains.

Mäpe jalum, mäpe k'abam
Let there not come falsehoods, let there not come blame

chirij kakän, kak'äb
behind our legs, our arms

ruc' wa' kamaestro, tajen cujutijoj
with him our teacher, who is just now teaching us

chi rech restudio utzij wa' tinimit, rech lengua Quiché.
the study of the idiom of this town, the Quiché language.

Caya' la pa ri kajolom.
You are giving it in our heads.

Quecubaxic ri nima k'atbaltzij, ch'uti k'atbaltzij
So that the large authorities, little authorities sit down

mujquimöxirisaj,
that they not cause us to become crazy,

are c'ut nutac'alibal, nupresenta
this then is my stake, my present

chiwäch la Tiox, chiwäch la Mundo
before you God, before you Earth

y xukijelo, ri comon Nantat, comon chuchkajawib.
and also, all ancestors, all diviners.

Quinc'amo wa' nuchak, nupatan
I am receiving my work, my service

nubaraj, nupunto
my mixing, my pointing

chiquiwäch comon chuchkajawib.
before them all diviners.

Are c'u wa', c'ambal rech nuchak, nupatan
Here then, receiving my work, my service

chiquiwäch comon chuchkajawib.
before them all diviners.

Are c'u wa', chiquiwäch comon (name)
Here then, before them all (name)

ta'bal mayij, tok'ob
is the offering for the the blessing, the favor

chi rech jun kachoch, chi rech jun kulew
for our house, for our land

chi rech jun kacarro, chi rech jun ka avión
for our car, for our airplane

chi rech ri katz'iak
for our clothes

ta'bal, tok'ob.
the offering, the favor.

Sachaj la numac, nujuyubal, nutak'ajal.
Pardon my sin, my mountains, my plains.

Jachtajic rech nuchak, nupatan
It is handed over my work, my service

nubaraj, nupunto.
my mixing, my pointing.

Prayer Before Untying the Baraj on Wajxakib Batz'

Tiox, sachaj la numac Tat.
God, pardon my sin Father.

Quinya'o jun pregunta chi kech wa' wijil, nutz'akat.
I am giving one question for this my neighbor, my companion.

Tiox, puxa c'o c'äx[12] quiquiriko
God, perhaps they will encounter pain

bäntäj recibir quichak, quipatan
having received their work, their service

quibaraj, quipunto.
their mixing, their pointing.

Pero, Tiox lal ta c'ut, Tat, y lal Mundo
But, God you give, Father, and you Earth

cuc'ataj la, caya la ri rajilal,
are being carried, you are giving its value,

uc'axelal chi kech wa' gasto.
its replacement for their money.

Xquisacho Tiox, lal caban la ri' tok'ob
That they be pardoned God, you are doing this favor

xukijelo ri Nantat.
also the ancestor.

Ay Tiox, faltalo ri oracion,
Oh God, we are lacking the prayer,

pero sí teren canök Tat, capetic cujlukojo.
but yes he left late Father, coming to worship for us.

Chic cujkojo chila' pa ri Sabal,
Already we were worshiping there at Sabal,

cujkoko chila' pa ri Nantat, cujkoko chila' pa ri Pila.
worshiping there at the Ancestor, worshiping there at the Spring.

Tiox, c'ambal rech quichak, quipatan
God, receiving their work, their service

jachtajic chirij cakän, chirij quik'äb.
it has been handed over behind their legs, behind their arms.

Pero Tiox, lal Tat, puxa c'o c'äx
But God, Father, perhaps there is to be pain

pa ri ja, c'olibal.
in the house, the place.

Sachaj la numac, Tiox.
Pardon my sin, God.

Prayer While Divining on Wajxakib Batz'

Tiox, sachaba' la numac.
God, cause my sin to be pardoned.

Cämic k'ij, cämic hora, Wajxakib Batz'
Now on this day, this hour, 8 Batz'

jachtajic quichak, quipatan
it is handed over their work, their service

chirij cakän, chirij quik'äb
behind their legs, behind their arms

c'amtajic cumal.
it has been received by them.

Quic'am ri k'ani baraj, saki baraj
They accept the yellow mixing, white mixing

k'ani punto, saki punto.
yellow pointing, white pointing.

Tiox, caya la ubixic cha kech.
God, you are giving a sign to us.

Y jelo, chi wa' la nujuyubal, chi wa' la nutak'ajal
And also, before you my mountains, before you my plains

Tiox, falta ujunabal, uwajxakibal, ubelejebal.
God, a one-place, eight-place, nine-place is lacking.

We c'u xemes c'utajic jun k'ij
If, in addition they had forgotten one day

jun nujunabal, jun nuwajxakibal, jun nubelejebal
one one-place, one eight-place, one nine-place

casach la quimac.
you are forgiving their sin.

Tiox, quivoluntad
God, with their will

quiquiya ri wa, quiquiya ri ja', che la Mundo.
they are giving food, they are giving water, for you Earth.

Cabixtaj la, "nujuyubal, nutak'ajal."
It has been said, "You are my mountains, my plains."

Sa'j la alcalte, sa'j la secretario.
Come here mayor, come here secretary.

Sa'j la ajregidores, sa'j la ajch'amiyab.
Come here councilmen, come here policemen.

Shrine Prayer

Sachaj la numac, Tiox. Sachaj la numac, Mundo.
Pardon my sin, God. Pardon my sin, Earth.

Sa'j la Ch'uti Sabal/Nima Sabal/K'ani Mar, Saki Mar[13]
Come here Little Sabal/Large Sabal/Yellow Sea, White Sea

K'ani Pila, Saki Pila
Yellow Spring, White Spring

ayin cho, ayin plo.
all lakes, all oceans.

S'aj la Ajaw Wajxakib K'anil/Belejib Batz'/Jun No'j.
Come here Lord 8 K'anil/9 Batz'/1 No'j.

Are c'u wa' nutac'alibal, nupresenta
Here is my stake, my present

chiquiwäch, nujuyubal, nutak'ajal
before them, my mountains, my plains

rech nuchak, nupatan
for my work, my service

nubaraj, nupunto
my mixing, my pointing

chiwäch la Tiox, chiwäch la Mundo
before you God, before you Earth

chiquiwäch ri nan, ri tat, comon chuchkajawib.
before them the mother, the father, common priest-shamans.

Sa'j la Mundo, K'ani Pila, Saki Pila
Come here Earth, Yellow Spring, White Spring

K'ani Mar, Saki Mar
Yellow Sea, White Sea

ayin cho, ayin plo.
all lakes, all oceans.

Chirelebal k'ij, chukajibal k'ij
At the rising of the sun (east), at the setting of the sun (west)

cajxucut kaj, cajxucut ulew
the four corners of sky (south), the four corners of earth (north)

ri nima juyub, ch'uti juyub
the large mountain, small mountain

ri nima loma, ch'uti loma
the large hill, small hill

ri nima xkanul, ch'uti xkanul
the large volcano, small volcano

ri nima liana, ch'uti liana
the large flat, small flat

ri nima tak'aj, ch'uti tak'aj.
the large plain, small plain.

C'ambal rech nuchak, nupatan
At the receiving place of my work, my service

nubaraj, nupunto
my mixing, my pointing

chila' ch'upum wi ri k'ani piley, saki piley
there were cut there the yellow beans, white beans

k'ani chok', saki chok'
yellow crystals, white crystals

pa ri Santa Catarina y Tzan Poklaj
at Santa Catarina and Tzan Poklaj

pa ri oriente, chirelebal k'ij.
at the east, at the rising of the sun.

Ch'upum tamom
The cutting chopping

ri k'ani chachal, saki chachal
of the yellow necklace, white necklace

pa ri Xiquinabaj Mundo.
at Stone Ear Mountain.

Xukijelo, chiquiwäch ri much'ulic bak, much'ulic ulew, much'ulic
    poklaj
Also, before them powdered bone, powdered clay, powdered sand

ri comon Nantat, comon chuchkajawib
the common ancestors, common priest-shamans

chiquiwäch ri kanan, katat
before them our mothers, our fathers

katit, kamam comon (name)
our grandmothers, our grandfathers common (name)

ban aläk tok'ob casilabaxic k'ani coyopa, saki coyopa
you sirs do the favor that the yellow sheet-lightning, white sheet-
    lightning be moved

chirelebal k'ij, chukajibal k'ij
at the rising of the sun (east), at the setting of the sun (west)

cajxucut kaj, cajxucut ulew.
four corners of sky (south), four corners of earth (north).

Catz'akatisaxic pa ri kajolom
That it be completed in our heads

che ri rajilabal k'ij.
for him/her the divining calendar.

Y je', ri chuchkajawib, ri xewacatic xo'l ja, xo'l c'olibal
And also, the diviners, the ones who passed among the houses,
    among the places

quich'aj taza, quich'aj china, quich'aj mulul rech chak, patan
washing the cups, washing the china, washing the gourd jars of the
    mixing, pointing

quech'awic chirech wa' k'ani coyopa, saki coyopa
they speak for this yellow sheet-lightning, white sheet-lightning

cuya ri sak, cuya ri k'alaj.
that it give the light, the clarity.

Y caya'ic jun kech ri k'an ilbal, sak ilbal
And to give us our yellow seeing instruments, white seeing
    instruments

chu xo'l wa' chok', wa' chachal
among these crystals, this necklace

c'o chu xo'l wa' nubaraj, wa' nupunto.
to be among this my mixing, this my pointing.

Wachic' cac'utunic
Dream that appears

pa ri k'ekum, pa ri ak'äb
in the obscurity, in the night

pa ri Ajaw Jun No'j.
on the Lord 1 No'j.

Jasa ri ucholaj?
What does it mean?

Catz'akatisaj aläk ri ubixic
You sirs are completing what is being said

pa ri k'ekum, pa ri ak'äb
in the obscurity, in the night

rech wachic'.
of his/her dream.

We c'o kanan, katat
If there is our mother, our father

cumol tzij chirij kakän kak'äb;
who unites words behind our legs our arms;

oj ri chirelebal k'ij, chukajibal k'ij
go to the place the sun comes from (east), to the place the sun falls
    (west)

cajxucut kaj, cajxucut ulew!
four corners of sky (south), four corners of earth (north)!

Ta'bal mayij, tok'ob
Here is the offering for the blessing, the favor

chi rech jun kachoch, chi rech jun kulew
for our house, for our land

chi rech ri estudio.
for the study.

Mäpetic jalum k'abäm chirij k'akän, kak'äb
Let there not come lies or blame among our legs, our arms (our
    family)

ruc' wa', kamaestro cujutijoj
with him, our teacher who is teaching us

rech wa' lengua Quiché
the Quiché language

rech wa' tinimit Santiago Chuwa Tz'ak.
of the town Santiago Momostenango.

Que' cubaxic ri nima k'atbaltzij, ch'uti k'atbaltzij
So that the large authorities, little authorities

mujquimöxirisaj.
not cause us to become crazy.

Are c'u wa' ta'bal tok'ob, mayij.
Here is the offering for the blessing, the favor.

Sachaj la numac Tiox. Sachaj la numac Mundo.
Pardon my sin God. Pardon my sin Earth.

Sachaj aläk nunan, nutat.
Pardon my sin my mother, my father.

Jachtajic rech nuchak, nupatan
It was handed over my work, my service

nubaraj, nupunto
my mixing, my pointing

chiwäch la Mundo.
before you Earth.

Diviner's Prayer for a Pregnant Woman

Sa'j la Mundo. Sa'j la Virgen Santa Ana.
Come here Earth. Come here Virgin Santa Ana.

Lal c'amal quibe ri iyomab,
You are the one who guides midwives,

caya la ri quichuk'ab.
you give their strength.

Y xukije, walcu'al
And also, my child

ximixobic rakän uk'äb,
whose legs and arms are bound (who is pregnant),

lal etam la jampa xopanic ri uk'ij.
you know when her day arrives.

Xa ta' jun hora o media hora
Only ask for an hour or half-hour of labor

cuya ri luz, cuya ri sak.
until she gives light, she gives birth.

Notes

Preface

1. Two key sources here are William F. Hanks and Don S. Rice, *Word and Image in Maya Culture*; and Linda Schele and David Freidel, *A Forest of Kings*.

2. Arlen F. Chase and Prudence M. Rice, *The Lowland Maya Postclassic*; Nancy M. Farriss, *Maya Society under Colonial Rule*; John W. Fox, *Maya Postclassic State Formation*; Robert Hill and John Monaghan, *Continuities in Highland Maya Social Organization*; Grant D. Jones, *Maya Resistance to Spanish Rule*; W. George Lovell, *Conquest and Survival in Colonial Guatemala*; and Carol A. Smith, *Guatemalan Indians and the State, 1540 to 1988*.

3. Communities like Momostenango, in Totonicapán, and Santiago Chimaltenango, in Huehuetenango, that were cohesive and well-organized fared better during the war than highly factionalized communities. See John M. Watanabe, "Enduring Yet Ineffable Community in the Western Periphery of Guatemala."

4. For arguments that the counterinsurgency attack on Mayan civilian populations was an attempt at genocide—defined by the general assembly of the United Nations as any act perpetrated with the intention of destroying totally or in part, a national, ethnic, racial, or religious group—see the resolution passed by the American Anthropological Association at its annual meeting in Washington, D.C., on December 7, 1982; Ricardo S. Falla, "We Charge Genocide"; Rigoberta Menchú, *I . . . Rigoberta Menchú: An Indian Woman in Guatemala*; Arturo Arias, "Changing Indian Identity: Guatemala's Violent Transition to Modernity"; and Richard N. Adams, "Conclusion: What Can We Know about the Harvest of Violence?" For an argument that it was also an example of attempted ethnocide—a term used by anthropologists to describe the damage caused to native cultures by war—see Carol A. Smith, "Destruction of the Material Bases for Indian Culture."

5. Robert M. Carmack, *Harvest of Violence*; Beatriz Manz, *Refugees of a Hidden War*; and Jean-Marie Simon, *Guatemala: Eternal Spring, Eternal Tyranny*.

Chapter 1

1. The orthography used for Quiché here is the practical one suggested by the Instituto Indigenista Nacional de Guatemala (see David G. Fox, *Lecciones elementales en Quiché*, pp. 15–18). Vowels are pronounced as in Spanish, except that ä is like the vowel in English "run," ë is like the vowel in English "met," and ö is like the vowel in English "foot." Consonants are also as in Spanish, with an equivalence between c (used before

a, o, u) and qu (before e, i), except for k, which is articulated with the tongue farther back than for c or qu; tz, which is like the German Zeit; w, which is like English w; x, which is like English sh; and b, which is a glottalized p. Other glottalizations are indicated by ', which indicates a plain glottal stop when it follows a vowel and a glottalized consonant in the following combinations: c' (or qu'), ch', k', t' and tz'.

2. Miguel León-Portilla, *Time and Reality in the Thought of the Maya*, pp. 17–20.

3. Sylvia Gronewold, "Did Frank Hamilton Cushing Go Native?" p. 48.

4. Gladys A. Reichard, *Spider Woman*.

5. Gary Witherspoon, *Language and Art in the Navajo Universe*, p. xiii.

6. Solon T. Kimball, "Learning a New Culture," pp. 191–92.

7. Bennetta Jules-Rosette, *African Apostles*, p. 21.

8. Victor Turner, Foreword to *African Apostles*, p. 8.

9. Johannes Fabian, "Language, History and Anthropology," p. 27.

10. Alfred J. Schutz, *The Phenomenology of the Social World*, pp. 97–138.

11. Pierre Bourdieu, *Outline of a Theory of Practice*, pp. 23–26, 4.

12. There are actually three calendars in this manuscript: one solar cycle and two divinatory cycles. I used a Xerox of the Newberry Library's photographic copy of the Berendt Manuscript located in the University of Pennsylvania Museum. The results of this part of my research will be published elsewhere.

13. Arnold van Gennep, *The Rites of Passage*; Max Gluckman, "Les rites de passage"; Victor Turner, *The Forest of Symbols* and *The Ritual Process*.

Chapter 2

1. In Guatemala, a *municipio* is a political, geographic, and administrative unit typically consisting of a city or town with outlying rural districts called *cantones*. A majority of the 325 *municipios* in the country have the demography of a largely rural New England township (e.g., Lincoln, Massachusetts) but the government of an incorporated city (e.g., Cambridge, Massachusetts). Thus, scholars who emphasize the demographic situation have chosen "township" as the English gloss, while those who emphasize governmental structure have chosen "municipality." A number of *municipios* make up a *departamento*, roughly equivalent (both demographically and politically) to a county, of which there are twenty-two in the entire nation.

2. According to Lyle Campbell (*Quichean Linguistic Prehistory*), the

particular Quiché dialect spoken in Momostenango is part of the south-western dialect group that includes Chichicastenango, Cunén, Santa Cruz del Quiché, Totonicapán, Nahualá, Santa Catarina Ixtahuacán, Quezalten-ango, Cuyotenango, Mazatenango, and San Antonio Suchitepequez. David G. Fox ("Review of *Quiché-English Dictionary,* by Munro Edmon-son"), however, breaks up this large dialect group into southwestern coastal, southwestern highland, central highland (including Momosten-ango), eastern, northeastern, and northern dialects, a division that corre-lates nicely with the ethnohistorical expansion of the Quiché nation.

3. For a few representative descriptions of the 8 Batz' ritual in Mo-mostenango, see S. K. Lothrop, "Further Notes on Indian Ceremonies in Guatemala"; Antonio Goubaud Carrera, "El 'Guajxaquíp Bátz'—ceremonia calendárica indígena"; Erna Fergusson, *Guatemala,* pp. 237–40; Marion Hollenbach, "An Ancient Quiché Ceremony"; Vera Kelsey and Lilly de Jongh Osborne, *Four Keys to Guatemala,* pp. 35–38; and Maurice Ries, "The Ritual of the Broken Pots."

4. For more detail about the militaristic Precolumbian Quiché state, see Robert M. Carmack's "The Documentary Sources, Ecology, and Cul-ture History of Prehispanic Quiche Maya," and "Toltec Influence on the Postclassic Culture History of Highland Guatemala"; and John W. Fox, *Quiché Conquest.*

5. The four principal lineages of the Quiché kingdom, according to the Franciscan friar Pedro de Betanzos ("Letter to the King in 1559"), were the Cawek, Nijaib, Ahaw Quiché, and Sakic.

6. The documents called Nijaib I and II, of which the first contains the account of the battle, were published (respectively) in Spanish and in facing-page Quiché and Spanish by Adrián Recinos, *Crónicas indígenas de Guatemala,* pp. 71–117. Nijaib III was published in Quiché and Span-ish, following the Quiché version located in the Archivo General de Centroamérica and a Spanish version located in the offices of the Auxiliary Organization in Momostenango, by Robert M. Carmack, *Quichean Civi-lization,* pp. 349–52. Nijaib IV, which exists in two Spanish versions in the Archivo General de Centroamérica, has been published only in Spanish by Carmack, ibid., pp. 352–55. Versions of Nijaib I and II were discovered in San Vicente Buenabaj by Carmack, ibid., pp. 33–34.

7. The two main sixteenth-century sources on Prehispanic Quiché social organization agree that there were four rulers at Utatlán. Bartolomé de Las Casas, *Apologetica historia de las Indias;* and Pedro de Betanzos, "Letter to the King in 1559." Las Casas, however, saw the political system as centralized, with a king, king-elect, and major and minor captains; while Betanzos saw it as decentralized, with four rulers representing the four lineages of the town. For the importance of *calpules* or *parcialidades* among the Quiché, see Francisco Ximénez, *Escolios a las historias del origen de los Indios,* pp. 8–9.

8. Material on the colonial period in Momostenango is scant. The majority of the primary documents are located in the Archivo General de Centroamérica and the Archivo Municipal de Momostenango. As Carmack has noted in *Quichean Civilization*, p. 158, this corpus of documents sheds little light on the perpetuation of traditional cultural patterns during the colonial period. However, it does show that early in the colonial period there were four sections of the community, each with its own patron saint, mayor, and alderman. The suggestion that the four *parcialidades*, or *calpules* were endogamous was made to me be a Momostecan elder who had served four years as mayor in the Auxiliary Organization, the traditional governing body of the municipality. He explained that before the community was divided into the cantons of today, there were *calpules*. He described the *calpul* as a group of people who all married each other and lived together on adjacent lands.

9. The Diego Vicente narrative was told by an elder in Momostenango on August 18, 1976, to Barbara and Dennis Tedlock (field tape Q72, in their possession). For a parallel oral narrative and a brief biography of Diego Vicente (pseudonym Diego Vico), see Carmack, *Historia social de los Quiches*, pp. 197–201.

10. The description of seventeenth-century Momostenango is based on Carmack, ibid.

11. The term *ladino*, meaning "the romance or new language" in Old Spanish, was applied in Spain to Moors who learned Castilian. Later, it was adopted by early Spanish colonists in the Americas as a derogatory term for Indians who learned Spanish and lived and worked in the cities as artisans. In colonial Guatemala, in addition to Indians, there were Spaniards, Negroes, mestizos (Indian-Spanish), mulattos (Negro-Spanish), and zambos (Negro-Indian); see Chester Lloyd Jones, *Guatemala, Past and Present*, p. 269. As late as the 1778 census, the term *ladino* described all persons of mixed blood, i.e., persons not classed as Spaniards, Indians, or Negroes. Later the term *Spaniard* disappeared and *ladino* meant any person with either Spanish ancestry or of Spanish cultural heritage. See Robert E. T. Roberts, "A Comparison of Ethnic Relations in Two Guatemalan Communities."

12. For an excellent review and discussion of the many Momostecan rebellions, see Carmack, "Motineros indígenas en tiempo de la independencia de Guatemala," pp. 49–66, and *Historia social de los Quiches*, pp. 215–44.

13. For more details on the history of the municipality of El Palmar, see Benson Saler, *The Road from El Palmar*, pp. 25–34.

14. For a discussion of the 8 Batz' cult in El Palmar see Saler, "Cultic Alternatives in a Guatemalan Village."

15. Francisco Rodríguez Rouanet, "Monografía del municipio de Momostenango," p. 16.

16. J. Steward Lincoln, "The Maya Calendar of the Ixil of Guatemala," p. 114.

17. Teodoro Cifuentes, although he was *ladino*, was very well thought of by indigenous Momostecans, and, according to local rumor, is said to have converted to, or at least to have participated in, the local Quiché religion. Carmack's Momostecan consultants even credit him with setting up the top two levels of the indigenous religious hierarchy—the town and canton priest-shamans, *Historia social de los Quiches*, p. 286; however, my own consultants do not.

18. For more information about the Momostecan Presidential Guard in Guatemala City, see Carmack, ibid., 289–90.

19. Richard N. Adams, *La Ladinización en Guatemala*.

20. J. Francisco Alonzo O., comp., *Censos VII de población y III de habitación*, p. 26.

21. For more detail about types of Guatemalan municipalities, see Sol Tax, "The Municipios of the Midwestern Highlands of Guatemala." When Tax classified Momostenango as a vacant center type of municipality, it had a population of only 25,704, with very few people living in the town center.

22. Carmack was the first scholar to discover and describe patriclans and patrilineages among present-day Quiché peoples; see "La perpetuación del clan patrilineal en Totonicapán"; "Ethnography and Ethnohistory: Their Application in Middle American Studies," pp. 138–39; and *Historia social de los Quiches*, pp. 239–40.

23. For the habitat of Momostenango, see Rodríguez, "Monografía del municipio de Momostenango"; and Robert M. Carmack, F. Sloane, and R. Stewart, "La pre- y proto-historia de Santiago Momostenango."

24. Pedro Cortés y Larraz, *Descripción geográfico-moral de la Diócesis de Goathemala*.

25. For the anthropological concept "status," see Ralph Linton, *The Study of Man*, and Meyer Fortes, "Ritual and Office in Tribal Society."

26. Why the twenty confraternities should be called *oxlajuj ch'ob* in Quiché is an interesting problem. Daniel G. Brinton believed that a *calpulli* type of organization consisting of thirteen divisions of a tribe was present in Precolumbian times among both the Cakchiquels and the Quiché (*The Annals of the Cakchiquels*, p. 34). The possible connection between this segmentation of the tribe, each section with is own deity (and later saint), is intriguing. However that may be, thirteen is a much-used number in indigenous religious matters.

27. The general pattern of Mesoamerican civil-religious hierarchies has been well defined and described by Sol Tax, "The Municipios of the Midwestern Highlands of Guatemala," pp. 442–44; and Fernando Cámera, "Religious and Political Organization." Frank Cancian provides the most thorough discussion of the operation of the system within a single com-

munity, *Economics and Prestige in a Maya Community*. The reputedly Precolumbian roots of the Mesoamerican civil-religious hierarchy have been explored by Pedro Carrasco, "The Civil-Religious Hierarchy in Mesoamerican Communities: Pre-Spanish Background and Colonial Development"; and denied by Marvin Harris, *Patterns of Race in the Americas*, pp. 25–43.

28. Rodríguez, "Monografía del municipio de Momostenango," p. 38.

29. For the various positive and negative effects of Catholic Action on the indigenous communities of Guatemala, see Richard N. Adams, *Crucifixion by Power;* Benjamin N. Colby and Pierre L. van den Berghe, *Ixil Country;* Ricardo S. Falla, *Quiché rebelde;* and Kay B. Warren, *The Symbolism of Subordination*.

30. The possible role of the current ladino priest in encouraging the *catequistas* to take over this symbolically important confraternity should be explored. Colby and van den Berghe report that a similar attempt in Chajul did, indeed, originate with the local priest *(Ixil Country*, p. 286).

31. Munro S. Edmonson, "Nativism, Syncretism and Anthropological Science." See also Barbara Tedlock, "A Phenomenological Approach to Religious Change in Highland Guatemala."

Chapter 3

1. For an example of the cultural distinction between priest and shaman, see E. Michael Mendelson, "Ritual and Mythology," p. 394.

2. Oliver La Farge, *Santa Eulalia*, p. 134.

3. Charles Wagley, *The Social and Religious Life of a Guatemalan Village*, pp. 68–71.

4. William Madsen, "Shamanism in Mexico."

5. Ibid., p. 48.

6. Peter T. Furst, "Shamanistic Survivals in Mesoamerican Religion."

7. Maud Oakes, *The Two Crosses of Todos Santos*, pp. 193–208.

8. Alfonso Villa Rojas, *The Maya of East Central Quintana Roo*, p. 74.

9. Madsen, "Shamanism," p. 57.

10. Charles Wisdom, *The Chortí Indians of Guatemala*, p. 344.

11. La Farge, *Santa Eulalia*, p. 161.

12. I have concentrated on the Maya here, but the existence of a complex shamanism among the Huichol should be noted as well: see Peter T. Furst, "To Find Our Life: Peyote among the Huichol Indians of Mexico"; and Barbara G. Myerhoff, *Peyote Hunt*.

13. Lois Paul and Benjamin D. Paul, "The Maya Midwife as Sacred Professional: A Guatemalan Case."

14. Evon Z. Vogt, "HƆiloletik: The Organization and Function of Shamanism in Zinacantan."

15. According to Daniel B. Silver, shamanic recruitment in Zinacantán can also take the following two forms: (1) the seer may be chosen before birth, a fact that is revealed during an illness later in life when a seer "pulses" the patient and divines from his blood that it is his destiny to be a seer; (2) the soul of the seer-to-be, during an "epileptic seizure," travels to the sacred mountain and receives curing instructions; see Daniel B. Silver, "Zinacanteco Shamanism," p. 28. In the follow-up study, Horacio Fabrega, Jr., and Daniel B. Silver pointed out that not all persons with seizures become seers and that many seers have no such history; see Horacio Fabrega, Jr., and Daniel B. Silver, *Illness and Shamanistic Curing in Zinacantan*, p. 32. With or without a seizure, shamanic recruitment in Zinacantán follows upon illness or dreams or both and thus fits the classical shamanic pattern.

16. Calixta Guiteras-Holmes, *Perils of the Soul,* p. 149.

17. Mircea Eliade, *Shamanism,* pp. 33–144.

18. Oakes, *The Two Crosses of Todos Santos,* pp. 56, 24, 257, 90.

19. Oliver La Farge and Douglas Byers, *The Year Bearer's People,* p. 143.

20. Manning Nash, "Cultural Persistence and Social Structure."

21. M. Nash's choice of Cantel as representative of midwestern Guatemalan communities is misleading; as Carmack has pointed out, "Cantel is so acculturated that aboriginal culture patterns are virtually absent." Robert M. Carmack, *Quichean Civilization,* p. 254.

22. Émile Durkheim, *The Elementary Forms of the Religious Life,* p. 405. Nash does not discuss the fact that the "priest" of Santa Eulalia engages in divination. See La Farge and Byers, *The Year Bearer's People,* p. 143.

23. W. Lloyd Warner, *A Black Civilization,* pp. 223–43.

24. J. Steward Lincoln, "The Maya Calendar of the Ixil of Guatemala," p. 121.

25. R. P. Francisco Vázquez, *Crónica de la provincia del Santísimo Nombre de Jesús de Guatemala* (as quoted in Gustavo Correa, "El Espíritu del mal en Guatemala," pp. 84–85).

26. Murdo J. MacLeod, *Spanish Central America,* p. 19.

27. Francisco Antonio de Fuentes y Guzmán, *Recordación Florida,* p. 158.

28. Erika Bourguignon, "World Distribution and Patterns of Possession States"; and Lewis Langness, "Hysterical Psychoses and Possessions." For more details on *cumatz* as a possible culture-specific syndrome, see Barbara Tedlock, "Mind, Body, and Cosmos in Highland Guatemala."

29. Ruth L. Bunzel, *Chichicastenango,* p. 287.

30. Ibid., pp. 299, 148–49.

31. Sol Tax, *Notes on Santo Tomás Chichicastenango (Nov. 1934–May 1935),* pp. 486, 399.

32. Flavio Rodas N., Ovidio Rodas C., and Lawrence F. Hawkins, *Chichicastenango, the Kiche Indians*, p. 68.

33. Leonhard Schultze Jena, *La vida y las creencias de los indígenas quichés de Guatemala*.

34. Carmack, "Ethnography and Ethnohistory," p. 139.

35. Agustín Estrada Monroy, ed., *Popol Vuh*, folio 3 vo., lines 35–36, 45–46; folio 4 ro., line 14.

36. Ibid., folio 4 ro., lines 18–20, 28.

37. Ibid., folio 1 ro., lines 14–15; folio 4 ro., line 7.

38. Ibid., folio 32 vo., lines 2–14.

Chapter 4

1. Sylvanus G. Morley, *The Ancient Maya*, p. 269; and Robert M. Carmack, *Quichean Civilization*, p. 160.

2. William Gates, in his "Review of *Archaeology of the Cayo District*, by J. Eric S. Thompson," takes credit for inventing the word *tzolkin* in 1921; and he modeled it after the Quiché Maya *ch'ol k'ij*, meaning "arranging" or "ordering of days," as a way of getting away from the use of the Aztec term.

3. Morley, *The Ancient Maya*, p. 301.

4. Alfonso Caso, "Zapotec Writing and Calendar," p. 931.

5. A highland origin for the calendar is favored by Alfred V. Kidder, "Archaeological Problems of the Highland Maya," p. 122. A lowland origin is favored by H. F. Gadow, *Through Southern Mexico*, p. 303.

6. For examples of colonial calendar wheels, see Charles P. Bowditch, *The Numeration, Calendar Systems and Astronomical Knowledge of the Maya*, pp. 326–31. Pecked cross and circle symbols are surveyed in Anthony F. Aveni, Horst Hartung, and Beth Buckingham, "The Pecked Cross Symbol in Ancient Mesoamerica."

7. Suzanna W. Miles, "An Analysis of Modern Middle American Calendars."

8. Gary H. Gossen, "A Chamula Solar Calendar Board from Chiapas, Mexico."

9. J. Steward Lincoln, "The Maya Calendar of the Ixil of Guatemala," p. 121.

10. J. Eric S. Thompson, *Maya Hieroglyphic Writing*, p. 99.

11. Zelia Nuttall, "Nouvelles lumières sur les civilisations américaines et le système du calendrier"; Ola Apenes, "Possible Derivation of the 260-day Period of the Maya Calendar"; Helga Larsen, "The 260-Day Period as Related to the Agricultural Life of the Ancient Indian"; R. H. Merrill, "Maya Sun Calendar Dictum Disproved," p. 307.

12. J. Eric S. Thompson, *The Rise and Fall of Maya Civilization*, p. 173.

13. Bowditch, *The Numeration, Calendar Systems*, p. 267; and Leonhard Schultze Jena, *La vida y las creencias de los indígenas quichés de Guatemala*, p. 75.

14. Thompson, *Maya Hieroglyphic Writing*, p. 98.

15. Exceptions to the central Mexican rule include the inhabitants of Teoca in Nicaragua and Meztitlán in Oaxaca, whose lists began with Acatl, the equivalent of Aj in Quiché. Eduard Seler, "Die Tageszeichen der aztekischen und der Maya-Handshriften und ihre Gottheiten," p. 418.

16. Morley, *An Introduction to the Study of the Maya Hieroglyphs*, p. 42.

17. Thompson, *Maya Hieroglyphic Writing*, p. 101.

18. Francisco Ximénez, *Historia de la provincia de San Vicente de Chiapas y Guatemala*, p. 101.

19. Adrián Recinos and Delia Goetz, trans., *The Annals of the Cakchiquels*, pp. 31–32.

20. The "objectivist" and "intersubjective" positions in anthropological inquiry are laid out by Pierre Bourdieu, *Outline of a Theory of Practice*, pp. 23–26.

21. Lincoln, "The Maya Calendar of the Ixil," p. 172.

22. Maud Oakes, *The Two Crosses*, p. 189.

23. Ruth L. Bunzel, *Chichicastenango*, p. 278.

24. Schultze Jena, *La vida y las creencias de los indígenas quichés*, pp. 29–30.

25. Antonio Goubaud Carrera, "The Guajxaquíp Báts," p. 7.

26. Benson Saler, *The Road from El Palmar*, pp. 114, 122.

27. Rafael Girard, *Los Mayas eternos*, p. 329. Girard nevertheless begins his own list of days with Imóx.

28. Philadelphia, University of Pennsylvania Museum Library, "Calendario de los Indios de Guatemala, 1722 Kiché." Copied by Berendt in 1877 from a manuscript in the Museo Nacional de Guatemala that is now lost.

29. Francisco Rodríguez Rouanet, "Monografía del municipio de Momostenango," pp. 92–94.

30. Bunzel, *Chichicastenango*, p. 277.

31. Thompson, *Maya Hieroglyphic Writing*, pp. 90, 88.

32. Karl Sapper, "Über Brujeria in Guatemala," p. 402. Schultze Jena, *La vida y las creencias de los indígenas quichés*, p. 29.

33. Rodríguez, "Monografía del municipio de Momostenango," p. 92.

34. Girard, *Los Mayas eternos*, p. 330.

35. Manning Nash, "Cultural Persistence and Social Structure," p. 151.

Chapter 5

1. Agustín Estrada Monroy, ed., *Popol Vuh*, folios 12 ro. to 32 vo.

2. J. Eric S. Thompson, *Maya Hieroglyphic Writing*, p. 66.

3. Ruth L. Bunzel, *Chichicastenango*, p. 283.

4. The word *nawal*, or *nagual*, has been assigned various meanings in the anthropological literature, the most frequent of which are "companion" or "guardian spirit" and "transforming witch." For an excellent review of the various definitions of *nawal*, see Benson Saler, "Nagual, Witch, and Sorcerer in a Quiché Village."

5. Thompson, *Maya Hieroglyphic Writing*, p. 70.

6. Paul Townsend, *We Have Come to Wake You, We Have Come to Rouse You Our Lords, Our Ladies*.

7. Ralph L. Roys, *The Book of Chilam Balam of Chumayel*, pp. 116–18.

8. Karl Sapper, "Über Brujería in Guatemala."

9. Leonhard Schultze Jena, *La vida y las creencias de los indígenas quichés de Guatemala*, p. 68.

10. Francisco Rodríguez Rouanet, "Monografía del municipio de Momostenango," p. 92.

11. Saler, *The Road from El Palmar*, p. 127.

12. Bunzel, *Chichicastenango*, p. 113.

13. Thompson, *A Commentary on the Dresden Codex*, p. 29.

14. Writing "logographically" means assigning one glyph per word rather than spelling words "phonetically," with a glyph for each phoneme, morpheme, or syllable. See David Kelley, *Deciphering the Maya Script*, p. 165.

15. For a somewhat different approach to the use of modern Mayan ethnographic materials for epigraphy, see Helen Neuenswander, "Vestiges of Early Maya Time Concepts in a Contemporary Maya (Cubulco Achi) Community."

Chapter 6

1. Maud Oakes, *The Two Crosses of Todos Santos*, p. 183.

2. J. Steward Lincoln, "The Maya Calendar of the Ixil of Guatemala," p. 121.

3. Benson Saler, "Sorcery in Santiago El Palmar," p. 136.

4. Ricardo S. Falla, *La conversión religiosa*, p. 81.

5. Ruth L. Bunzel, *Chichicastenango*, p. 290.

6. Sol Tax, *Notes on Santo Tomás Chichicastenango*, p. 517.

7. Flavio Rodas N., Ovidio Rodas C., and Lawrence F. Hawkins, *Chichicastenango, the Kiche Indians*, p. 71.

8. Leonhard Schultze Jena, *La vida y las creencias de los indígenas quichés de Guatemala*, p. 95.

9. Sheila Cosminsky, "Knowledge and Body Concepts of Traditional Guatemalan Midwives," p. 3.

10. Robert E. Hinshaw, *Panajachel*, p. 128.

11. Charles Wisdom, *The Chortí Indians of Guatemala*, p. 344.

12. Leon A. Valladares, *El hombre y la maíz*, p. 219.

13. Charles Wagley, *The Social and Religious Life of a Guatemalan Village*, p. 126.

14. Oliver La Farge, *Santa Eulalia*, p. 182.

15. Isabel Kelly, *Santiago Tuxtla, Veracruz Culture and Health*, p. 68.

16. Ralph L. Beals, "Ethnology of Western Mixe," p. 97.

17. C. Mak, "Mixtec Medical Beliefs and Practices," p. 140.

18. Elsie Clews Parsons, *Mitla*, p. 137.

19. Evon Z. Vogt, *Zinacantán*, p. 422.

20. Horacio Fabrega, Jr., and Daniel B. Silver, *Illness and Shamanistic Curing in Zinacantan*, p. 151.

21. June Nash, "The Logic of Behavior," pp. 133, 134, 132.

22. Albert L. Wahrhaftig, "Witchcraft and Curing in two Tzeltal Communities," p. 14.

23. M. Esther Hermitte, "Supernatural Power and Social Control in a Modern Mayan Village," p. 94.

24. Duane Metzger and Gerald Williams, "Tenejapa Medicine," pp. 217, 222, 223.

25. Alfonso Villa Rojas, "Kinship and Nagualism in a Tzeltal Community," p. 584.

26. Hermitte, "Supernatural Power," p. 83n.

27. William Holland, "Highland Maya Folk Medicine: A Study of Culture Change," pp. 139, 135.

28. Victor Turner, *Revelation and Divination in Ndembu Ritual*, pp. 15–16.

29. James Boster, "K'ekchi' Maya Curing Practices in British Honduras," pp. 166, 155.

30. David Fox, "Review of *Quiché-English Dictionary,* by Munro Edmonson," pp. 191–97; and Sol Tax, *Notes on Santo Tomás Chichicastenango*, p. 517.

31. Schultze Jena, *La vida y las creencias de los indígenas quichés*, p. 96. Rodas N., Rodas C., and Hawkins, *Chichicastenango*, p. 71.

32. In the ancient "language of Zuyua," the secret religious language of the Yucatec priesthood that was recorded in the Chumayel document, we find the following riddle: "Go and call your companions to me. These are the old man with nine sons and the old woman with nine children." The answer is "The old man with nine sons . . . it is his great toe . . . The old woman . . . it is his thumb" (Ralph L. Roys, *The Book of Chilam Balam of*

Chumayel, p. 94). Here, the principle of age linked to large thumb and toe is the same as with the Quiché, but the male/female dichotomy is an up/down rather than a right/left dichotomy.

33. Turner, *Revelation and Divination*, pp. 15–16.

34. Barbara Bode, "The Dance of the Conquest of Guatemala," p. 213.

35. Pedro Cortés y Larraz, *Descripción geográfico-moral de la Diócesis de Goathemala*.

36. Adrián Recinos and Delia Goetz, *The Annals of the Cakchiquels*, pp. 61–62.

37. Munro S. Edmonson, *The Book of Counsel: The Popol Vuh of the Quiche Maya of Guatemala*, pp. 180–81.

38. Sol Tax, *Notes on Santo Tomás Chichicastenango*, p. 471.

Chapter 7

1. The *Popol Vuh*, in its description of a calendar diviner's actions, refers to *ucahic* (*ukajic* in the present orthography, "his [her] borrowing") using the same stem as appears in *quinkajaxtaj* ("I am borrowing").

2. Ruth Bunzel, *Chichicastenango*, p. 114.

3. Benson Saler, *The Road from El Palmar*, p. 128.

4. Leonhard Schultze Jena, *La vida y las creencias de los indígenas quichés*, p. 22.

5. Charles Wagley, *The Social and Religious Life of a Guatemalan Village*, pp. 68–75; La Farge, *Santa Eulalia*, pp. 182–83.

6. Saler, *The Road from El Palmar*, p. 82.

Chapter 8

1. The passage of the sun across the zenith is a phenomenon that occurs only in tropical latitudes, where there are two such passages annually, equally spaced about the solstices; one occurs on the day the sun crosses the zenith as it goes northward along the ecliptic and the other as it returns southward.

2. Clemency C. Coggins, "The Shape of Time."

3. Victoria Bricker, "Directional Glyphs in Maya Inscriptions and Codices"; and R. E. W. Adams and G. F. Mobley, "Rio Azul." For a discussion of the ben-ich superfix, see David Humiston Kelley, *Deciphering the Maya Script*, p. 206.

4. Brian Stross, "Classic Maya Directional Glyphs."

5. Linda Schele, David Stuart, and Nikolai Grube, "A Commentary on the Restoration and Reading of the Glyphic Panels from Temple 11";

and Linda Schele and Nikolai Grube, "A Preliminary Inventory of Place Names in the Copán Inscriptions."

6. Colonial Yucatec terms are found in Alfredo Barrera Vásquez, *Diccionario maya cordemex, maya-español, español-maya*; and J. Martínez Hernández, *Diccionario de Motul, maya español*. Linguists and ethnographers who have focused on the problem of Mayan directional terms are John R. Sosa, *The Maya Sky, the Maya World*; Barbara Tedlock, "Earth Rites and Moon Cycles,"; Evon Z. Vogt, "Cardinal Directions and Ceremonial Circuits in Mayan and Southwestern Cosmology"; John M. Watanabe, "In the World of the Sun"; Brian Stross, "Classic Maya Directional Glyphs."

7. Kekchí terms for the directions can be found in Esteban Haeserijn V., *Diccionario k'ekchi' español*, pp. 461, 467, 479, 481; and Sandra Pinkerton, *Studies in K'ekchi*, pp. 110, 131, 144, 148, 151, 153.

8. Tzeltal directional terms are to be found in John M. Dienhart, *The Mayan Languages*, pp. 211, 597, 690, 713; and in June Nash, *In the Eyes of the Ancestors*, p. 293.

9. H. Wilbur Aulie and Evelyn W. de Aulie, *Diccionario ch'ol-español español-ch'ol*; J. Kathryn Josserand and Nicholas A. Hopkins, "Chol (Mayan) Dictionary Database, Part III"; John M. Dienhart, *The Mayan Languages*; E. Matthew Ulrich and Rosemary Dixon de Ulrich, *Diccionario Maya Mopan/Español Español/Maya Mopan*; John R. Sosa, "Cosmological, Symbolic and Cultural Complexity among the Contemporary Maya of Yucatan"; and Martínez Hernández, *Diccionario de Motul, maya español*. The statements about Mopán are partly based on my own recent fieldwork in Belize.

10. For Tzotzil directions see Gary H. Gossen, *Chamulas in the World of the Sun*, p. 31; Robert M. Laughlin, *The Great Tzotzil Dictionary of San Lorenzo Zinacantán*, pp. 432, 474, 508; and Evon Z. Vogt, *Tortillas for the Gods*, p. 16. Mam directional terms are to be found in Nora C. England, *A Grammar of Mam, a Mayan Language*, p. 341; and John M. Watanabe, "In the World of the Sun," p. 712.

11. Helen Neuenswander, "Vestiges of Early Maya Time Concepts in a Contemporary Maya (Cubulco Achi) Community"; Robert M. Carmack, *Quichean Civilization*, p. 317.

12. Note that fig. 26, p. 141, is from the point of view of a person facing the sun.

13. Weldon W. Lamb, "Star Lore in the Yucatec Maya Dictionaries"; and Fermín Joseph Tirado, "Vocabulario de lengua Kiche."

14. For the connection between meteors and cigars, see Alfred M. Tozzer, *A Comparative Study of the Mayas and the Lacandones*, p. 158; and Rafael Girard, *Los mayas*, p. 74. Past and present use of obsidian blades in human sacrifice, bleeding, and surgery is discussed by

Don E. Crabtree, "Mesoamerican Polyhedral Cores and Prismatic Blades";
Sandra L. Orellana, *Indian Medicine in Highland Guatemala*, pp. 72–75;
and Francis Robicsek and Donald M. Hales, "Maya Heart Sacrifice: Cultural Perspective and Surgical Technique."

15. Robert Burnham, *Burnham's Celestial Handbook*, p. 1320;
Thomas C. Harrison, "The Orion Nebula: Where in History Is It?"; and
John R. Sosa, *The Maya Sky, the Maya World*, p. 431. Sosa links Aldebaran to the Pleiades, but it is the brightest star in the Hyades.

16. Alfredo Barrera Vásquez, *Diccionario maya cordemex, maya-español, español-maya*, p. 896.

17. See Robert M. Laughlin, *The Great Tzotzil Dictionary of San Lorenzo Zinacantán*, p. 58; June Nash, *In the Eyes of the Ancestors*, pp. 92–93; Maud Oakes, *The Two Crosses of Todos Santos*, p. 56; Victor Perera and Robert D. Bruce, *The Last Lords of Palenque*, p. 230; and Charles Wagley, *The Social and Religious Life of a Guatemalan Village*, p. 76.

18. Dennis Tedlock, *Popol Vuh*, pp. 134, 365; and Pantaleón de Guzmán, "Compendio de nombres en lengua Cakchiquel." For a comparison of the plumage and habits of black hawks and Swainson's hawks, see Arthur Cleveland Bent, *Life Histories of North American Birds of Prey*, pp. 259–64; John Farrand, *The Audubon Society Master Guide to Birding*, pp. 233–34; Michael Harwood, *Proceedings of the North American Hawk Migration Conference*, p. 128; and Hugh C. Land, *Birds of Guatemala*, pp. 69–70.

19. Arthur Cleveland Bent, *Life Histories of North American Birds of Prey*, pp. 222–34; Leslie Brown, *Birds of Prey*, p. 132; John Farrand, *The Audubon Society Master Guide to Birding*, p. 240; Ludlow Griscom, "The Distribution of Bird-Life in Guatemala"; and Alexander Wetmore, *Water, Prey, and Game Birds of North America*, p. 230.

20. Jean Dorst, *The Migrations of Birds*, pp. 361–62; John R. Haugh, "Local Ephemeral Weather Conditions and Their Effects on Hawk Migration Routes," pp. 72, 77–81; and Donald S. Heintzelman, *A Manual for Bird Watching in the Americas*, pp. 122–23.

21. Hugh C. Land, *Birds of Guatemala*, p. 67.

22. Judith A. Remington, "Current Astronomical Practices among the Maya," pp. 85–87.

23. John Farrand, *The Audubon Society Master Guide to Birding*, p. 240; and Michael Harwood, *Proceedings of the North American Hawk Migration Conference*, p. 128.

24. Rafael Girard, *Los mayas*, p. 121.

25. Dieter Dütting and Matthias Schramm, "The Sidereal Period of the Moon in Maya Calendrical Astronomy"; and Harvey M. Bricker and Victoria R. Bricker, "Zodiacal References in the Maya Codices."

Chapter 9

1. For a discussion of intersubjectivity see Alfred J. Schutz, *The Phenomenology of the Social World*. The most influential book on the importance of practical knowledge is Pierre Bourdieu, *Outline of a Theory of Practice*. For a discussion of the emergence and development of practice theory in American anthropology during the 1980s, see Sherry B. Ortner, "Theory in Anthropology Since the Sixties," pp. 144–57. The central role of feminist thought and practice in the development of "practice theory" is discussed in Jane Collier and Sylvia Yanagisako, "Theory in Anthropology Since Feminist Practice."

2. Pierre Bourdieu, *Outline of a Theory of Practice*, p. 22.

3. Pierre Bourdieu, *Outline of a Theory of Practice*, p. 27.

4. The separation of divination from revelation has been laid out by Victor Turner, *Revelation and Divination in Ndembu Ritual*.

5. Alfred M. Tozzer, *Landa's Relación de las Cosas de Yucatán*, p. 168.

Afterword

1. Munro S. Edmonson, *The Book of the Year*, p. 176; Benjamin N. Colby and Lore M. Colby, *The Daykeeper*, pp. 224–25.

2. Adrián Recinos and Delia Goetz, *The Annals of the Cakchiquels*, p. 120.

3. According to a report by AVANCSO, *Política institucional hacia el desplazado interno en Guatemala*, nearly 80 percent of the inhabitants of the departments of El Quiché, Huehuetenango, Chimaltenango, and Alta Verapaz had to leave their homes during the height of the violence in 1981 and 1982. Benjamin N. Colby, "Cognitive Economy, Coherence, and Divination in Three Civilizations," reported that Ixil daykeepers were forbidden by the military to go into the mountains in order to practice their rituals. Diane M. Nelson, "The Reconstruction of Mayan Identity," p. 6, reported that in the late seventies, there were thirty daykeepers in Nebaj, while today, after the counterinsurgency army violence of the early eighties, there are only ten left.

4. David Stoll, "Evangelicals, Guerrillas, and the Army," p. 91; Thomas R. Melville, "The Catholic Church in Guatemala," p. 27.

5. Americas Watch, *Guatemala: A Nation of Prisoners*, p. 253, and Beatriz Manz, *Refugees of a Hidden War*, pp. 35, 98–99.

6. Robert M. Carmack, *Harvest of Violence*, pp. xv–xvi.

7. The situation in the weaving industry in Momostenango is appar-

ently the opposite of that in the nearby community of San Miguel Totonicapán, where younger women no longer wear traditional dress and there
is little demand for native cloth; Carol A. Smith, "Destruction of the Material Bases for Indian Culture," p. 229.

8. Beatriz Manz, *Refugees of a Hidden War*, pp. 30, 209.

9. The use of the term "diaspora" for dispersals outside of the Jewish
and Armenian contexts is currently advocated by scholars from several
disciplines, and a new journal, *Diaspora*, has been founded, in order to
discuss transnational communities. See Khachig Tölölyan, "The Nation-
State and Its Others," in the first issue of *Diaspora*.

10. In all my publications, since 1988, I have adopted the new orthography. However, since I could not change the orthography throughout this volume, I have retained the earlier one, suggested by the Instituto Indigenista Nacional de Guatemala (see n. 1, chapter 1). The only
changes that the new Quiché orthography makes are that the glottalized
b (or p) sound is now represented as b' rather than simply as b; wherever
there was either a "c" or a "qu" before, there is now a "k"; and what was
written with a "k" previously is now written with a "q."

11. This discussion of the current situation among the Mopán Maya
in Belize is based upon my recent fieldwork in San Antonio, Toledo District, during 1990 and 1991. See also Jacqueline Wiora Sletto and Bjorn
Sletto, "Cultural and Economic Revival: Toledo Maya," and the statements made by The Toledo Maya Cultural Council to the World Council
of Indigenous People, published in the IWGIA Newsletter during 1984,
1985, and 1986.

12. The Kekchí earth deity Tzuultak'a ("Mountain-Valley") is the
same as the Quiché earth deity Juyubtak'aj ("Mountain-Valley"). During
our recent research in Belize, Dennis Tedlock and I were able to record
and translate, with the help of a catechist Kekchí speaker from San Pedro
Columbia, a long prophetic narrative centering on Tzuultak'a, recorded
in Guatemala, and currently circulating among Mayans in the Toledo District. For a discussion of the importance of Tzuultak'a among Kekchí
speakers, see Jon Schackt, "The Tzuultak'a: Religious Lore and Cultural
Processes among the Kekchi," and Richard Wilson, "Machine Guns and
Mountain Spirits."

13. Diane M. Nelson, "The Reconstruction of Mayan Identity,"
p. 14.

Appendix A

1. The narrator of this story was both the head of the Auxiliary Organization and the *síndico segundo* of the Municipal Corporation,
1974–78. He was also a lineage priest-shaman and an *ajnawal mesa*.

Appendix B

1. Edmonson, *The Book of Counsel: The Popol Vuh of the Quiche Maya of Guatemala,* pp. xi–xii.

2. For a discussion of the full complexity of Quiché versification, see Dennis Tedlock, "Las formas del verso quiché de la paleografía a la grabadora."

3. The term *kajuyubal* is simultaneously an epithet for the Mundo and a metaphor for our own human bodies.

4. Here the deceased mothers and fathers (diviners) are being referred to.

5. The "united work united service" refers to the union between the diviner and his/her divining seeds. This union is considered a close one. Some male diviners refer to their divining equipment as "my second wife." In this context it also refers to the joint intiation of a husband and wife.

6. Here "his birthday" refers to the birthday of a woman's divining seeds and crystals that are of the opposite sex.

7. Here *ne'* means to begin something brand new. This word also means a baby boy or girl.

8. A *chuchkajaw* plants himself/herself firmly in the earth when he/she accepts the status.

9. Here the place names of the locales where the divining seeds and crystals were collected are used.

10. The wife "looks after" *(ilol wech)* what is needed for lunch and tells the husband she also "listens to" *(tal wech)* what he needs (e.g., pants that need ironing). The husband "listens to" *(tal wech)* what is needed and he "looks after" *(ilol wech)* earning the money for these necessities.

11. *Wa kuqui'a* is a synecdoche for all food and all drink.

12. Just as the receiving of the *patan* can relieve, even cure, serious illnesses, so it can also bring these same illnesses to newly received members.

13. The order of the shrines Ch'uti Sabal, Nima Sabal and K'ani Mar Saki Mar, also called K'ani Pila Saki Pila, depends upon whether it is a one, eight, or nine day. If it were a one day, then one would begin the list of shrines with the *ujunabal* ("its-one-place") or K'ani Mar Saki Mar.

Bibliography

Academia de las Lenguas Mayas de Guatemala. *Lenguas mayas de Guatemala: documento de referencia para la pronunciación de los nuevos alfabetos oficiales.* Guatemala: Instituto Indigenista Nacional, 1988.

Adams, R. E. W., and Mobley, G. F. "Rio Azul: Lost City of the Maya." *National Geographic* 169(1986):420–51.

Adams, Richard N. *La Ladinización en Guatemala.* Seminario de Integración Social Guatemalteca, Publicación no. 9, Guatemala, 1959.

———. *Crucifixion by Power: Essays on Guatemalan National Social Structure, 1944–1966. Austin: University of Texas Press, 1970.*

———. *"Conclusions: What Can We Know about the Harvest of Violence?" In Harvest of Violence.* Edited by Robert M. Carmack, pp. 274–91. Norman: University of Oklahoma Press, 1988.

Alcorn, Janis B. *Huastec Mayan Ethnobotany.* Austin: University of Texas Press, 1984.

Alonzo O., J. Francisco, comp. *Censos VII de población y III de habitación.* Guatemala: Dirección General de Estadistica, Ministerio de Economía, 1973.

Americas Watch. *Guatemala: A Nation of Prisoners.* New York: Americas Watch, 1983.

Andrews, E. Wyllys. "Chronology and Astronomy in the Maya Area." In *The Maya and Their Neighbors.* Edited by C. L. Hay and others, pp. 150–61. New York: Appleton-Century, 1940.

Annis, Sheldon. *God and Production in a Guatemalan Town.* Austin: University of Texas Press, 1987.

———. "Story from a Peaceful Town: San Antonio Aguas Calientes." In *Harvest of Violence.* Edited by Robert M. Carmack, pp. 155–73. Norman: University of Oklahoma Press, 1988.

Apenes, Ola. "Possible Derivation of the 260-day Period of the Maya Calendar." *Ethnos* 1(1936):5–8.

Arias, Arturo. "Changing Indian Identity: Guatemala's Violent Transition to Modernity." In *Guatemalan Indians and the State, 1540 to 1988.* Edited by Carol A. Smith, pp. 230–57. Austin: University of Texas Press, 1988.

Aulie, H. Wilbur, and Aulie, Evelyn W. de. *Diccionario ch'ol-español español-ch'ol.* Mexico: Instituto Lingüístico de Verano, 1978.

AVANCSO. *Política institutional hacia el desplazado interno en Guatemala.* Guatemala: Inforpress, 1990.

Aveni, Anthony F. "The Moon and the Venus Table: An Example of Commensuration in the Maya Calendar." Paper delivered at the International Conference on Ethnoastronomy, National Air and Space Museum, Washington, D.C., 1983.

Aveni, Anthony F.; Hartung, Horst; and Buckingham, Beth. "The Pecked Cross Symbol in Ancient Mesoamerica." *Science* 202(1978):267–79.

Baroco, John. "Notas sobre el uso de nombres calendáricos durante el siglo VXI." In *Ensayos de antropología de la zona central de Chiapas*. Edited by Norman A. McQuown and Julian Pitt-Rivers. Mexico: Instituto Nacional Indigenista, *Colección de Antropologia Social* 8(1970): 135–48.

Barrera Vásquez, Alfredo. *Diccionario maya cordemex, maya-español, español-maya*. Mérida: Ediciones Cordemex, 1980.

Beals, Ralph L. "Ethnology of Western Mixe." *University of California Publications in American Archaeology and Ethnology* 42(1945):1–176.

Bent, Arthur Cleveland. *Life Histories of North American Birds of Prey*, part 1. New York: Dover, 1961.

Berger, Peter L., and Luckmann, Thomas. *The Social Construction of Reality*. New York: Doubleday, 1966.

Berryman, Phillip. *The Religious Roots of Rebellion: Christians in Central American Revolutions*. Maryknoll, New York: Orbis, 1984.

Betanzos, Pedro de. "Letter to the King in 1559." In "Don Juan Cortes, Cacique de Santa Cruz Quiché." *Estudios de Cultura Maya* 6(1967): 251–66.

Black, George; Jamail, Milton; and Stoltz Chinchilla, Norma. *Garrison Guatemala*. New York: Monthly Review Press, 1984.

Bode, Barbara. "The Dance of the Conquest of Guatemala." In *The Native Theatre in Middle America*. Middle American Research Institute, Publication no. 27(1961):205–92. New Orleans: Tulane University.

Boster, James. "K'ekchi' Maya Curing Practices in British Honduras." Senior honors thesis, Harvard University, 1973.

Bourdieu, Pierre. *Outline of a Theory of Practice*. Translated by Richard Nice. Cambridge: Cambridge University Press, 1977.

Bourguignon, Erika. "World Distribution and Patterns of Possession States." In *Trance and Possession States*. Edited by R. M. Prince. Montreal: R. M. Bucke Memorial Society, 1968.

Bowditch, Charles P. *The Numeration, Calendar Systems and Astronomical Knowledge of the Mayas*. Cambridge, Mass.: Harvard University Press, 1910.

Bricker, Harvey M., and Bricker, Victoria R. "Zodiacal References in the Maya Codices." Paper presented at Colgate University in the conference "Astronomy in the Maya Codices," 1989.

Bricker, Victoria R. "El hombre, la carga y el camino: Antiguos conceptos mayas sobre tiempo y espacio, y el sistema zinacanteco." In *Los Zinacantecos*. Edited by Evon Z. Vogt, pp. 355–70. Mexico: Instituto Nacional Indigenista, 1966.

———. "Directional Glyphs in Maya Inscriptions and Codices." *American Antiquity* 48(1983):347–53.

———. "A Phonetic Glyph for Zenith: Reply to Closs." *American Antiquity* 53(1988):394–400.

Brintnall, Douglas E. *Revolt against the Dead: The Modernization of a Maya Community in the Highlands of Guatemala.* New York: Gordon and Breach, 1979.

Brinton, Daniel G. *The Annals of the Cakchiquels.* Brinton's Library of Aboriginal American Literature, no. 6. Philadelphia, 1885.

Brown, Leslie. *Birds of Prey: Their Biology and Ecology.* London: Hamlyn, 1976.

Bunzel, Rith L. *Chichicastenango: A Guatemalan Village.* American Ethnological Society, Publication no. 22. Seattle: University of Washington Press, 1952.

Burnett, Virginia Garrard. "Protestantism in Rural Guatemala, 1872–1954. "*Latin American Research Review* 3(1989):127–45.

Burnham, Robert. *Burnham's Celestial Handbook*, vol. 2. New York: Dover, 1978.

Cámara, Fernando. "Religious and Political Organization." In *Heritage of Conquest.* Edited by Sol Tax, pp. 142–73. Glencoe, Illinois: Free Press, 1952.

Campbell, Lyle. *Quichean Linguistic Prehistory.* University of California Publications in Linguistics, no. 81. Berkeley and Los Angeles: University of California Press, 1977.

Cancian, Frank. *Economics and Prestige in a Maya Community: The Religious Cargo System in Zinacantan.* Stanford: Stanford University Press, 1965.

Carmack, Robert M. "Motineros indígenas en tiempo de la independencia de Guatemala." *Estudios Sociales* 9(1963):49–66.

———. "The Documentary Sources, Ecology, and Culture History of Prehispanic Quiche Maya." Ph.D. dissertation, University of California at Los Angeles, 1965.

———. "La perpetuación del clan patrilineal en Totonicapán." *Antropologia e Historia de Guatemala* 18(1966):43–60.

———. "Toltec Influence on the Postclassic Culture History of Highland Guatemala." Middle American Research Institute, Publication no. 26(1968):52–92. New Orleans: Tulane University.

———. "Ethnography and Ethnohistory: Their Application in Middle American Studies." *Ethnohistory* 18(1971):127–45.

———. *Quichean Civilization: The Ethnohistoric, Ethnographic, and Archaeological Sources.* Berkeley and Los Angeles: University of California Press, 1973.

———. "Estratificación y cambio social en las tierras altas occidentales de Guatemala: El caso de Tecpanaco." *América Indígena* 36(1976):253–301.

———. *Historia social de los Quiches.* Seminario de Integración Social Guatemalteca, Publicación no. 38. Guatemala, 1979.

————. *Harvest of Violence: The Maya Indians and the Guatemalan Crisis*. Norman: University of Oklahoma Press, 1988.

————. "State and Community in Nineteenth-Century Guatemala: The Momostenango Case." In *Guatemalan Indians and the State*. Edited by Carol A. Smith, pp. 116–36. Austin: University of Texas Press, 1990.

Carmack, Robert M.; Fox, John; and Stewart, R. *La formación del reino quiché: Según la arqueología y etnología*. Instituto Nacional de Antropología e Historia de Guatemala, Publicación Especial, no. 7. Guatemala, 1975.

Carmack, Robert M.; Sloane, F.; and Stewart, R. "La pre- y proto-historia de Santiago Momostenango." *Guatemala Indígena* 7(1972):5–21.

Carrasco, Pedro. "The Civil-Religious Hierarchy in Mesoamerican Communities: Pre-Spanish Background and Colonial Development." *American Anthropologist* 63(1961):483–97.

Caso, Alfonso. "Zapotec Writing and Calendar." In *Handbook of Middle American Indians*. Edited by Robert Wauchope. Austin: University of Texas Press, 1964–76. Vol. 3, *Archaeology of Southern Mesoamerica*, edited by Gordon R. Willey, 1965, pp. 931–47.

————. *Los Calendarios Prehispánicos*. Instituto de Investigaciones Históricas. Mexico: Universidad Nacional Autónoma de Mexico, 1967.

Cerezo D., Hugo. "El indígena en un documento del siglo XVIII: Notas preliminaries." *Antropología e Historia de Guatemala* 3(1941):37–40.

Chase, Arlen F., and Rice, Prudence M. *The Lowland Maya Postclassic*. Austin: University of Texas Press, 1985.

Chinchilla Aguilar, Ernesto. "El Mundo mágico en un catecismo quiché-español del siglo XVII." In *La danza del sacrificio y otros estudios*. Edited by Ernesto Chinchilla Aguilar, pp. 65–76. Guatemala: Editorial "José de Pineda Ibarra," 1963.

Coe, Michael D. *The Maya*. New York: Praeger, 1966.

Coggins, Clemency C. "The Shape of Time: Some Political Implications of a Four-Part Figure." *American Antiquity* 45(1980):727–39.

Colby, Benjamin N. "The Anomalous Ixil—Bypassed by the Postclassic?" *American Antiquity* 41(1976):74–80.

————. "Cognitive Economy, Coherence, and Divination in Three Civilizations." In *Ethnographic Encounters in Southern Mesoamerica*. Edited by Victoria R. Bricker and Gary H. Gossen, pp. 275–85. Albany: Institute for Mesoamerican Studies, 1989.

Colby, Benjamin N., and Berghe, Pierre L. van den. *Ixil Country: A Plural Society in Highland Guatemala*. Berkeley and Los Angeles: University of California Press, 1969.

Colby, Benjamin N., and Colby, Lore M. *The Daykeeper: The Life and Discourse of an Ixil Diviner*. Cambridge, Mass.: Harvard University Press, 1981.

Collier, Jane, and Yanagisako, Sylvia. "Theory in Anthropology Since Feminist Practice." *Critique of Anthropology* 9(1989):21–27.

Correa, Gustavo. "El Espíritu del mal en Guatemala." In *Nativism and Syncretism*. Middle American Research Institute, Publication no. 19(1960):37–104. New Orleans: Tulane University.

Cortés y Larraz, Pedro. *Descripción geográfico-moral de la Diócesis de Goathemala*, 2 vols. Biblioteca "Goathemala," vol. 22. Guatemala: Sociedad de Geografía e Historia de Guatemala, 1958.

Cosminsky, Sheila. "Knowledge and Body Concepts of Traditional Guatemalan Midwives: Implications for Training and Health Care." Paper read at the 76th Annual Meeting of the American Anthropological Association, November 1977, at Houston. Mimeographed.

Crabtree, Don E. "Mesoamerican Polyhedral Cores and Prismatic Blades." *American Antiquity* 33(1968):446–78.

Davis, Shelton H. "Introduction: Sowing the Seeds of Violence." In *Harvest of Violence*. Edited by Robert M. Carmack, pp. 3–36. Norman: University of Oklahoma Press, 1988.

Davis, Shelton H., and Hodson, Julie. *Witnesses to Political Violence in Guatemala: The Suppression of a Rural Development Movement*. Boston: Oxfam America, 1982.

Dienhart, John M. *The Mayan Languages: A Comparative Vocabulary*, 3 vols. Denmark: Odense University Press, 1989.

Dorst, Jean. *The Migrations of Birds*. Translated by C. D. Sherman. Boston: Houghton Mifflin, 1962.

Durán, Diego. *Book of the Gods and Rites and the Ancient Calendar*. Translated and edited by Fernando Horcasitas and Doris Heyden. Norman: University of Oklahoma Press, 1971.

Durkheim, Émile. *The Elementary Forms of the Religious Life*. Translated by Joseph Ward Swain. New York: Collier Books, 1961.

Dütting, Dieter, and Schramm, Matthias. "The Sidereal Period of the Moon in Maya Calendrical Astronomy." *Tribus* 37(1988):139–73.

Earle, Duncan M. "The Metaphor of the Day in Quiche: Notes on the Nature of Everyday Life." In *Symbols beyond the Closed Community*. Edited by Gary Gossen, pp. 155–72. Albany: Institute for Mesoamerican Studies, 1986.

———. "Mayas Aiding Mayas: Guatemalan Refugees in Chiapas, Mexico." In *Harvest of Violence*. Edited by Robert M. Carmack, pp. 256–73. Norman: University of Oklahoma Press, 1988.

Edmonson, Munro S. "Nativism, Syncretism and Anthropological Science." In *Nativism and Syncretism*. Middle American Research Institute, Publication no. 19(1960):181–204. New Orleans: Tulane University.

———. *The Book of Counsel: The Popol Vuh of the Quiche Maya of*

Guatemala. Middle American Research Institute, Publication no. 35(1971). New Orleans: Tulane University.

————. *The Book of the Year: Middle American Calendrical Systems*. Salt Lake City: University of Utah Press, 1988.

Eggan, Fred. "Social Anthropology and the Method of Controlled Comparison." *American Anthropologist* 56(1954):743–63.

Eliade, Mircea. *Shamanism: Archaic Techniques of Ecstacy*. Translated by Willard R. Trask. New York: Pantheon Books, 1964.

England, Nora C. *A Grammar of Mam, a Mayan Language*. Austin: University of Texas Press, 1983.

Estrada Monroy, Agustín, ed. *Popol Vuh: Traducido de la lengua quiché a la castellana por el R. P. fray Francisco Ximénez (Paleografía parcialmente modernizada y notas por Monroy)*. Guatemala: Editorial "José de Pineda Ibarra," 1973.

Fabian, Johannes. "Language, History and Anthropology." *Philosophy of the Social Sciences* 1(1971):19–47.

Fabrega, Horacio, Jr., and Silver, Daniel B. *Illness and Shamanistic Curing in Zinacantan: Anb Ethnomedical Analysis*. Stanford: Stanford University Press, 1973.

Falla, Ricardo S. *La conversión religiosa: Estudio sobre un movimiento rebelde a las creencias tradicionales en San Antonio Ilotenango, Quiché, Guatemala (1948–1970)*. Ann Arbor, Mich.: University Microfilms, 1975.

————. *Quiché rebelde*. Colección "Realidad Nuestra," vol. 7, Guatemala: Editorial Universitaria de Guatemala, 1978.

————. "We Charge Genocide." In *Guatemala Tyranny on Trial: Testimony of the Permanent People's Tribunal*. Edited by Susanne Jonas; Ed McCaughan; and Elizabeth Sutherland Martínez, pp. 112–19. San Francisco: Synthesis Publications, 1984.

————. "Struggle for Survival in the Mountains: Hunger and Other Privations Inflicted on Internal Refugees from the Central Highlands." In *Harvest of Violence*. Edited by Robert M. Carmack, pp. 235–55. Norman: University of Oklahoma Press, 1988.

Farrand, John. *The Audubon Society Master Guide to Birding*, part 1. New York: Alfred A. Knopf, 1983.

Farriss, Nancy M. *Maya Society under Colonial Rule: The Collective Enterprise of Survival*. Princeton: Princeton University Press, 1984.

Fergusson, Erna. *Guatemala*. New York: Alfred A. Knopf, 1936.

Fortes, Meyer. "Ritual and Office in Tribal Society." In *Essays on the Ritual of Social Relations*. Edited by Max Gluckman, pp. 53–88. Manchester: Manchester University Press, 1962.

Foster, George. "Nagualism in Mexico and Guatemala." *Acta America* 2(1944):85–103.

Fox, David G. "Review of *Quiché-English Dictionary,* by Munro Edmonson." *Language* 44(1968): 191–97.

———. *Lecciones elementales en Quiché.* Guatemala: Instituto Linguistico de Verano, 1973.

Fox, John W. *Quiché Conquest: Centralism and Regionalism in Highland Guatemalan State Development.* Albuquerque: University of New Mexico Press, 1978.

———. *Maya Postclassic State Formation: Segmentary Lineage Migration in Advancing Frontiers.* Cambridge: Cambridge University Press, 1987.

Fuentes y Guzmán, Francisco Antonio de. *Recordación florida: Discurso historial y demonstración natural, material, militar y política del reyno de Guatemala.* Biblioteca "Goathemala," vols. 6–8. Guatemala: Sociedad de Geografía e Historia de Guatemala, 1932–33.

Furst, Peter T. "To Find Our Life: Peyote among the Huichol Indians of Mexico." In *Flesh of the Gods.* Edited by Peter T. Furst, pp. 136–84. New York: Praeger, 1972.

———. "Shamanistic Survivals in Mesoamerican Religion," *Actas del 41 Congreso Internacional de Americanistas, México, 1974,* vol. 3(1976): 149–57. Mexico: Instituto Nacional de Antropología e Historia.

Gadamer, Hans-Georg. *Philosophical Hermeneutics.* Berkeley and Los Angeles: University of California Press, 1976.

Gadow, H. F. *Through Southern Mexico.* New York: Charles Scribner's Sons, 1908.

Gates, William. "Review of *Archaeology of the Cayo District,* by J. Eric S. Thompson." *Maya Society Quarterly* 1(1931): 37–44.

Geertz, Clifford. *The Interpretation of Cultures.* New York: Basic Books, 1973.

Gennep, Arnold van. *The Rites of Passage.* Translated by B. Vizedom and Gabrielle L. Caffe. London: Routledge and Kegan Paul, 1960.

Gillin, John. "Parallel Cultures and the Inhibitions to Acculturation in a Guatemalan Community." *Social Forces* 24(1945)1–14.

Girard, Rafael. *Los Mayas eternos.* Mexico: Antigua Librería Robredo, 1962.

———. *Los mayas.* Mexico: Libro Mex, 1966.

Gluckman, Max. "Les rites de passage." In *Essays on the Ritual of Social Relations.* Edited by Max Gluckman, pp. 1–52. Manchester: Manchester University Press, 1962.

Goldstein, Leon J. "The Phenomenological and Naturalistic Approaches to the Social." In *Theory in Anthropology.* Edited by Robert A. Manners and David Kaplan, pp. 97–104. Chicago: Aldine Publishing Co., 1968.

Gossen, Gary H. "Temporal and Spatial Equivalents in Chamula Ritual

Symbolism." In *Reader in Comparative Religion: An Anthropological Approach*. Edited by William Lessa and Evon Z. Vogt. New York: Harper & Row, 1972.

———. "A Chamula Solar Calendar Board from Chiapas, Mexico." In *Mesoamerican Archaeology: New Approaches*. Edited by Norman Hammond, pp. 217–53. London: Duckworth, 1974.

———. *Chamulas in the World of the Sun: Time and Space in a Maya Oral Tradition*. Cambridge, Mass.: Harvard University Press, 1974.

Goubaud Carrera, Antonio. "El 'Guajxaquíp Báts'—Ceremonia calendárica indígena." *Anales de la Sociedad de Geografía e Historia de Guatemala* 12(1935):39–52.

———. *The Guajxaquíp Báts: An Indian Ceremony of Guatemala*. Guatemala: Centro Editorial, 1937.

Gregory, James R. "On Being Indian in Southern Belize: A Research Note." *Belizean Studies* 8 no. 4(1980):1–9.

Griscom, Ludlow. "The Distribution of Bird-Life in Guatemala." *Bulletin of the American Museum of Natural History* 64(1932):15–77.

Gronewold, Sylvia. "Did Frank Hamilton Cushing Go Native?" In *Crossing Cultural Boundaries: The Anthropological Experience*. Edited by Solon T. Kimball and James B. Watson, pp. 33–50. San Francisco: Chandler Publishing Co., 1972.

Guerrilla Army of the Poor (EGP). *Compañero*. Guatemala: Solidarity Publications, 1982.

Guiteras-Holmes, Calixta. *Perils of the Soul: The World View of a Tzotzil Indian*. New York: Free Press of Glencoe, 1961.

Gurvitch, Georges. *The Spectrum of Social Time*. Translated by Phillip Bosserman. Boston: Reidel, 1964.

Guzmán, Pantaleón de. "Compendio de nombres en lengua Cakchiquel." Manuscript in the collection of E. G. Squier. Photocopy in Gates collection, in the library at Brigham Young University, Provo, Utah, 1704.

Haeserijn V., Esteban. *Diccionario k'ekchi' español*. Guatemala: Piedra Santa, 1979.

Hall, Edward T., Jr. "A Microcultural Analysis of Time." In *Men and Cultures*. Edited by Anthony F. C. Wallace, pp. 118–22. Philadelphia: University of Pennsylvania Press, 1960.

Hallowell, A. Irving. "Temporal Orientation in Western Civilization and in a Preliterate Society." *American Anthropologist* 39(1937):647–70.

Hammond, Norman, and Willey, Gordon R., eds. *Maya Archaeology and Ethnohistory*. Austin: University of Texas Press, 1979.

Hanks, William F., and Rice, Don S. *Word and Image in Maya Culture: Explorations in Language, Writing, and Representation*. Salt Lake City: University of Utah Press, 1989.

Harris, Marvin. *Patterns of Race in the Americas*. New York: W. W. Norton & Co., 1964.

Harrison, Thomas C. "The Orion Nebula: Where in History Is It?" *Quarterly Journal of the Royal Astronomical Society* 25(1984):65–79.

Harwood, Michael. *Proceedings of the North American Hawk Migration Conference, Syracuse, New York, April 18–21, 1974.* Washington Depot, Conn.: The Hawk Migration Association of North America, 1975.

Haugh, John R. "Local Ephemeral Weather Conditions and Their Effects on Hawk Migration Routes." In *Proceedings of the North American Hawk Migration Conference.* Edited by Michael Harwood, pp. 72–84. Washington Depot, Conn.: The Hawk Migration Association of North America, 1975.

Hawkins, John. *Inverse Images: The Meaning of Culture, Ethnicity, and Family in Postcolonial Guatemala.* Albuquerque: University of New Mexico Press, 1984.

Heintzelman, Donald S. *A Manual for Bird Watching in the Americas.* New York: Universe Books, 1979.

Henderson, John S. "Origin of the 260-Day Cycle in Mesoamerica." *Science* 185(1974):542–43.

Hermitte, M. Esther. "Supernatural Power and Social Control in a Modern Mayan Village." Ph.D. dissertation, University of Chicago, 1964.

Hernández Spina, Vicente. "Ixtlavacan Quiche Calendar of 1854." Translated by Ethel-Jane W. Bunting. *Maya Society Quarterly* 1(1932): 72–77.

Hill, Robert, and Monaghan, John. *Continuities in Highland Maya Social Organization: Ethnohistory in Sacapulas, Guatemala.* Philadelphia: University of Pennsylvania Press, 1987.

Hinshaw, Robert E. *Panajachel: A Guatemalan Town in Thirty-Year Perspective.* Pittsburgh: University of Pittsburgh Press, 1975.

———. "Tourist Town amid the Violence: Panajachel." In *Harvest of Violence.* Edited by Robert M. Carmack, pp. 195–205. Norman: University of Oklahoma Press, 1988.

Holland, William Robert. "Highland Maya Folk Medicine: A Study of Culture Change." Ph.D. dissertation, University of Arizona, 1962.

Hollenbach, Marion. "An Ancient Quiché Ceremony." *El Palacio* 42(1937): 80–84.

Hood, Mantle. "Within the Context." In *Musicology.* Edited by Frank Ll. Harrison, Mantle Hood, and Claude V. Palisca, pp. 260–89. Englewood Cliffs, N.J.: Prentice-Hall, 1963.

Hunt, Eva. *The Transformation of the Hummingbird: Cultural Roots of a Zinacantecan Mythical Poem.* Ithaca: Cornell University Press, 1977.

Ingham, John. "Time and Space in Ancient Mexico: The Symbolic Dimensions of Clanship." *Man* n.s. 6(1971):615–30.

Jiménez Moreno, Wigberto. "Religión o religiones mesoamericanas?" In *Simposium sobre religiones mesoamericanas.* Verhandlungen des 38

Internationalen Amerikanisten Kongresses, Stuttgart-Munich, 3(1968):
201–6.

Jones, Chester Lloyd. *Guatemala, Past and Present*. Minneapolis: University of Minnesota Press, 1940.

Jones, Grant D. *Maya Resistance to Spanish Rule: Time and History on a Colonial Frontier*. Albuquerque: University of New Mexico Press, 1989.

Josserand, J. Kathryn, and Hopkins, Nicholas A. "Chol (Mayan) Dictionary Database, Part III." Final performance report for the National Endowment for the Humanities, 1988.

Jules-Rosette, Bennetta. *African Apostles: Ritual and Conversion in the Church of John Maranke*. Ithaca: Cornell University Press, 1975.

Kelley, David Humiston. *Deciphering the Maya Script*. Austin: University of Texas Press, 1976.

Kelly, Isabel. *Santiago Tuxtla, Veracruz Culture and Health*. Mexico: Institute of Inter-American Affairs, 1956.

———. *Folk Practices in North Mexico: Birth Customs, Folk Medicine, and Spiritualism in the Laguna Zone*. Austin: University of Texas Press, 1965.

Kelsey, Vera, and Jongh Osborne, Lilly de. *Four Keys to Guatemala*. New York: Funk & Wagnalls Co., 1939.

Kendall, Carl; Hawkins, John; and Bossen, Laurel. *Heritage of Conquest: Thirty Years Later*. Albuquerque: University of New Mexico Press, 1983.

Kidder, Alfred V. "Archaeological Problems of the Highland Maya." In *The Maya and Their Neighbors*. Edited by C. L. Hay and others, pp. 117–25. New York: Appleton-Century Co., 1940.

Kimball, Solon T. "Learning a New Culture." In *Crossing Cultural Boundaries: The Anthropological Experience*. Edited by Solon T. Kimball and James B. Watson, pp. 182–92. San Francisco: Chandler Publishing Co., 1972.

Koizumi, Junji. *Symbol and Context: A Study of Self and Action in a Guatemalan Culture*. Ann Arbor: University Microfilms, 1981.

La Farge, Oliver. "Maya Ethnology: The Sequence of Cultures." In *The Maya and Their Neighbors*. Edited by C. L. Hay and others, pp. 281–91. New York: Appleton-Century Co., 1940.

———. *Santa Eulalia: The Religion of a Cuchumatán Indian Town*. Chicago: University of Chicago Press, 1947.

La Farge, Oliver, and Byers, Douglas. *The Year Bearer's People*. Middle American Research Institute, Publication no. 3. New Orleans: Tulane University, 1931.

Lamb, Weldon W. "Star Lore in the Yucatec Maya Dictionaries." In *Archaeoastronomy in the Americas*. Edited by Ray A. Williamson, pp. 233–48. Los Altos, California: Ballena Press, 1981.

Land, Hugh C. *Birds of Guatemala*. Wynnewood, Pennsylvania: Livingston Publishing, 1970.

Langness, Lewis. "Hysterical Psychoses and Possessions." In *Culture-Bound Syndromes, Ethnopsychiatry, and Alternate Therapies*. Edited by William P. Lebra, pp. 56–67. Honolulu: University Press of Hawaii, 1976.

Larsen, Helga. "The 260-Day Period as Related to the Agricultural Life of the Ancient Indian." *Ethnos* 1(1936):9–12.

Las Casas, Bartolomé de. *Apologetica Historia de las Indias*. 2 vols. Nueva Biblioteca de Autores Españoles, vol. 13. Madrid, 1909.

Laughlin, Robert M. *The Great Tzotzil Dictionary of San Lorenzo Zinacantán*. Smithsonian Contributions to Anthropology, No. 19. Washington, D.C.: Smithsonian Institution Press, 1975.

Leach, Edmund. "Two Essays Concerning the Symbolic Representation of Time." In *Rethinking Anthropology*. Edited by Edmund Leach, pp. 124–36. London: The Athlone Press, 1961.

Lehmann, Walter. "Der Kalender der Quiché-Indianer Guatemalas." *Anthropos* 6(1911):403–10.

Leonard, Sister Blanche M. "Ontological Categories of the Gods of Yucatan." Mimeographed. Cambridge, Mass.: Harvard University, 1964–65.

León-Portilla, Miguel. *Time and Reality in the Thought of the Maya*. Boston: Beacon Press, 1973.

Lincoln, J. Steward. "The Maya Calendar of the Ixil of Guatemala." *Contributions to American Anthropology and History* 38(1942):99–128.

Linton, Ralph. *The Study of Man*. New York: Appleton-Century Co., 1936.

Long, Richard C. E. "Some Maya Time Periods." In *Proceedings of the International Congress of Americanists, The Hague, 1921*, vol. 1(1924): 574–81.

Lothrop, S. K. "Further Notes on Indian Ceremonies in Guatemala." *Indian Notes* 6(1929):1–25.

———. "A Modern Survival of the Ancient Maya Calendar." In *Proceedings of the 23rd International Congress of Americanists, New York, 1928*, vol. 1(1930):652–55.

Lounsbury, Floyd G. "Maya Numeration, Computation and Calendrical Astronomy." *Dictionary of Scientific Biography*. Edited by Charles Coulston Gillispie, vol. 15, suppl. 1(1978):759–818.

Lovell, W. George. *Conquest and Survival in Colonial Guatemala: A Historical Geography of the Cuchumatán Highlands 1500–1821*. Montreal: McGill-Queen's University Press, 1985.

———. "From Conquest to Counter-Insurgency." *Cultural Survival Quarterly* 9(1985):46–49.

———. "Surviving Conquest: The Maya of Guatemala in Historical Perspective." *Latin American Research Review* 23 no. 2 (1988):25–57.

MacLeod, Murdo J. *Spanish Central America: A Socioeconomic History, 1520–1720.* Berkeley and Los Angeles: University of California Press, 1973.

McArthur, Harry, and McArthur, Lucille. "Notas sobre el calendario ceremonial de Aguacatán, Huehuetenango." *Folklore de Guatemala* 2(1965):23–38.

Madsen, William. "Shamanism in Mexico." *Southwestern Journal of Anthropology* 11(1955):48–57.

Mak, C. "Mixtec Medical Beliefs and Practices," *América Indígena* 19 (1959):125–51.

Malmstrom, Vincent H. "Origin of the Mesoamerican 260-Day Calendar." *Science* 181(1973):939–41.

Manz, Beatriz. *Refugees of a Hidden War: The Aftermath of Counterinsurgency in Guatemala.* Albany: State University of New York Press, 1988.

Martínez Hernández, J. *Diccionario de Motul, maya español, atribuido a fray Antonio de Ciudad Real y arte de lengua maya por fray Juan Coronel.* Mérida: Tipográfica Yucateca, 1930.

Melville, Thomas R. "The Catholic Church in Guatemala, 1944–1982." *Cultural Survival Quarterly* 7(1983):23–27.

Menchú, Rigoberta. *I . . . Rigoberta Menchú: An Indian Woman in Guatemala.* Edited and introduced by Elizabeth Burgos-Debray. London: British Library, 1984.

———. *Indian Guatemala: Path to Liberation.* Washington, D.C.: EPICA Task Force, 1984.

Mendelson, E. Michael. *Los escándalos de Maximón.* Seminario de Integración Social Guatemalteca, Publicación no. 19. Guatemala, 1965.

———. "Ritual and Mythology." In *Handbook of the Middle American Indians.* Edited by Robert Wauchope. Austin: University of Texas Press, 1964–76. Vol. 6, *Social Anthropology,* edited by Manning Nash, 1967, pp. 392–415.

Merrill, R. H. "Maya Sun Calendar Dictum Disproved," *American Antiquity* 10(1945):307–11.

Metzger, Duane, and Williams, Gerald. "Tenejapa Medicine I: The Curer," *Southwestern Journal of Anthropology* 19(1963):216–34.

Miles, Suzanna W. "An Analysis of Modern Middle American Calendars: A Study in Conservation." In *Acculturation in the Americas.* Edited by Sol Tax, pp. 273–84. Chicago: University of Chicago Press, 1952.

———. "The Sixteenth Century Pokom-Maya." *Transactions of the American Philosophical Society,* vol. 47, part 4(1957):735–81.

Mondloch, James. "Sincretismo religioso maya-cristiano en la tradición oral de una comunidad quiché." *Mesoamérica* 3(1982):107–23.

Montejo, Victor. *Testimony: Death of a Guatemalan Village.* Willimantic, Conn.: Curbstone Press, 1987.

Morley, Sylvanus G. *An Introduction to the Study of the Maya Hiero-glyphs*. Bulletin 57 of the Bureau of American Ethnology. Washington, D.C., 1915.

————. *The Ancient Maya*. Stanford: Stanford University Press, 1946.

Myerhoff, Barbara G. *Peyote Hunt: The Sacred Journey of the Huichol Indians*. Ithaca: Cornell University Press, 1974.

Nash, June. "The Logic of Behavior: Curing in a Maya Indian Town." *Human Organization* 26 (1967):132–40.

————. *In the Eyes of the Ancestors: Belief and Behavior in a Maya Community*. New Haven: Yale University Press, 1970.

Nash, Manning. "Cultural Persistence and Social Structure: The Meso-american Calendar Survivals." *Southwestern Journal of Anthropology* 13(1957):149–55.

————. *Machine Age Maya*. American Anthropological Association, Memoir no. 87. Menasha, Wisc.: American Anthropological Association, 1958.

Natanson, M. A., ed. *Phenomenology and the Social Sciences*. 2 vols. Evanston: Northwestern University Press, 1973.

Nelson, Diane M. "The Reconstruction of Mayan Identity." *Report on Guatemala* 12 no. 2(1991):6–7, 14.

Neuenswander, Helen. "Vestiges of Early Maya Time Concepts in a Contemporary Maya (Cubulco Achi) Community: Implications for Epigraphy." Mimeographed. Guatemala: Summer Institute of Linguistics, 1978.

Nuttall, Zelia. "Nouvelles lumières sur les civilisations américaines et le système du calendrier." *Proceedings of the 22nd International Congress of Americanists, Rome, 1926*, vol. 1(1928):119–48.

Oakes, Maud. *The Two Crosses of Todos Santos: Survivals of Mayan Religious Ritual*. Bollingen Series, no. 27. New Jersey: Princeton University Press, 1951.

Ordóñez, J. Martín. "Religión, magia y folklore en Chichicastenango." *Guatemala Indígena* 4(1969):180–204.

Orellana, Sandra L. *Indian Medicine in Highland Guatemala: The Pre-Hispanic and Colonial Periods*. Albuquerque: University of New Mexico Press, 1987.

Ortiz, Alfonso. *Tewa World: Space, Time, Being, and Becoming in a Pueblo Society*. Chicago: University of Chicago Press, 1969.

Ortner, Sherry B. "Theory in Anthropology Since the Sixties." *Society for the Comparative Study of Society and History* 26(1984):126–66.

Parsons, Elsie Clews, *Mitla: Town of the Souls*. Chicago: Chicago University Press, 1936.

Paul, Benjamin D., and Demarest, William J. "The Operation of a Death Squad in San Pedro la Laguna." In *Harvest of Violence*. Edited by

Robert M. Carmack, pp. 119–54. Norman: University of Oklahoma Press, 1988.

Paul, Lois, and Paul, Benjamin D. "The Maya Midwife as Sacred Professional: A Guatemalan Case." *American Ethnologist* 2(1975):707–26.

Perera, Victor, and Bruce, Robert D. *The Last Lords of Palenque: The Lacandon Mayas of the Mexican Rain Forest.* Berkeley and Los Angeles: University of California Press, 1982.

Philadelphia, University of Pennsylvania Museum Library. "Calendario de los Indios de Guatemala, 1722 Kiché."

Pinkerton, Sandra. *Studies in K'ekchi.* Texas Linguistic Forum no., 3. Austin: University of Texas, 1976.

Pitt-Rivers, Julian. "Spiritual Power in Central America: The Naguals of Chiapas." In *Witchcraft Confessions and Accusations.* Edited by Mary Douglas, pp. 183–206. London: Tavistock Publications, 1970.

Price, William J. "Time is of the Gods." *Practical Anthropology* 11(1964): 266–72.

Recinos, Adrián. *Crónicas indígenas de Guatemala.* Guatemala: Editorial Universitaria, 1957.

Recinos, Adrián, and Goetz, Delia, trans. *The Annals of the Cakchiquels.* Norman: University of Oklahoma Press, 1953.

Reichard, Gladys A. *Spider Woman: A Story of Navajo Weavers and Chanters.* New York: Macmillan, 1934.

Reina, Ruben E. *The Law of the Saints: A Pokomam Pueblo and its Community Culture.* New York: Bobbs-Merrill Co., 1966.

Remington, Judith A. "Current Astronomical Practices among the Maya." In *Native American Astronomy.* Edited by Anthony F. Aveni, pp. 75–88. Austin: University of Texas Press, 1977.

Richards, M. "Cosmopolitan World View and Counterinsurgency in Guatemala." *Anthropological Quarterly* 3(1986):90–107.

Ricoeur, Paul. *Interpretation Theory: Discourse and the Surplus of Meaning.* Fort Worth: The Texas Christian University Press, 1976.

Ries, Maurice. "The Ritual of the Broken Pots." *América Indígena* 5(1943):245–52.

Roberts, Robert E. T. "A Comparison of Ethnic Relations in Two Guatemalan Communities." *Acta Americana* 6(1948):135–51.

Robicsek, Francis, and Hales, Donald M. "Maya Heart Sacrifice: Cultural Perspective and Surgical Technique." In *Ritual Human Sacrifice in Mesoamerica.* Edited by Elizabeth H. Boone, pp. 49–90. Washington, D.C.: Dumbarton Oaks, 1984.

Rodas N., Flavio: Rodas C., Ovidio; and Hawkins, Lawrence F. *Chichicastenango, the Kiche Indians: Their History and Culture, Sacred Symbols of their Dress and Textiles.* Guatemala: Unión Tipográfica, 1940.

Rodríguez Rouanet, Francisco. "La ceremonia del Wakxakib Bats y el 'Dios Mundo' en Momostenango," *Folklore de Guatemala* 3(1967): 77–80.

————. "Monografía del municipio de Momostenango: Departamento de Totonicapán." *Guatemala Indígena* 5(1971): 11–99.

Roys, Ralph L. *The Book of Chilam Balam of Chumayel.* Norman: University of Oklahoma Press, 1967.

Rubel, Arthur J. "Prognosticative Calendar Systems." *American Anthropologist* 67(1965): 107–10.

Saler, Benson. *The Road from El Palmar: Change, Continuity, and Conservatism in a Quiché Community.* Ann Arbor: University Microfilms, 1960.

————. "Nagual, Witch, and Sorcerer in a Quiché Village," *Ethnology* 3(1964): 305–28.

————. "Sorcery in Santiago El Palmar." In *Systems of North American Witchcraft and Sorcery.* Edited by Deward Walker, pp. 125–46. Anthropological Monographs of the University of Idaho, no. 1. Moscow, Idaho: University of Idaho, 1970.

————. "Cultic Alternatives in a Guatemalan Village." Paper read at the Association of Social Anthropologists, Conference on Regional Cults, 1976, Manchester, England. Mimeographed.

Sanders, William T., and Price, Barbara J. *Mesoamerica: The Evolution of a Civilization.* New York: Random House, 1968.

Sapper, Karl. "Über Brujeria in Guatemala." *Proceedings of the 21st International Congress of Americanists, Göteborg, 1924,* vol. 1(1925): 391–405.

Schackt, Jon. "The Tzuultak'a: Religious Lore and Cultural Processes among the Kekchi." *Belizean Studies* 12 no. 5(1984): 16–29.

Schele, Linda, and Freidel, David. *A Forest of Kings: The Untold Story of the Ancient Maya.* New York: William Morrow, 1990.

Schele, Linda, and Grube, Nikolai. "A Preliminary Inventory of Place Names in the Copán Inscriptions." *Copán Notes* no. 93, 1990.

Schele, Linda; Stuart, David; and Grube, Nikolai. "A Commentary on the Restoration and Reading of the Glyphic Panels from Temple 11." *Copán Notes* no. 64, 1989.

Scholte, Bob. "Dwelling on the Everyday World: Phenomenological Analyses and Social Reality." *American Anthropologist* 78(1976): 585–89.

Schultze Jena, Leonhard. *La vida y las creencias de los indígenas quichés de Guatemala.* Biblioteca de Cultura Popular, vol. 49. Translated by Antonio Goubaud Carrera and Herbert D. Sapper. Guatemala: Ministerio de Educación Pública, 1954.

Schutz, Alfred J. *The Phenomenology of the Social World.* Translated by

George Walsh and Frederick Lehnert. Evanston: Northwestern University Press, 1967.

Sedat S., Guillermo. *Nuevo diccionario de las lenguas k'ekchi' y española*. Chamelco, Alta Verapaz, Guatemala, 1955.

Seler, Eduard. "Die Tageszeichen der aztekischen und der Maya-Handshriften and ihre Gottheiten." In *Gesammelte Abhandlungen zur Amerikanischen Sprach und Altertumskunde*, vol. 1, pp. 417–503. Graz: Akademische Druck und Verlagsanstalt, 1888.

Sexton, James. *Son of Tecún Umán: A Maya Indian Tells His Life Story*. Tucson: University of Arizona Press, 1981.

———. *Campesino: The Diary of a Guatemalan Indian*. Tucson: University of Arizona Press, 1985.

Shaw, Mary, ed. *According to Our Ancestors: Folk Texts from Guatemala and Honduras*. Guatemala: Instituto Lingüístico de Verano en Centro América, 1971.

Siegel, Morris. "Religion in Western Guatemala: A Product of Acculturation." *American Anthropologist* 43(1941):62–76.

Silver, Daniel B. "Zinacanteco Shamanism." Ph.D. dissertation, Harvard University, 1966.

Simon, Jean-Marie. *Guatemala: Eternal Spring, Eternal Tyranny*. New York: W. W. Norton, 1987.

Sletto, Jacqueline Wiora, and Sletto, Bjorn. "Cultural and Economic Revival: Toledo Maya." *Native Peoples* 4(1990):38–44.

Smith, Carol A. "Local History in Global Context: Social and Economic Transitions in Western Guatemala." In *Micro and Macro Levels of Analysis in Anthropology: Issues in Theory and Research*. Edited by Billie R. De Walt and Pertti J. Pelto, pp. 83–120. Westview Press: Boulder, 1985.

———. "Destruction of the Material Bases for Indian Culture: Economic Changes in Totonicapán." In *Harvest of Violence*. Edited by Robert M. Carmack, pp. 206–31. Norman: University of Oklahoma Press, 1988.

———, ed. *Guatemalan Indians and the State, 1540 to 1988*. Austin: University of Texas Press, 1990.

———. "Class Position and Class Consciousness in an Indian Community: Totonicapán in the 1970s." In *Guatemalan Indians and the State*. Edited by Carol A. Smith, pp. 205–29. Austin: University of Texas Press, 1990.

Solano Pérez-Lila, Francisco. *Los Mayas del siglo XVIII; Pervivencia y transformación de la sociedad indígena guatemalteca durante la administración borbonica*. Madrid: Ediciones Cultura Hispanica, 1974.

Sosa, John R. *The Maya Sky, the Maya World: A Symbolic Analysis of Yucatec Maya Cosmology*. Ann Arbor: University Microfilms, 1985.

———. "Cosmological, Symbolic and Cultural Complexity among the

Contemporary Maya of Yucatan." In *World Archaeoastronomy*. Edited by A. F. Aveni, pp. 130–42. Cambridge: Cambridge University Press, 1989.

Spinden, Herbert J. "Central American Calendars and the Gregorian Day." *Proceedings of the National Academy of Science* 6(1920):56–59.

Stoll, David. "Evangelicals, Guerrillas, and the Army: The Ixil Triangle Under Ríos Montt." In *Harvest of Violence*. Edited by Robert M. Carmack, pp. 90–116. Norman: University of Oklahoma Press, 1988.

Stross, Brian. "Classic Maya Directional Glyphs." *Journal of Linguistic Anthropology* 1(1991):97–114.

Tax, Sol. "The Municipios of the Midwestern Highlands of Guatemala." *American Anthropologist* 39(1937):423–44.

———. *Notes on Santo Tomás Chichicastenango (Nov. 1934–May 1935)*. Microfilm collection of manuscripts in Middle American Cultural Anthropology, no. 16. Chicago: University of Chicago Library, 1947.

———. *Heritage of Conquest: The Ethnology of Middle America*. Glencoe, Illinois: Free Press, 1952.

———. "Cultural Differences in the Maya Area: A 20th Century Perspective." In *Desarrollo cultural de los Mayas*. Edited by Evon Z. Vogt and Alberto Ruiz L., pp. 279–328. Mexico: Universidad Nacional Autónoma de Mexico, 1964.

Tedlock, Barbara. "A Phenomenological Approach to Religious Change in Highland Guatemala." In *Heritage of Conquest: Thirty Years Later*. Edited by Carl Kendall and John Hawkins, pp. 235–46. Albuquerque: University of New Mexico Press, 1983.

———. "Earth Rites and Moon Cycles: Mayan Synodic and Sidereal Lunar Reckoning." Paper delivered at the International Conference on Ethnoastronomy, National Air and Space Museum, Washington, D.C., 1983.

Tedlock, Dennis. "Las formas del verso quiché de la paleografía a la grabadora." In *Nuevas perspectivas sobre el Popol Vuh*. Edited by Roberto Carmack, pp. 123–32. Guatemala: Piedra Santa, 1983.

———. *Popol Vuh*. New York: Simon and Schuster, 1985.

Teeple, John E. *Maya Astronomy*. Carnegie Institute of Washington Publication no. 403, Contributions to American Archaeology vol. 1, no. 2, Washington, D.C., 1931.

Tenzel, James H. "Shamanism and Concepts of Disease in a Mayan Indian Community." *Psychiatry* 33(1970):372–80.

Thompson, Donald E. "Maya Paganism and Christianity: A History of the Fusion of Two Religions." In *Nativism and Syncretism*. Middle American Research Institute, Publication No. 19(1960):5–34. New Orleans: Tulane University.

Thompson, J. Eric S. *Maya Hieroglyphic Writing: An Introduction*. Norman: University of Oklahoma Press, 1950.

―――. *The Rise and Fall of Maya Civilization*. Norman: University of Oklahoma Press, 1954.

―――. *A Commentary on the Dresden Codex: A Maya Hieroglyphic Book*. Memoirs of the American Philosophical Society, no. 93. Philadelphia: American Philosophical Society, 1972.

Tirado, Fermín Joseph. "Vocabulario de lengua Kiche." Photocopy of manuscript located in the Tozzer Library, Harvard University, Cambridge, Mass., 1787.

Toledo Maya Cultural Council (TMCC). "Mopan and Kektchi Indians Fight for Their Culture." *IWGIA Newsletter* 37(1984):18–21.

―――. "The Mayas Call for Help and Solidarity." *IWGIA Newsletter* 41(1985):46–51.

―――. "The Toledo Maya Homeland." *IWGIA Newsletter* 46(1986): 17–20.

Tölölyan, Khachig. "The Nation-State and Its Others." *Diaspora* 1(1991): 3–7.

Townsend, Paul. *We Have Come To Wake You, We Have Come to Rouse You Our Lords, Our Ladies: Ritual Rhetoric from Cotzal*. Computer Program Printout, no. 8179. Guatemala: Summer Institute of Linguistics, 1979.

Tozzer, Alfred M. *A Comparative Study of the Mayas and the Lacandones*. New York: Macmillan Co., 1907.

―――. *Landa's Relación de las Cosas de Yucatán*. Papers of the Peabody Museum of Archaeology and Ethnology, vol. 18. Cambridge, Mass.: Harvard University, 1941.

Turner, Victor. *The Forest of Symbols: Aspects of Ndembu Ritual*. Ithaca: Cornell University Press, 1967.

―――. *The Ritual Process: Structure and Anti-Structure*. Ithaca: Cornell University Press, 1969.

―――. Foreword to *African Apostles: Ritual and Conversion in the Church of John Maranke*, by Bennetta Jules-Rosette. Ithaca: Cornell University Press, 1975.

―――. *Revelation and Divination in Ndembu Ritual*. Ithaca: Cornell University Press, 1975.

Ulrich, E. Matthew, and Ulrich, Rosemary Dixon de. *Diccionario Maya Mopan/Español Español/Maya Mopan*. Guatemala: Instituto Lingüístico de Verano, 1976.

Valladares, Leon A. *El hombre y la maíz: etnografía y etnopsicología de Colotenango, Guatemala*. Guatemala, 1957.

Vázquez, R. P. fray Francisco. *Crónica de la provincia del Santísimo Nombre de Jesús de Guatemala*. 2nd edition, 4 vols. Guatemala, 1937–44.

Villa Rojas, Alfonso. *The Maya of East Central Quintana Roo.* Carnegie Institution of Washington, Publication no. 559. Washington, D.C., 1945.

————. "Kinship and Nagualism in a Tzeltal Community (Tenejapa)." *American Anthropologist* 49(1947):578–87.

————. "The Concepts of Space and Time Among the Contemporary Maya." In *Time and Reality in the Thought of the Maya.* Edited by Miguel León-Portilla, pp. 113–59. Boston: Beacon Press, 1973.

Vogt, Evon Z. "H?iloletik: The Organization and Function of Shamanism in Zinacantan." In *Summa Antropológica en homenaje a Roberto J. Weitlaner,* pp. 359–69. Mexico: Instituto Nacional de Antropología e Historia, 1966.

————. *Zinacantán: A Maya Community in the Highlands of Chiapas.* Cambridge, Mass.: Harvard University Press, Belknap Press, 1969.

————. *Tortillas for the Gods: A Symbolic Analysis of Zinacanteco Rituals.* Cambridge, Mass.: Harvard University Press, 1976.

————. "Cardinal Directions and Ceremonial Circuits in Mayan and Southwestern Cosmology." *National Geographic Society Research Reports* 21(1985):487–96.

Wachtel, Nathan. *The Vision of the Vanquished: The Spanish Conquest of Peru through Indian Eyes 1530–1570.* New York: Harper & Row, 1977.

Wagley, Charles. *The Social and Religious Life of a Guatemalan Village.* American Anthropological Association, Memoir no. 71. Menasha, Wisc.: American Anthropological Association, 1949.

Wahrhaftig, Albert L. "Witchcraft and Curing in Two Tzeltal Communities." Master's Thesis, University of Chicago, 1960.

Warner, W. Lloyd. *A Black Civilization: A Social Study of an Australian Tribe.* New York: Harper and Brothers, 1937.

Warren, Kay B. *The Symbolism of Subordination: Indian Identity in a Guatemalan Town.* Austin: University of Texas Press, 1978.

Watanabe, John M. "In the World of the Sun: A Cognitive Model of Mayan Cosmology." *Man* 18(1983):710–28.

————. "Enduring Yet Ineffable Community in the Western Periphery of Guatemala." In *Guatemalan Indians and the State, 1540 to 1988.* Edited by Carol A. Smith, pp. 183–204. Austin: University of Texas Press, 1988.

————. "Elusive Essences: Souls and Social Identity in Two Highland Maya Communities." In *Ethnographic Encounters in Southern Mesoamerica.* Edited by Victoria R. Bricker and Gary H. Gossen, pp. 263–74. Albany: Institute for Mesoamerican Studies, 1989.

Wetmore, Alexander. *Water, Prey, and Game Birds of North America.* Washington, D.C.: National Geographic Society, 1965.

Wilson, Richard. "Machine Guns and Mountain Spirits: The Cultural Effects of State Repression among the Q'eqchi' of Guatemala." *Critique of Anthropology* 11(1991):33–61.

Wisdom, Charles. *The Chortí Indians of Guatemala*. Chicago: University of Chicago Press, 1940.

——. "The Supernatural World and Curing." In *Heritage of Conquest*. Edited by Sol Tax, pp. 119–41. Glencoe, Illinois: Free Press, 1952.

Witherspoon, Gary. *Language and Art in the Navajo Universe*. Ann Arbor: University of Michigan Press, 1977.

Ximénez, fray Francisco. "El calendario k'iché." *Revista de Etnología, Arqueología y Lingüística* 1(1926):251–57.

——. *Historia de la provincia de San Vicente de Chiapas y Guatemala*. Biblioteca "Goathemala," vols. 1–3. Guatemala, 1929–31.

——. *Escolios a las historias del origen de los Indios*. Sociedad de Geografía e Historia de Guatemala, pub. 13, 1967,

Index

288

ethnocide, xiii, 247 n.4
ethnohistorical documents, 1, 6, 7, 96, 176,
179, 180, 248 n.12. *See also* Annals of
the Cakchiquels, Calendario de los Indios de Guatemala, 1722 Kiché, Chilam
Balam of Chumayel, Dresden Codex,
Madrid Codex, Paris Codex, Popol Vuh,
Título C'oyoi

Fabian Johannes, 5
Fabrega, Horacio, Jr., 135
factionalism, 40, 247 n.3
Falla, Ricardo S., 133
Federation of Central America, 20
fireworks, 66, 101, 118
Fuentes y Guzmán, Francisco Antonio de,
57
Furst, Peter T., 48

Gemini, 181, 182, 189. *See also* Castor;
Pollux
genocide, xiii, 247 n.4
Girard, Rafael, 96, 99
Gossen, Gary H., 92, 178
Goubaud Carrera, Antonio, 95
grabbing, the, 153, 160, 162, 163, 165, 167
Great Nebula, M42, 181
Gronewold, Sylvia, 4
Guatemalan nation state, xiii, xiv, 1, 2, 51,
91, 136, 211; relations with Momoste-
cans, 19–22, 33, 112
Guatemala City, xiv, 21, 22, 31
Guatemala Scholars Network, xiv
Guerrilla Army of the Poor (EGP), xiii
Guiteras-Holmes, Calixta, 50

haab, 89
Hawkins, Lawrence F., 84, 134
hawk migration, 185–89, 190, 204
heredity. *See* inheritance
hero twins, 181. *See also* Hunahpu;
Xbalanque
Hermitte, M. Esther, 136
hieroglyphic script, 1, 212, 256 n.14; decipherment of, xiii, 127–31, 173–76
Highland Maya, 1–2, 89, 96, 97, 104, 199
h'ilol, 50, 135
Hinshaw, Robert E., 134
h'men, 49
Holland, William Robert, 136
Hood, Mantle, 4
house building, 120, 153
Huehuetenango, 14, 20, 28, 38, 209,
261 n.3; Ixcán Grande area, 27
huipil, 22, 28, 29, 57, 210
Hunahpu, 186. *See also* hero twins;
Xbalanque

Hyades, 181, 182
hysterical psychoses, 57

Ik', 89, 92, 96, 99, 100, 101, 103, 127–28,
130, 147, 148, 154, 159, 192, 193, 194,
195, 205, 217; day description for,
126–27
illness, 7, 40, 42, 50, 54–58, 64, 76, 108,
111, 113, 119, 128, 129, 146, 154, 156,
162, 199, 202, 230, 263 n.12. *See also*
sickness
ilol katinimit. See political organization,
mayor
imbrication. *See* time
Imöx, 89, 94, 95, 96, 97, 103, 118, 193; day
description for, 125–26
incense, 38, 62, 66, 76, 81, 82, 101, 110,
111, 114, 118, 128; burning of, 65, 69,
70, 148, 169, 191, 192
inheritance, 49, 50
initiation, days for, 59, 117; finances of, 66,
69; ritual for, 116
Integración de Indígenas Mayas (IXIM),
212
intersubjectivity, xi, 5, 95, 199, 261 n.1
Itzep Chanchavac, Rigoberto, 211
Ix, 53, 76, 77, 80, 81, 82, 89, 98, 103, 107,
139, 148, 193, 194, 218; day description
for, 119–20
Ixil Maya, 1, 13, 21, 27, 54, 92, 95, 127,
133, 261 n.3. *See also* Chajul; Cotzal;
Nebaj

Jacaltec Maya, 51
Joyan, 100, 101, 102, 217
Jules-Rosette, Bennetta, 5
Junajpu, 60, 71, 82, 89, 103, 107, 130, 140,
141, 142, 163, 167, 168, 180, 191, 193,
203; day description for, 124–25
Jutacaj, 17, 19. *See also* social organization,
cantons
juyubal, 223, 235, 263 n.3

Kanhobal Maya, 47, 49, 134, 212. *See also*
Santa Eulalia
K'ani Pila, Saki Pila; K'ani Mar, Saki Mar.
See Paja'
K'anil, 53, 76, 80, 82, 89, 98, 103, 130,
139, 166, 168, 191, 193, 194, 218, 239;
day description for, 114–15
katun, 203
Kekchí Maya, 13, 137, 146, 176, 212
Kelly, Isabel, 135
k'ij ("day" in Quiché Maya), 2–3
Kimball, Solon T., 5
kin ("day" in Yucatec Maya), 2